China-Focused Cases

CEIBS Case Center
Editor

China-Focused Cases

Selected Winners of the CEIBS Global Case Contest II

東方出版中心
Orient publishing center

Springer

Editor
CEIBS Case Center
Case Center
China Europe International Business School
Shanghai, China

ISBN 978-981-97-8582-7 ISBN 978-981-97-8580-3 (eBook)
https://doi.org/10.1007/978-981-97-8580-3

Jointly published with Orient Publishing Center
The print edition is not for sale in China (Mainland). Customers from China (Mainland) please order the print book from: Orient Publishing Center.
ISBN of the Co-Publisher's edition: 978-7-5473-2517-9

This Springer imprint is published by the registered company Springer Nature Singapore Pte Ltd.
The registered company address is: 152 Beach Road, #21-01/04 Gateway East, Singapore 189721, Singapore

Foreword

In the 1990s, China began its transition to a market economy, creating a nationwide demand for entrepreneurs and professional managers. After a meeting between the P.R.C. leader Deng Xiaoping and President of the European Commission Jacques Delors, Li Lanqing, former Vice Premier of the State Council, proposed "the establishment of a business school in China that would provide students with a truly international education without requiring them to go abroad". As a result, China Europe International Business School (CEIBS) was founded in 1994 with the efforts of many world-class management educators. Today, thanks to the tireless efforts of its entire community over the past 30 years, CEIBS is proud to be recognized as one of the world's top business schools.

CEIBS would not be where it is today without its unwavering commitment to both its motto of "Conscientiousness, Innovation and Excellence" and its positioning of "China Depth, Global Breadth". The school has always given top priority to high-quality teaching. Its signature pedagogical method, the case study, has been seamlessly woven into the fabric of every curriculum and used in most courses since the school's inception.

For a long time, CEIBS, like most business schools around the world, relied heavily on the case libraries of leading Western business schools for its teaching. However, due to China's ever-changing environment and the cultural differences between East and West, many Western management concepts and experiences may not be fully applicable to Chinese companies. Chinese entrepreneurs and their Western counterparts in China often find themselves having to make decisions in business environments that are rarely found in other markets. In addition, China's rapid economic growth has attracted global attention, driving demand for China-focused cases from business schools around the world. As a role model among Chinese business schools, CEIBS felt the need to share the China story with the rest of the world, not only to meet its own teaching needs, but also to satisfy the global demand from other schools for China-focused cases.

In a relatively short period of time, thanks to the dedication of the CEIBS research and teaching community, the school has made great strides in case development. Currently, we develop more than 100 China-themed cases, annually. Leveraging these high-quality cases, we have launched a series of "Real Situation Learning Method" (RSLM)-based courses that immerse students in real-life business decision-making. This innovative approach is designed to give our participants the experience to make a better contribution to management practices. CEIBS also works with firms on case studies to encourage their executives to reflect on their own practices. This collaboration has had a positive and far-reaching social impact, enhancing the thought leadership and visibility of CEIBS and its faculty, in China as well as around the world.

In addition to their use in CEIBS classrooms, these high-quality CEIBS cases are also available through world-renowned business case platforms such as Harvard Business Publishing-Education, Ivey Publishing, and The Case Centre to disseminate the distinctive Chinese business practices globally. CEIBS is committed to shaping and sharing Chinese management knowledge in the era of globalization, an embodiment of its positioning of "China Depth, Global Breadth".

Commissioned and supported by the Shanghai Municipal Government and the Shanghai Municipal Education Commission, CEIBS, in cooperation with partner institutions, has established and currently operates the "Global Platform of China Cases" ("ChinaCases.Org"). Following the guiding principle of "focusing on management issues in the Chinese business context", "ChinaCases.Org" has collected nearly 3,000 China-themed cases to date.

To mark the 30th anniversary of CEIBS, the CEIBS Case Center has compiled a series of books featuring classic CEIBS cases, its experience in case development, and the progress in building "ChinaCases.Org". These achievements are the result of not only the concerted efforts of the CEIBS community, but more importantly, the evolution and development of China's management education over the past 30 years.

We hope that this collection of case books will give you a glimpse into the rise of CEIBS over the past 30 years, which epitomizes the significant changes that have taken place in China over the same period.

Shanghai, China

Prof. Wang Hong
CEIBS President

Prof. Dominique Turpin
CEIBS President (European)

Contents

Freshippo: Data-Driven Business Model Innovation 1

Daddy Lab: A Chinese Social Enterprise's Dilemma 15

SHEIN: Redefining Global Fast Fashion 33

A Dispute Over Year-End Bonuses (a) 55

Navigating EtonHouse Through Crises: The Paradoxical Leadership of Ng Gim Choo 65

Antigal: Strategy and Succession Challenges in a Family-Owned Vineyard with Global Ambitions 81

Geek+: Challenges and Growth in the World of Autonomous Warehouse Robotics 97

AstraZeneca (China): Promoting Social Innovation with Holistic Disease Management Solutions Throughout the Patient Journey 119

Midea in India 137

Alibaba versus JD.Com: Strategies, Business Models, and Financial Statements 151

Being United and Working Together: Qiangda Chilli Leads to a Win–Win Outcomes 165

KFC China: Building Competitive Advantages Through Digitalization 179

Winner Technology: Big Data Disruption in the Retail Industry 199

Appendix 215

Freshippo: Data-Driven Business Model Innovation

In January 2016, the first Freshippo grocery store opened in Shanghai, China. Starting in the second half of 2017, Freshippo entered an era of rapid expansion, opening one store every six days on average. By June 2018, it had already opened 46 stores in 13 cities across the country.[1] Before the birth of Freshippo, customers could only choose between two shopping channels: supermarkets and e-commerce platforms. However, Freshippo had freed customers from the yoke of these limited choices. Apart from grocery shopping, they could even have fresh food cooked in- store to eat on the spot. If they didn't want to carry their groceries home, they could scan the QR codes with the Freshippo app and then have Freshippo deliver to their homes. The app also allowed customers outside stores to place orders online.

Hou Yi, Freshippo's Founder and CEO, had been infusing Freshippo's name with concepts like "omnichannel" and "mobile e-commerce" that previously had nothing to do with traditional offline stores. The creation of such a new platform straddling the boundary of online and offline retail and its driving business model evolution, according to Hou Yi, could be attributed to technological innovation.[2]

Technologies such as mobile Internet, cloud computing, big data, and artificial intelligence (see Exhibit 1) had all played a vital role in Freshippo's business model innovation. First, technologies helped Freshippo reinforce interactions between customers, product locations, and stores anytime, anywhere, online and offline, so that Freshippo could collect large amounts of data. Second, cloud computing made it convenient for Freshippo to build its business operation system around Ali Cloud. Third, through big data and artificial intelligence, Freshippo had established a set of unified standards for both online and offline retailing in terms of its membership system, product prices, inventory, marketing channels, and accounting procedures.

Professor Vincent Chang and Senior Case Researcher ZHU Qiong of China Europe International Business School developed this case. The case aims to provide the basis for classroom discussion rather than illustrate effective or ineffective handling of a management situation. This case was the Best Case Award winner of 2018 Global Contest for the Best China-Focused Cases.

China-Focused Cases, https://doi.org/10.1007/978-981-97-8580-3_1

Technology	Content
Cloud Computing	This was an Internet-based computing method through which shared resources and information of both hardware and software could be provided to computers and other devices as needed. Cloud computing allowed its users to reduce the cost of technology application, keep up with the latest technology trends, and enhance collaboration. There were three categories of cloud computing services: IaaS (Infrastructure-as-a-Service), PaaS (Platform-as-a-Service), and SaaS (Software-as-a-Service). Along with the development of mobile Internet, mobile cloud computing technologies had also been evolving. People could gain access to infrastructure, platforms and software they needed via mobile Internet in an on-demand.
Big Data	This referred to myriad diversified information assets with high growth rates. Because in the past these assets could not be processed to create commercial value by traditional data-processing methods, big data technologies that could exploit data to create value emerged. These technologies included data collection and storage, data filtering, algorithm analysis and prediction, data security, data analysis results display, to name just a few.
Artificial Intelligence	This was a way to intelligently process big data, mainly used in fields like fingerprint recognition, facial recognition, image and language recognition, and intelligent control. AI technologies mainly included natural language generation, machine learning, deep learning, and biometrics. To adopting AI applications, a large amount of data was required for training and optimizing the corresponding algorithms.

Exhibit 1 Emerging technologies used by Freshippo *Source* Compiled by authors according to "what is the Difference and Connection Between Data Center, Cloud Computing, and Big Data?" Sohu, January 12, accessed July 5,2018, https://www.sohu.com/a/216330788_100,012,035

Following Alibaba's "One Data"[1] Strategy, Freshippo's entire enterprise system and information technology (IT) architecture were built around Alibaba Cloud.[3]

Would Freshippo benefit further from the advent of the 5G era and from the gradual maturity of emerging technologies? How should it leverage emerging technologies to evolve into a more competitive and profitable platform?

[1] Alibaba's 'One Data' Strategy was launched at the end of 2015, which aimed at building an organizational and business mechanism characterized by a big "One Data" platform. With this strategy, the front-end business unit can become more responsive to the ever-changing market, while the one data platform integrates the entire group's capabilities on operational data and product technologies to strongly support the businesses at the front end. Quoted from "In-Depth Analysis on Alibaba's 'One Data' Strategy", Sohu, 2017.05.30, accessed on September 12, 2018. https://www.sohu.com/a/144689936_488677.

1 Data-Driven Business Model

Freshippo had started as a chain of brick-and-mortar stores mainly selling fresh produce—with fresh seafood as its signature product—supplemented by in-store catering and online retail businesses. To shop at Freshippo, customers had to download the Freshippo app, which was linked to Alipay. Freshippo offered 30 min grocery delivery within a radius of three kilometers.

Even before Freshippo was born, the founding team had already decided that Alibaba's big data analysis could lead to what they called "top-level design". This design laid the foundation for setting key performance indicator (KPI)-based objectives for Freshippo's business model. First, the revenue from online transactions should be greater than that from offline transactions; second, each store should generate more than 5,000 orders per day online; third, the Freshippo app should be able to survive independently without support from other online traffic; and fourth, the stores should offer 30 min delivery while keeping logistics costs under control.

Guided by these objectives, Freshippo determined that 20-to-45-year-old female white-collar workers who used Alipay would be its target customers. According to findings from Alipay's data, most customers in this group had families to take care of. They also lived a fast-paced life, enjoyed a moderate to high level of spending power, and attached importance to quality of life. Fresh foods and healthy diets were their needs, and once they had trust in the products offered by Freshippo, they would naturally choose the Freshippo app for their online purchases if they were unable to visit stores.

The operation's results demonstrated Freshippo's high brand visibility shortly after it started selling fresh seafood. This was largely owing to the willingness and financial ability of the aforementioned customer group to consume seafood that was not commonly found elsewhere. Meanwhile, the cleanliness of the seafood section in Freshippo stores was greatly attractive to them. These customers not only contributed to consumption, but spread word-of-mouth on social media as well. The quick rise of the Freshippo brand and customers' brand awareness had everything to do with this demographic.

It was also data that pushed forward the creation of the F2 (Fast & Fresh) convenience stores, Freshippo Cloud Supermarket, and the Hexiaoma stores.

The F2 convenience stores were created after Freshippo identified the pain points around the breakfast and lunch of office workers: food hygiene concerns and time wasted in queues. Therefore, F2 stores were positioned as providers of breakfast, lunch, and afternoon tea for office workers. Customers could place orders via the Freshippo app and the stores would prepare the food for them. Customers could then go to the stores at the appointed time to either pick up their food or eat it on the spot.

The first F2 store opened in December 2017, with very similar furnishings and product categories to Freshippo. Seafood was also the main product that attracted customers. The only difference was that the store had floor space of 500 square meters and served customers located within a 500 m radius.

Freshippo Cloud Supermarket, launched on April 1, 2018, was an online retail business formed in order to offer products unavailable in Freshippo's brick-and-mortar stores. Carefully selected based on data on consumer needs, the 20,000 stock-keeping units (SKUs) sold at Freshippo Cloud Supermarket were products offering the best value from 10 categories, including staple and non-staple foods, maternal and child supplies, adult products, and daily necessities. The overnight delivery service offered by Freshippo Cloud Supermarket used customer data to reduce the cost of order fulfillment. Through data analysis, the company realized that short delivery times were not necessarily the only factor in creating the best fast-moving consumer goods shopping experience. Customers demanded fast delivery only when they had no concern about price.[4]

Opened in Suzhou in June 2018, Hexiaoma was a type of Freshippo supermarket jointly run by Freshippo and RT-Mart, an offline supermarket chain acquired by Alibaba. It had floor space of about 800 square meters. Like Freshippo, Hexiaoma integrated its stores and warehouses as well as its online business. The stores had a fresh produce section that occupied 50% of the entire floor space, but they offered neither fresh seafood, dining, nor on-site food preparation services. While still offering delivery within a 3 km radius, Hexiaoma only promised delivery within an hour and offered free delivery only for a customer's first order. Contributors to Hexiaoma's differentiation included data-driven site selection, product selection, and data marketing supported by Alibaba's big data resources and algorithms. In addition, Hexiaoma combined Freshippo's experience in data-driven operations with RT-Mart's experience in brick-and-mortar store management.[5]

Key technologies such as big data and artificial intelligence had also driven Freshippo to iterate its fresh store business model as well. Nearly one year after its first store launched in Shanghai in January 2016, it opened the third store, which was clearly distinct compared to the first two. The store area was doubled, with dining and retail space each taking up half of the store area. This was to expand the warehousing and distribution capacities of the store, and to strengthen the ability of the store to attract customers and direct them online.

To address the issue of long wait times for meals,[6] for which Freshippo had been widely criticized, Freshippo opened the Freshippo Nanxiang Store in February 2018. It was a brick-and-mortar store that combined an automated restaurant and a supermarket in one. Customers first chose their seats on the screen at the restaurant entrance, and then followed the instructions from the system to get seated. Next, they scanned the QR code on the table with their Freshippo app to order dishes. Beside the table, there was a track for robots to deliver dishes. From customer ordering to preparation in the kitchen to dish delivery, all activities were managed by the system and displayed on the screen beside the table. In this store, it was robots that delivered dishes and even cooked some standard dishes. The robotic dish delivery system and equipment, developed by Freshippo itself, adopted a variety of hybrid sensing technologies and deep learning techniques involving sounds and images. According to Freshippo, with this system, it took a robot about 40 s on average to deliver a dish once it was ready.[7] However, the store had still been receiving customer complaints, including some related to long wait times and stale and lackluster food.[8]

2 Data-Driven Core Competencies

Freshippo's operational efficiency could be attributed to its mature data- processing and application technologies. With these technologies, Freshippo could create business models supported by various data-driven core competencies.

2.1 *Data-Driven Site Selection*

To open a brick-and-mortar store, the first issue to address was siteselection. The primary basis of Freshippo's siteselection was the big data profiles of Alipay users. When Freshippo considered a location, it would conduct big data analysis of active Alipay users within a three-kilometer radius. The data might be from Alipay or from the third-party platforms such as WeChat and Weibo. The reason why Freshippo opened its first store in Chengdu in Hongpailou District rather than the traditional Chunxi Road Shopping District was that according to its big data analysis, there were more online shoppers in Hongpailou District, with higher online transaction volumes and spending per order.[9] In addition to data on user profiles, Freshippo would also gauge whether local real-estate companies would cooperate and whether local property management companies were qualified service providers. Without their support, Freshippo could hardly find enough parking spaces, cost- effective warehousing, and store space to offer customers an optimized offline shopping experience and efficient online order delivery.

Freshippo did not always open its stores in central areas as traditional supermarkets often did. It would sometimes choose relatively distant locations. For example, Freshippo Dacheng Road Store in Beijing was not centrally located at all. Neither was its Yizhuang Store (in Beijing). Although the Yizhuang area was a relatively remote place, data showed that it was home to many executives of Fortune 500 companies.

2.2 *Online Traffic Guided by Brick-And-Mortar Stores*

According to the original plan of the Freshippo project, brick-and-mortar stores were supposed to provide customers with enjoyable experiences to build their trust and loyalty. The ultimate goal was to boost online traffic by guiding customers to shop on its app. Therefore, while Freshippo opened its stores, it also launched its online retail business via its app.

The Freshippo app played a vital role in converting offline traffic to online traffic. For Freshippo, all channels and shopping scenarios served to guide traffic to the Freshippo app. First, customers had to use the app to make payments in offline stores. Second, as Freshippo's online platform and stores offered products of the same category, quality, and price, customers could use the app to scan product barcodes in-store and then place orders online for home delivery. Third, customers could scan products on a self-checkout machine in a store and then pay via the app, which saved time waiting inline. Fourth, if customers ordered food in the dining area of a store, they would receive a message from the app when the food was ready. In the meantime, they could shop around.

2.3 Personalized Marketing

Because all the customers, no matter online or offline, had to make payments via the Freshippo app, Freshippo was able to turn all of them into its members and had full access to information on their consumption needs and habits. Based on this data and with Alibaba's personalized recommendation technology, the Freshippo app was able to perform one-on-one marketing to thousands of different customers. The interactive marketing venues ranged from events at stores to different forms of promotion online. For example, Freshippo would invite children of a similar age and their parents to parties in stores; when there was a product promotion, Freshippo would send the information directly to customers in need of such a product.

Freshippo had developed extensive profiles of its customers. When it created scene-based advertising content, it used these profiles to determine which content might resonate most with specific customers. For example, in 2018, the brand content of Freshippo changed from "fresh food" to "fresh elements in daily life". Correspondingly, the video ads of Freshippo comprised five scenes based on customer data: (1) a husband, who was a senior executive at work, ordered large lobsters from Freshippo for his wife; (2) a daughter who studied overseas ordered king crabs for her parents in China; (3) children became friends as they got together at Freshippo to observe the seafood they liked, which made their mothers beam with smiles; (4) neighbors shared "Daily Fresh" chicken stew with one another; and (5) white-collar workers got to know each other because of a bowl of dumplings made with their hometown flavor.[2]

2.4 Supply Chain Management

The supply chain of Fre shippo—from procurement, warehousing, and logistics to distribution (see Exhibit 2)—was fully managed with new technologies and equipment. Freshippo's supply chain management system was built around the Alibaba

[2] This was a private-label brand launched by Freshippo in August 2017, which included goods like vegetables, meat, and milk. These goods were directly purchased from production bases or suppliers and had to be sold at its stores within 24 h. Those that were near the end of their shelf life would be either sold at a discount via the Freshippo app or used as ingredients for dishes offered to consumers.

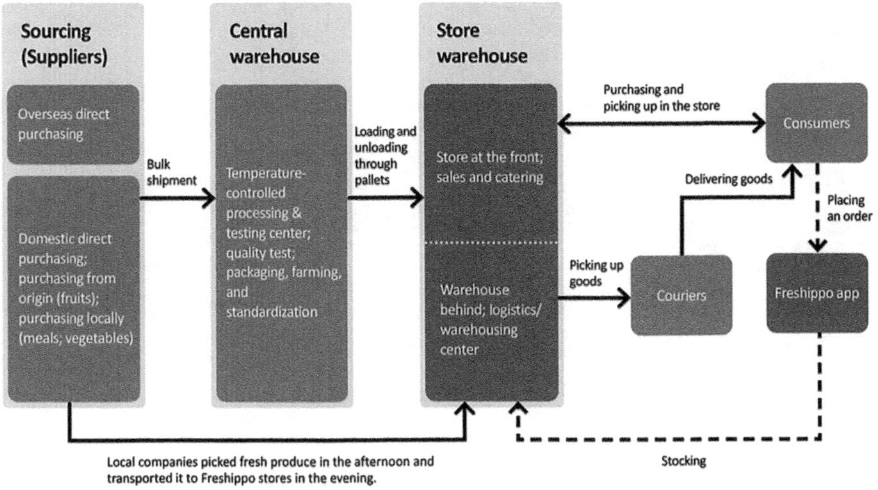

Exhibit 2 Freshippo's supply chain. *Note* The solid line represents logistics; the dotted line represents information flows. *Source* Adapted from "A probe into Freshippo's Logistics System", www.yidianzixun.com, April 17, 2018, accessed May 29, 2018, http://www.yidianzixun.com/article/0Ip5R82a

Cloud platform, which included the enterprise resource planning system, the point-of-sale system, the logistics system, the distribution system, and the app system. It took Freshippo and Alibaba 1.5 years and 500 software engineers to develop a system suite that fully realized digital management over Freshippo's memberships, goods, marketing, transactions, supply chain, and store operations. The data thus generated, together with the external data of Freshippo and the support of technologies such as those in the fields of deep learning, image recognition, speech recognition, temperature recognition, geographical positioning, had helped Freshippo build an intelligent algorithm model to enhance its supply chain operations and management capability in productselection, warehouse management, store operations, order fulfillment, and delivery (see Exhibit 3).

3 Data-Driven Product Selection

As for procurement forecasting, Freshippo made product selection and procurement plans for each store and allocated stock accordingly based on big data from Alibaba and its own customers.

Thanks to big data, Freshippo's product selection capability had been continuously improving. When a store was not yet opened, Freshippo collected data from Alipay user profiles and product supplier information. After a store was opened, the company added the operations data. In the first two months after a store was opened, Freshippo tracked the sales of each SKU to decide whether a certain kind of product should be

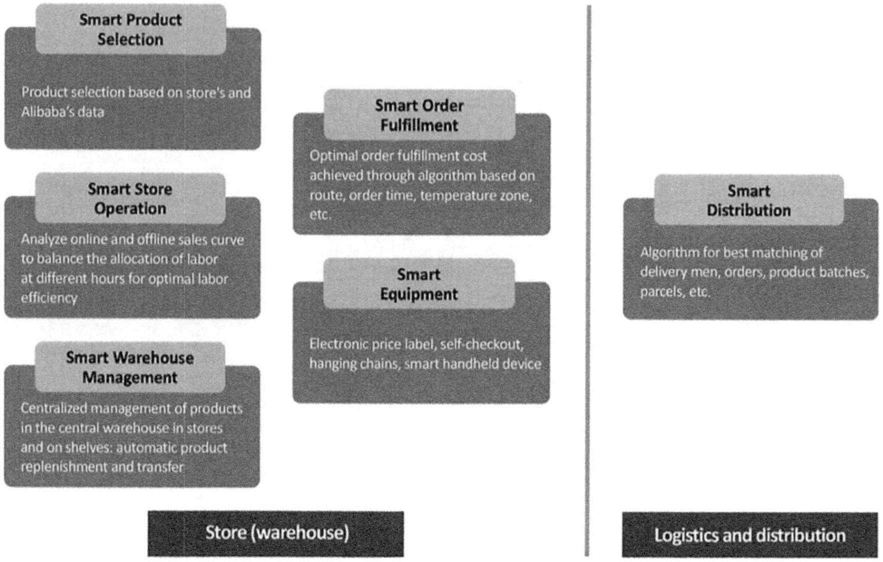

Exhibit 3 Operation management and capability algorithm of Freshippo's supply chain. *Source* Adapted from "A probe into Freshippo's Logistics System", www.yidianzixun.com, April 17, 2018, accessed May 29, 2018, http://www.yidianzixun.com/article/0Ip5R82a

stocked. If so, Freshippo then decided the frequency and quantity of the orders. Two months after a store was opened, the SKU's product category and customers' ordering patterns would normally fall into place. After that, Freshippo would continue to track customers' shopping preferences, purchase frequency, and product reviews through its app, through Wi-Fi, and through its product QR code in order to further optimize its product selection algorithm.

Freshippo sold produce from both its private label and from third parties. Since its inception, Freshippo had built an R&D team for its private-label brands such as "Freshippo Taste" and "Daily Fresh." By early 2018, Freshippo had already created more than 300 private-label brands.[10] Products under the private-label brands were purchased through the "buyers system" directly from domestic or overseas production bases. For example, Freshippo found a partner with fishing rights in Alaskan waters for king crabs and placed orders directly with this partner. The partner then packed the king crabs in coolers. After that, Freshippo was responsible for cold-chain transportation to send the crabs to the Freshippo processing and testing center. Finally, the crabs were delivered to the stores.

"Daily Fresh" products, on the other hand, were purchased via the fresh produce supply chain that Freshippo had built with local farms. The quantity of the order for each store was fed into Freshippo's system by noon every day, and product purchase plans were forwarded to farms by 2 pm. Picking would be done on the farms before 3 pm, and all the fresh produce would be delivered to stores after 5 pm. For vegetables, the time from picking to putting on sale was strictly kept within 18 h. During the process, the system performed real-time monitoring through Wi-Fi cameras, temperature sensors, GPS, and so on. Freshippo also required fresh produce suppliers to set up processing plants near their farms that were equipped with cold-chain temperature control, prepackaging production lines, and Wi-Fi cameras. The cold-chain transportation vehicles were also equipped with temperature sensors, GPS, and so on.[11]

Products of third-party brands were selected based on Freshippo's big data. So as to make the prices more reasonable, Freshippo did not charge entry fees, promotion fees, or other kinds of marketing fees to third-party suppliers.

4 Warehouse Management

There were two levels of warehouses at Freshippo. The first level was the central warehouse, which also performed functions like quality inspection, product standardization, and live seafood farming. Store warehouses were the second level. "Daily Fresh" products were delivered directly from farms to store warehouses, while all other products were delivered in bulk on pallets by trucks first from their origins or suppliers to the central warehouse, and then to the store warehouses. "Daily Fresh" products were only transported in small packages in the final three kilometers from stores to customers. The warehouse management algorithm for the central warehouse and store warehouses was built on operational data from the stores and the Alibaba systems.

By means of electronic shelf labels[3] and product barcodes, Freshippo implemented a real-time and unified pricing and inventory management system both online and offline. All the product information was consistent, no matter whether the products were in the central warehouses, in the store warehouses, or on store shelves. Therefore, whenever a product was out of stock or moving slowly in a store warehouse or on a shelf, automatic replenishment or promotion would be triggered in the warehouse management system. For example, if "Daily Fresh" products were left on shelves near the end of the day, the system would target customers interested in such products and would push promotions to them. From the beginning of such a promotion, the system would adjust the promotional plan according to the sales performance at regular intervals (say, every other hour) in order to achieve more effective results.

[3] An electronic price label, which could replace traditional paper price tags, was an electronic display device with information-sending and information-receiving functions. When connected to a back-end database through a wired or wireless network, the label could display the latest product information and ensure price consistency between the checkout counter and the shelf.

5 Store Operation

Because every product had an electronic shelf label and a barcode, the store employees could identify products with handheld intelligent devices. With the help of the system, they could perform other tasks—including receiving goods, shelving, order picking, packaging, and distribution—in an efficient manner. For example, they could determine which products were put on shelves and at what time, the number of times a product was replenished, and even how many fish were killed.

Furthermore, the store operation system was able to assign tasks to employees that were accurate to the minute, so as to ensure not only a balanced distribution of work in stores but also optimal human efficiency and sales per square meter.

For example, when an online order was generated, the system broke down the order items into different tasks based on products' locations in the warehouse, product sorters' locations, and their workload. Each task was assigned to the nearest product sorter so that a product-picking task could be accomplished within three minutes. The conveyor belts hanging on store ceilings were designed to facilitate efficient product picking and delivery. Product-picking bags moved along the conveyor belts to the product-gathering area, where the products were packed. In sum, the whole order-generation process did not take more than 10 min.

6 Order Fulfillment

The algorithm for order fulfillment at Freshippo was based on information regarding product production routes, order sequences, temperature zones required by ordered products, warehouse sections where products were stored, and so on. This was to ensure the highest efficiency of product production and distribution, as well as the best consumption experience at the lowest fulfillment cost.

Take the promise of fulfilling an order within 30 min as an example. At Freshippo, product picking was not done by an individual employee for each order. Instead, the Freshippo system consolidated the same products in different orders and then assigned tasks to store employees nearby. Each employee did his or her part of the picking job with the help of a handheld device. Products picked would be put into bags, hung on conveyor belts on store ceilings, and then transferred to the warehouses at the backs of stores.

The product picking time for each employee was controlled by the system to stay within three minutes. Once product-picking bags were hung on the conveyor belts, it also took less than three minutes for them to be transferred to the store warehouses. The final packing was also limited to within three minutes. The system automatically grouped and combined products according to order composition, adjacency of order time and customer locations, and similarity in delivery routes. Products for each order were then manually packed, sent to the logistics center through the vertical lift system, and ready for delivery. The time left for delivery men to do their job was 20 min.

7 Logistics and Distribution

It was through system optimization that Freshippo was able to deliver orders within 20 min. First, based on information like order time and delivery address, the Freshippo system would combine different orders into delivery batches. Then, based on information including the order batch, the order category (normal temperature or cold chain), delivery men's familiarity with the distribution area, and delivery men's locations at that time, the system would calculate the best delivery route and assign delivery to the most appropriate delivery man.

On the other side, the logistics and distribution system at Freshippo Cloud Supermarket was different. In order to reduce the cost of order fulfillment, orders would accumulate to a certain quantity and then the best outbound route would be determined according to the order quantity and product types. Orders on the same distribution route would be integrated according to the maximum workload with which a delivery man could cope. Then the integrated orders would be transported during the night from the central warehouse to the stores. The next day, delivery men would pickup parcels of the integrated orders during relatively less busy store hours. After a delivery man reached a customer, he would sort out the customer's parcels according to the order information.

8 Other Technology-Driven New Retailers

Freshippo was not the only technology-driven New Retailer around the world. Amazon Go had appeared in the U.S. market, and the Chinese market included unmanned convenience stores and unattended shelves.

8.1 Amazon Go

Amazon Go was a brick-and-mortar cashier-free convenience store created by Amazon, the world's largest e-commerce retail company. By leveraging technologies such as computer vision, deep learning, and sensor fusion, Amazon Go had eliminated cashier checkout in traditional convenience stores, allowing customers to "take and just go".[12] Customers could download the Amazon Go app on their mobile devices and then enter an Amazon Go store by scanning the code at the store entrance. Whenever customers took an item off the shelf, the item "would be" added to a virtual shopping cart. If it was put back on the shelf, the item would automatically disappear from the shopping cart. After customers had selected what they needed, they could go straight out of the store. Within a few minutes of exiting the store, an electronic receipt would be pushed to their mobile phones and they would be charged on their Amazon accounts. The electronic receipt showed not only shopping details, but also the length of time the customer had stayed in the store.[13]

Amazon Go was run on a trial basis on the first floor at the Amazon headquarters in Seattle in December 2016, serving only Amazon employees. It was intended to be officially open to the public in early 2017. However, during the trial operation period, it was found that when there were more than 20 people in the store or when customers took products off shelves too fast, the tracking devices in the store were unable to accurately track customers and products.[14] It took Amazon a year to tackle this problem. Hence, Amazon Go was not officially open to the public until January 22, 2018. However, Amazon planned to open five more stores in 2018.[15]

8.2 Unattended Convenience Stores and Unattended Shelves

The first unattended convenience store in China was BingoBox, opened in Guangzhou in August 2016. It kicked offits large-scale expansion through franchising in Shanghai in June 2017. By January 2018, it had already entered nearly 30 cities across China.[16]

The entry of BingoBox into Shanghai had led to the creation of a series of unattended convenience stores under other brands. Having seen the trend, investors threw themselves into this field one after another. On June 28, 2017, F5 Future Store received A+ round investment of ¥30[4] million. On July 3, BingoBox completed its Series A financing of more than ¥100 million. Then on July 8, Tao Café, Alibaba's version of Amazon Go, made its debut at Taobao Creation Festival in Hangzhou.

However, industry experts had noted that compared with Amazon Go, the unattended convenience stores in China were still not truly of a "take and just go" model. Most of the products in these stores had RFID labels,[5] which required customers to scan QR codes to pay upon the completion of shopping.[17]

Apart from convenience stores, unattended shelves focusing on the office market were another New Retail application scenario that caught the eyes of venture capitalists in 2017. As by the end of September that year, at least 16 brands of unattended shelves received financing of a combined total of over ¥2.5 billion, according to the third-party data. However, since the beginning of 2018, this retail segment had reported negative news such as layoffs and store closures. Therefore, the sustainability and profitability of the business model of unattended shelves had been questioned.

---

[4] ¥ = CNY = Chinese yuan renminbi; ¥ 1 = approximately US$0.1470 in June, 2020.

[5] This was a kind of non-contact automatic identification technology that automatically identified a target object and acquired relevant data through radio-frequency signals. The identification work did not require manual intervention.

9 The Future of Freshippo

With the advent of the 5G era, Freshippo realized that more data sources would be found and hence more business opportunities would emerge. The company hoped to further reinforce its online and offline channel development by leveraging Internet of Things technology. With its strengths in channel development, Freshippo could increase its bargaining power and pricing power across the value chain.[18]

On the online side, other e-commerce channels of Alibaba—such as Taobao.com and ele.me—would also push traffic to Freshippo. On the offline side, apart from its own stores, Freshippo had been trying to empower its strategic partners and turn their channels into its own. Hexiaoma stores were just the first attempt of Freshippo in this regard. The integration of online and offline channels and their expansion benefited Freshippo not only with a sizeable market but also with a tremendous amount of real-time data. This would bring Freshippo more bargaining power with suppliers.

In the face of a larger market, Freshippo expected to build many more private labels based on existing data resources and the application of emerging technologies. This strategy could help Freshippo increase its pricing power by redefining product attributes under its private-label brands. One of the examples of following strategy was its "Daily Fresh" brand. To implement this strategy, Freshippo had established plant standards for its partnering farms, and instituted environmental requirements, such as the use of pollution-free and hazard-free resources, including land and water.

Would innovative initiatives like "Daily Fresh" and Hexiaoma ultimately help Freshippo grow into an influential player with strong bargaining power across the value chain in the New Retail industry? Could Freshippo's operational shortcomings exposed during its past development be properly addressed through data- and technology-driven innovation? How could Freshippo better leverage emerging technologies to become more competitive in the 5G era?

Endnotes

1. Dong Ye. "Freshippo Opened 46 Stores," pintu360.com, April 26, 2018, accessed May 29, 2018, www.sohu.com/a/229549090_363549.
2. Hema Xiansheng CEO Hou Yi: What We Have Learnt from Amazon Go: Technology Drives New Retail," iYiou, December 11, 2016, accessed July 5, 2018. https://www.iyiou.com/ p/35888#0-tsina-1–10,554-397232819ff9a47a7b7e80a40613cfe1.
3. "The Secret of New Logistics at Freshippo: What Is Special About It?" Sohu, May 2, 2018, accessed July 5, 2018, www.sohu.com/a/230194576_650513.
4. Ibid.
5. "Data Mindset Behind Hexiaoma Shocks Traditional Businesses," uMeng Data, June 6, 2018, accessed July 5, 2018, http://www.investorscn.com/2018/06/06/69124.
6. "Hidden Risks in Hema's Operating Model," Sohu, April 24, 2017, accessed July 5, 2018, 24, www.sohu.com/a/136085005_479244.

7. Wang Shiqi, "The Secret Behind Hema Automatic Restaurant: Dish Delivery in 40 Seconds on Average," rich.online.sh.cn, June 13, 2018, accessed July 5, 2018, https://rich.online.sh.cn/ rich/gb/content/2018–06/13/content_8929852.htm.
8. Dianping.com, accessed July 5, 2018, http://m.dianping.com/shop/98652528/review_all.
9. Wang Dan, "Freshippo Xiansheng to Open 10 Stores in Chengdu This Year," Sichuan Online, May 8, 2018,accessed July 5, 2018, http://news.winshang.com/html/063/8471.html.
10. "First Freshippo Store in Chengdu Opens," winshang.com, February 6, 2018, accessed May 25, 2018, http://news.winshang.com/html/063/3994.html.
11. Ibid.
12. Michael Kasavana, "Amazon Go's Impact on Payments, Self-Checkout," Louisville, January 31, 2017, accessed June 29, 2018, https://www.retailcustomerexperience.com/blogs/amazon- gos-impact-on-payments-self-checkout-2.
13. Ibid.
14. "After More Than 20 Years of E-Commerce, What Is Special About Amazon Go?" QDaily, March 5, 2018, accessed July 5, 2018, http://new.qq.com/omn/20180305/20180305A0U8EM. html.
15. "Amazon Plans to Open 6 Amazon Go Grocery Stores," Sohu, February 24, 2018, accessed July 5, 2018, https://www.sohu.com/a/223829910_223764.
16. "Fosun Nurtures New Species of Unmanned Retail by Leading BingoBox Round B Financing," China.com.cn, January 17, 2018, accessed July 5, 2018, www.xinhuanet.com/ itown/2018–01/17/c_ 136,902,370.htm.
17. "Unmanned Retail in China from the Perspective of Amazon Go Is a Double-Edged Sword," Daily Economic News, October 24, 2017, accessed July 5, 2018, http://tech.sina.com.cn/ it/2017–10-24/doc-ifymzzpw0432445.shtml.
18. "Freshippo Xiansheng CEO Hou Yi: What Kind of New Retail Do We Want to Create?"Pintu Business Review, October 15, 2017, accessed July 5, 2018, http://tech.ifeng.com/ a/20171015/44716331_0.shtml.

Daddy Lab: A Chinese Social Enterprise's Dilemma

It was August 2019, and the fall school semester was just around the corner. After encasing his daughter's new textbooks in plastic covers, Wenfeng Wei picked up his phone to check on Hangzhou Daddy Lab Technology Co., Ltd.'s ("Daddy Lab") online store. Each time his daughter prepared to go back to school, Wei would recall his challenging but fulfilling journey over the prior years.

Wei started Daddy Lab in August 2015 to raise awareness of potentially harmful plastic book covers that millions of Chinese students used each day. He wanted to fight poor-quality, hazardous consumer products head-on. Wei became an internet celebrity overnight after his short video on the unsafe book covers went viral. He racked up thousands of followers on WeChat under the moniker "Daddy Wei." Followers swelled to 500,000 in 2017 before hitting 1.65 million by 2018. In September 2018, Daddy Lab was one of only a dozen companies to gain China Gold Social Enterprise certification from the China Charity Fair. Wei felt incredibly honored to receive such recognition.

"Love, not profit, is the key to our success ", said Wei when introducing Daddy Lab. Its business model involved identifying, testing and reporting potentially hazardous products to the public via social media . It would also recommend and sell high-quality, non-hazardous products for profit via e-commerce platforms. However, Wei wondered if Daddy Lab should continue as both a "reviewer" and a "seller" and how these dual roles could affect follower and consumer trust. As a social entrepreneur, he grappled with trying to make the world a safer place for children and their families while also requiring sufficient profits to sustain this purpose.

Professor Daniel Han Ming Chng, Senior Case Researcher Dr. ZHAO Liman, Professor Byron Lee, Professor Peter Moran, and Research Assistant SUN Heming of China Europe International Business School developed this case with the helpful cooperation and support of the case company. The case aims to provide the basis for classroom discussion rather than illustrate effective or ineffective handling of a management situation.

This case was the Best Award winner of 2020 Global Contest for the Best China-Focused Cases.

China-Focused Cases, https://doi.org/10.1007/978-981-97-8580-3_2

As Wei considered Daddy Lab's future, the following questions kept him awake at night: Was Daddy Lab's current business model effective in achieving its social and financial goals? How could Daddy Lab better manage its dual roles as a "reviewer" and a "seller"? How could Daddy Lab become more sustainable in the future?

1 Founder: Wenfeng Wei

Wei graduated from the prestigious Zhejiang University in 1998 with a ... degree in physics. Then he worked at the Zhejiang Entry-Exit Inspection and Quarantine Bureau for over ten years. His primary responsibility was product safety testing and certification. It was a stable job that allowed him ample time to spend with his young family.

In 2009, he stepped down from the bureau to start the REACH24H Consulting Group in Hangzhou, Zhejiang provincial capital. The venture provided REACH[1] compliance solutions in China. By 2014, the company had established branches in the US, Europe, and Taiwan, with annual revenue exceeding ¥50 million.[2] It employed more than 150 employees and provided chemical safety and toxicology risk assessment services to over 3,000 companies.

Just as Wei had started planning the company's aggressive expansion, a piece of plastic used to wrap books changed his career plan and life.

2 Discovering and Solving a Social Problem

A few days before the spring semester in February 2015, Wei's daughter, a second-grader, asked him to wrap her new textbooks with plastic book covers. With his years of experience in product testing, he instinctively questioned the cover's quality due to its pungent smell. He went out to buy more from various bookshops and found they all had the same odor. He told his daughter that the plastic was likely hazardous, and suggested that she used paper covers instead. However, the school informed that students had to use transparent plastic covers. He then realized that millions of students in China might be exposed to unsafe products.

As government inspection bureaus in China did not provide testing services for private individuals, Wei tried encouraging authorities to test these potentially hazardous covers. He posted on microblogging platform Weibo, made phone calls

---

[1] Registration, Evaluation, Authorisation and Restriction of *Chemicals* (REACH) is an EU regulation aimed at protecting human health and the environment from the risks posed by chemicals that came into effect in June 2007. It promotes alternative methods for chemical hazard assessment to reduce tests on animals.

[2] ¥ = CNY = Chinese Yuan Renminbi, ¥1 = approximately US$0.1611, US$1539 as of December 31, 2014 and 2015, ¥1 = approximately US$0.1520, US$0.1439 as of January 31 and December 31, 2016, ¥1 = approximately US$0.1453 as of December 31, 2018.

to the industrial, commercial, and education authorities, and even brought the plastic book covers to education officials in person. However, he failed to make progress. "Many of the officials I contacted simply passed the buck on to others without taking any action," Wei said. "Thus, I decided to make a 'scene' that was too big for them to ignore."

In June 2015, Wei invested ¥1 million of his own money to launch Daddy Lab, an enterprise to detect poor-quality and hazardous consumer products used by children and families in China.[3] " The name Daddy Lab cannot be more suitable. What else can better describe the things we are doing right now?" Wei said.[1] His first goal was to fight unsafe plastic book covers sold throughout China. Wei also believed that Daddy Lab could help relieve product safety problems in China and help consumers (see Exhibit 1: China's Institutional Environment of Product Safety and Product Testing).

Daddy Lab spent ¥9,500 to test book cover material at the National Center of Supervision and Inspection for Fine Chemicals Quality in Taizhou, Jiangsu province. The results showed that all seven samples contained unsafe amounts of two compounds—polycyclic aromatic hydrocarbon (PAHs) and diethylhexyl phthalate (DEHP). Various international health agencies classified the former as a probable carcinogen. The latter was believed to cause endocrine disruption in males that could have lasting effects on reproduction. The plastic covers were manufactured according to national test standards at that time, but they did not include tests for hazardous substances like PAHs and DEHP. Wei said, "Our mission is to detect the hazardous substances that have passed standard testing procedures so that we can better protect our children."

To raise awareness, Wei spent ¥100,000 to make a short video about the unsafe plastic book covers and posted it on Daddy Lab's official WeChat account. Released on August 25, 2015, the video went viral via WeChat Moments—a social media feature similar to Facebook's News Feed. National media, including state broadcaster CCTV and the People's Daily, picked up the video, and spread nationwide.[4]

Wei leveraged WeChat's group chat function to drum up support. When a group reached the 500-member limit, he would create a new one.[5] To nurture productive relationships with local government and manufacturers, Wei invited them to the groups to discuss how to improve product standards and ensure those sold in China were safe.

[3] Wei had registered a company in January 2015, planning to do cross-border e-commerce, but changed its strategic direction and. When he was asked to sell book covers by the company's name to parents, he sold them through this company. In June 2016, this company was renamed as Hangzhou Daddy Lab Technology Co., Ltd. in June 2015.

[4] By mid-2019, the video had accumulated 2 million views.

[5] By the end of June 2017, Daddy Lab had 13 WeChat groups, the classification of which was not based on members' geographical location, occupation, or identity.

3 Voluntary Testing Through Crowdfunding

Following Daddy Lab's report on plastic book covers, many parents asked Wei to test other products used by their children at school (such as pencils, erasers, plastic files, and glues) and by families at home (such as kettles, chopping boards, water purifiers, and insect-repelling bracelets). Daddy Lab became a fully-fledged social enterprise for detecting and communicating accurate information to the public to raise awareness of hazardous products.

Wei joked, "I used to think that I would make money from product testing for the rest of my life. It never occurred to me that one day I would spend money on testing." Faced with a vast number of testing requests, Wei worried about Daddy Lab's future. Although some parents would consciously support Daddy Lab via online donations when submitting testing requests, it was not enough to cover the testing fee and operating cost. By October 2015, the company had run up a ¥700,000 deficit. His initial investment was running out, threatening the firm with insolvency. Wei considered charging parents who sent him testing requests to continue testing, but he quickly gave up that idea, as such expenses were far beyond what any individual was willing to pay. Under financial distress, he announced to his WeChat groups in late 2015 that Daddy Lab would only be able to continue for a few more months before it had to cease operations.

To Wei's surprise, thousands of parents came to his aid. One of them said, "Daddy Wei, as long as you don't forget your original purpose and continue to do more testing for us, we will standby your side forever." Many supporters tried to donate money via WeChat immediately after hearing the news; some gave as much as ¥20,000. However, Daddy Lab was not allowed to receive such donations as it was registered as a for-profit business enterprise.

To continue, Wei decided his best option was to invite at least 500 of his followers to invest at least ¥3,000 each to raise ¥1.5 million in exchange for a combined 10% stake in Daddy Lab. However, Zhejiang Equity Exchange informed him that equity-based crowdfunding involving more than 200 investors was not permitted.

Wei redesigned his plan by raising the minimum investment to ¥10,000 to stay within the limit. To his delight, the increased amount did not dampen his supporters' enthusiasm. In January 2016, Daddy Lab released details of the funding plan (see Exhibit 2).[6] Wei recalled, "I tried to remind them that an investment like this is risky. Some replied that it wasn't a problem, and they just wanted to support me without thinking about a return. I was really touched by their kindness." Daddy Lab raised ¥2 million from 112 parents, who collectively received a 10%[7] stake. The new funding

[6] Daddy Lab's investment from small (individual) shareholders was equity-based. Investors were expected to have a certain level of risk tolerance. The company did not impose any requirements on investors' qualifications but entrusted the job to Dream Move out of legal compliance considerations.

[7] The target was ¥1.7 million as mentioned in Exhibit 1, but Daddy Lab raised ¥2 million in total thus transferred 10% of shares. By February 2018, Wei held 90% of shares, including 15% on behalf of the management team. Lead investor Shanghai Niejing Investment Management held

energized operations. With this demonstration of trust from his followers, Wei was even more determined to expand Daddy Lab's product testing.

Daddy Lab followed a systematic approach when selecting products for testing. Parents could submit candidate products online (see Exhibit 3), and Daddy Lab's team of ten chemical engineers would evaluate each request. They would select popular consumer products that a typical family uses, determine substances used during manufacturing and identify their toxicity risks before choosing a relevant testing standard based on the REACH and hazardous chemicals databases. Daddy Lab's minimum requirements for all tests followed the most recent international standards. Parents bought the products themselves and sent them to the lab to ensure authenticity.

Manufacturers could also submit their products to Daddy Lab for testing and certification. Daddy Lab's team would similarly evaluate these requests. For these products, the firm would buy them on the open market rather than using their samples. To remain impartial, it did not receive any payment from manufacturers and would submit all products to a qualified third party for testing.

To fund these tests, Daddy Lab continued with a crowdfunding model. It would announce the specific products selected to all followers who voluntarily donated funds via online tipping to test them. By January 2016, 1,944 followers had crowd-funded ¥60,847, racking up testing costs of ¥96,883. By the end of 2016, Daddy Lab had raised ¥240,472 from 4,660 followers on WeChat's crowdfunding platform and supported 23 testing projects. After completing the tests, Daddy Lab would upload invoices to their official account on WeChat.

When Daddy Lab crossed the breakeven point around mid-2017, it stopped accepting donations from its followers. In 2018, it founded Daddy Lab Charity Foundation. It donated ¥1 million, of which about 35% was crowdsourced from previous years. The Foundation provided public lectures and created the Daddy Lab Fund to reward parents who identified potential hazardous products or children's health problems.

4 "Internet Celebrity + E-commerce" Model

> Please don't call me a philanthropist because others are likely to impose a moral judgment on me. Even when doing social work, we should be able to survive and be sustainable.
>
> —Wenfeng Wei[2]

Though Daddy Lab was positioned as a social enterprise dedicated to addressing a social problem, Wei understood that it had to find a sustainable business model if the enterprise was to survive. Hence, he adopted an "internet celebrity + e-commerce" model to balance social contributions with financial sustainability.

2.5%. Hangzhou Judao Investment Management Company represented 110 small shareholders, holding 6.5%. Another individual investor held 1%.

Wei recalled, "After watching the plastic book covers video, more and more parents in our WeChat groups started requesting safe book covers. They asked, 'Daddy Wei, can you please tell us which are good, instead of which products are hazardous?'" To Wei, finding the problem was one thing, but solving it was another. To find high-quality, non-hazardous plastic book covers, Wei visited many manufacturers. After multiple comparisons, he chose a firm in Shanghai that followed a relatively good manufacturing process. Wei showed the manager his test report and explained that it would help children if book covers were produced using food-grade plastics. However, the manager said this was not possible because of the high material cost.

As Wei knew that the manager had a son in kindergarten, he paid a second visit. He asked the manager how he could continue to produce unsafe products when he knew his son was using them every day. Wei offered to purchase the book covers if the manager would switch to using food-grade plastics that passed the Daddy Lab's higher safety standard. The manager was moved by his words and agreed to produce samples of the new covers. After they received positive test results, Wei put in an order.

Daddy Lab started selling the new covers online on its "Daddy's Recommendations" online store on Youzan,[8] at the price of product cost plus logistic cost. Within a week, it received more than 5,000 group purchase orders and sold most of its inventory.[9] Following this initial positive reception from parents, Daddy Lab started selling more high-quality, safe products requested by followers on its online store. By October 2015, Daddy Lab's monthly revenue was about ¥300,000.

In June 2016, Wei won first prize at the 4th Social Entrepreneurs Star Competition. He became more determined to apply the "internet celebrity + e-commerce" model to support his social mission. By the end of 2016, more than 40,000 parents had made purchases on Daddy Lab's online store. In March 2017, Daddy Lab opened its online store on Taobao and started to sell more products from more categories (see Exhibit 4).

However, in contrast to many other online stores that sold many types of items in each product category, it followed four basic rules.

First, Daddy Lab would never accept cooperation that was purely commercial or that might undermine Wei's control and jeopardize its social purpose. For example, a well-known brand wanted Daddy Lab to recommend and sell its product. This brand's profile would guarantee more sales, but Wei saw it as a purely commercial activity that could weaken his control over the safety and quality of its products sold. He refused the proposal.

---

8 Youzan was an internet and mobile retail service provider that aimed to provide business owners with micro-stores and complete mobile retail solutions.

9 At the beginning of the spring semester in February 2016, the Quality and Technology Supervision Bureau in Shanghai and Jiangsu conducted special examinations on plastic book covers and included PAHs and DEHP in tests.

Second, Daddy Lab would include the test report from the independent institutions and the manufacturer's website for each product they offered for sale. Wei believed that the key to high-quality non-hazardous products was not related to laboratory testing but stemmed from "honest" manufacturers. The third-party testing report validated the impartiality of Daddy Lab's certifications and emphasized its commitment to identifying and working with "honest" manufacturers.

Third, Daddy Lab only chose to sell one of all qualified products that passed the laboratory tests for a particular category. It would still recommend the other qualified products to consumers. When choosing among these qualified products, the primary consideration was safety. For example, while Daddy Lab tested 32 brands of sunblock, finding that 10% contained harmful chemical substances and only five were safe and effective as claimed. Daddy Lab would recommend all five, but among these, it would choose one to sell—usually the most profitable—on its e-commerce platform.

Fourth, Wei knew that most of his customers were already followers and their needs were his priority. To better maintain a good relationship with them, Daddy Lab set up several customer-friendly rules. For example, if a customer did not like one of Daddy Lab's products, they could unconditionally return it. To avoid losing their support after an unsatisfactory purchasing experience, the company used special cards to make returns and exchanges easy (see Exhibit 5). A customer once filed a complaint to Daddy Lab's after-sales team that a batch of its table lamps had quality problems. Daddy Lab conducted a thorough test and verified the issues raised. Then it communicated these problems to the manufacturer and recalled all lamps in the same batch. To Wei, those customers served as another layer of quality control.

5 Establishing Standards and Driving Social Reform

From Wei's perspective, Daddy Lab's role was to determine which consumer products were hazardous and make them known to supervising authorities to push for more robust regulatory action and improved standards.

For example, in the middle of 2016, many parents requested testing of synthetic running tracks used in schools. Daddy Lab's team conducted on-site inspections and tested samples from 14 schools. It detected seven hazardous substances exceeding the maximum acceptable standard in the tracks. Daddy Lab's report drew widespread public attention. Subsequently, the Zhejiang provincial education department sent an investigation team to the school. After confirming that the tracks contained excessive amounts of hazardous substances, they ordered their dismantling. Many other provinces released new standards for synthetic running tracks to regulate the industry. In November 2016, the Ministry of Education also updated standards to test for more hazardous substances.[3]

Nevertheless, there were voices of skepticism. A raw material supplier for running tracks snapped at Wei during a call, "The tire granules we purchased have already passed safety testing. How can you tell such a blatant lie?"[4] However, as Wei explained, "Track-related standards only include tests for eight chemicals in the production and application process, manufacturers may add other hazardous substances." In other words, though raw materials passed tests and met national standards, it did not mean the final product was safe.

Wei said, "We should not blame the government for this. The process of change has to be gradual. We are faced with an astonishing variety of products due to the rapid development of science and technologies. One of the most effective ways for better supervision is to update existing standards. However, the tremendous number of products in the vast Chinese market makes it impossible to rely solely on government supervision. Industries should regulate themselves, and consumers should be able to differentiate the good from the bad. Enterprises like us can work as a supplemental force pushing the market into a virtuous circle."[5]

Even so, some laboratories that had previously accepted Daddy Lab's testing requests refused further requests over concerns the tests could affect future business with large corporate clients. Wei also received several threatening phone calls from manufacturers. "Sometimes when I received a call from an unknown number, the voice would say 'if you continue like this, it will not end well. ' Before hanging up, they would remind me to watch my back," he said. "It is lucky that I have my followers' support. Some of them volunteered their services to act as my legal counsel, giving me invaluable advice and assistance."

To maintain good relations with manufacturers and local authorities, Daddy Lab only released its post-test analysis (including the date, expenses, methods, chemical content analysis, and recommendations) without details of the brands or manufacturers involved. Wei said, "It is the government's duty to expose poor- quality brands."[6] In January 2018, Zhejiang Provincial Administration of Quality and Technology Supervision named the social enterprise one of 16 authorized institutions to test product quality and safety.

6 Amplifying Social Impact

> When you are doing something right, you feel that everyone in the world is standing by your side.
>
> —Wenfeng Wei

Knowing that Daddy Lab was winning the trust of more and more parents, Wei sought more ways to benefit his followers. He noticed that some were attempting to raise funds for children with leukemia via WeChat Moments. Many parents believed that newly renovated homes were a major cause of leukemia in children. Daddy Lab wanted to provide portable high-accuracy formaldehyde detectors to help them measure formaldehyde concentration in their homes. Since a single device cost far more than what an average family could afford, he raised ¥50,000 through crowd-funding from 487 parents and bought three detectors. In July 2016, Daddy Lab launched a formaldehyde detector lending program nationwide.

Followers who had recently renovated their home could apply to use the device free of charge, without paying a deposit or signing any agreement. They would leave a message in the lending diary via the WeChat account to apply to use them. The diary's title page read, "Be simple, and the world will be a fairyland." The program was hailed as a trust experiment online and gained immediate popularity. Later, another 100 detectors were purchased and put into use. By January 2017, the program had reached over 6,000 families (30,000+ rooms) in 29 provinces, and 39% of those rooms had formaldehyde concentration exceeding standards. All users took good care of the devices, and none were lost or broken. Through this project, Daddy Lab attracted 500,000 additional followers.

To better meet the high demand and market opportunities created by this service, Daddy Lab officially launched the "Love Drifting" WeChat mini- program[10] in July 2018 and created a similar applet on Douyin, China's localized version of TikTok.[11] In addition to providing free testing for followers who applied in advance, the mini-program allowed followers who urgently needed to use a device to pay ¥100 for quick access.[12] This project was a great success, accumulating more than 1.5 million users by the end of 2018. In terms of Daddy Lab's social mission, the project helped users test over 60,000 rooms, of which 44% exceeded the acceptable rate of formaldehyde concentration. By the end of 2018, some 5,377 customers had donated between ¥10 and ¥50 to sponsor the project's operations. This resulted in a total project income of ¥3.1 million, against a total expenditure of ¥3.4 million.

[10] WeChat Mini-programs are powerful small applications directly integrated inside WeChat messaging application. Daddy Lab's Love Drifting mini-program was developed to serve more needs of detecting formaldehyde concentration.

[11] Launched in September 2016, Douyin is a Chinese viral video-sharing social network. TikTok is the platform's international version.

[12] When it was launched, the fee was ¥200 each time, within one year the fee reduced to ¥100 each time.

Daddy Lab also launched a series of charity events through its WeChat groups and online store. For example, in February 2017, Daddy Lab donated over 400 pieces of stationery in the name of its parent-supporters to Xintian Primary School in Bijie, Guizhou, one of China's poorest provinces.

7 Daddy Lab's Dilemma

The social enterprise attracted widespread attention with its mission. In 2018, total views of its WeChat articles and videos hit 20 million while followers exceeded 1.7 million. Cumulative Douyin views reached 60.3 million, with the number of followers reaching 6.9 million by the end of 2018. Its influence across China's social media landscape continued to expand (see Exhibit 6).

The year 2018 saw rising revenue, product categories and repeat customer rate. About 10% of followers were online customers. By the end of the year, it had 50 employees, with an expanded management team and an increasing number of shareholders (see Exhibit 7).

Daddy Lab's success attracted potential investors, and its financial stability provided Wei with greater bargaining power in negotiations. Given his social mission and the need to maintain company control, Wei opted for bank loans. "If we get ¥10 million from investors for 10% of shares, we will lose 10% of control over our business. If we borrow money from the bank, we will not lose any control, and often we can get preferential interest rates," he explained.

Despite its achievements, Daddy Lab faced many uncertainties. "Our biggest challenge is the dilemma of being a 'reviewer' and a 'seller.'" Wei said. Daddy Lab's purpose was to protect children and their families from potentially hazardous consumer products by testing (i.e., being a "reviewer"). Meanwhile, to have a long-term social impact, it applied the e-commerce model to generate a sustainable source of revenue and profits (i.e., being a "seller"). Although the firm had been economically sustainable through product sales since 2017, Wei wondered how Daddy Lab's model of selling more products would impact its credibility as a neutral and impartial reviewer. Some suppliers (who had received unfavorable reviews) and even some customers questioned the impartiality of its testing methods and results. They argued that although it sent products for third-party testing, the selection process of products and institutions was not transparent. Moreover, they had to rely on Daddy Lab's interpretations and recommendations. Could they trust the enterprise as a neutral and impartial reviewer?

This dual roles dilemma was intertwined with Daddy Lab's dual social and financial goals. For example, when potential investors suggested that Daddy Lab should serve manufacturers as a specialized testing and certification center to earn more money, Wei worried that it would undermine his social mission. He believed that it would be difficult to stay neutral if Daddy Lab conducted tests for business clients and charged fees for domestic certifications. Wei continually searched for the right balance between Daddy Lab's social mission and its for-profit online business to ensure sustainability. Wei was aware that breaking the equilibrium between social or financial aims could jeopardize Daddy Lab's long-term future. Moving forward, could the enterprise maintain its credibility among followers as an impartial reviewer while also seeking profits? How could Wei develop a more sustainable model?

Exhibit 1 China's Institutional Environment for Product Safety and Product Testing Industry

China has its own product quality law.[13] The PRC National People's Congress and the State Council assigned various agencies specific tasks to regulate and supervise product quality and safety. The AQSIQ (Administration of Quality Supervision, Inspection, and Quarantine) offices oversaw and regulated the quality and safety of products manufactured in China and those imported into China at central and local levels. The State Administration for Industry and Commerce and its local offices oversee any quality and safety issues. Other relevant authorities have the power to supervise product quality and safety in their own industrial sectors. Under PRC law, manufacturers must comply with compulsory state and industrial product safety standards concerning food, agricultural products, containers, drugs, and other relevant products. Manufacturers must obtain permits from the government to produce or distribute certain regulated products. They are also liable for consumer injuries or property damage caused byproduct defects.

- China's product safety laws and standards were relatively lax compared with those of many developed countries. For example, multiple international brands (e.g., Starbucks, Subway and McDonald) were found in 2014 to have used a chemical substance known as azodicarbonamide in their products in China. Some even claimed that its use as a food additive was fully compliant with local food safety regulations. However, Singapore, Australia, Japan and the EU had already banned azodicarbonamide's use in food production long before this time due to potential hazards.

[13] URL: http://english.mofcom.gov.cn/article/policyrelease/Businessregulations/201303/20130300046024.shtml.

Table 1 Number of Product Testing Organizations and Their Revenues in China

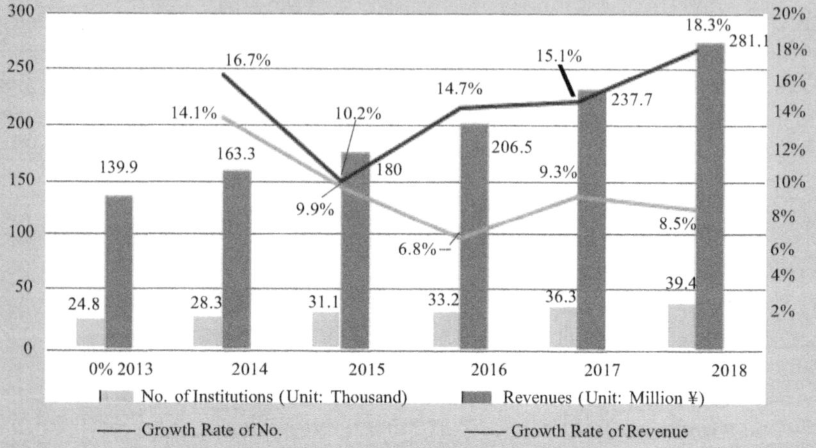

When consumers got injured, they could file a complaint to the China Consumer Association (CCA) as well as local and grassroots associations nationwide. The CCA monitored goods and services to protect consumer rights and interests. The CCA provided up-to-date consumer information and advice on its website. However, these protections often only covered aftersales scenarios.

From 2013, more and more product testing organizations emerged in China (see Table 1). Most provided services for businesses rather than individuals, as individual testing services were very costly. About 52% of these organizations focused on industrial testing, 22% on life science, food and environment, and only 9% on consumer products. Barriers to entry were high amid low market concentration and fierce competition. In 2016, about 55% of these organizations were state-owned institutions, and 43% were private. Among the 39,472 testing organizations in 2018, 79% were small (with 10–100 employees),and only 1% had more than 500 employees.

Source USCBC, "Overview of China's Product Safety Regime," China Business Review, January 1, 2010, accessed April 28, 2021, https://www.chinabusinessreview.com/overview-of-chinas-product-safety-regime/; "Starbucks confirms the use of chemical food additive in Chinese mainland, Subway and McDonald's say otherwise," Global Times, February 10, 2014, accessed April 28, 2021, https://www.globaltimes.cn/content/841686.shtml. "Anlysis on Market Size and the Five Development Opportunities of the Third-party Product Testing Institutions in China," www.chyxx.com, October 23, 2019, accessed April 28, 2021, https://www.chyxx.com/industry/201910/796153.html. "Status Quo and Prospect of China's Testing Industry in 2019; The Market Size was Expected to Expand to Reach 650 billion in 2024," Qianzhan.com,

December 26, 2019, accessed April 28, 2021, https://bg.qianzhan.com/ trends/ detail/506/191226-92997c31.html.

Exhibit 2

Daddy Lab's Announcement for Small Shareholders in the First Round of Crowdfunding

Dear friends who have supported Daddy Lab for the past four months:

How time flies! It's been four-and-a-half months since Daddy Lab was born on August 25. As I write this announcement, many WeChat group members who knew of my plan in advance have already signed up for crowdfunding, and places quickly ran out. My team and I are delighted to hear this news.

In the past four months, I have got to know hundreds of parents. We created a WeChat group full of love. We built many other groups, including those for technical exchanges, publicity, food safety, and a special hospital- themed group headed by a doctor. We tested many products, from student supplies and daily necessities to food. Anything that might contain hazardous substances fell into one of our testing categories.

This decision dates back to October when some group members joked that they could donate money to become Daddy Lab shareholders. I thought about it thoroughly. The platform was initially intended to serve them, and I thought it might be possible to do it together. Then I began getting down to it, and it took until now to finally put everything in place. I am very sorry for making you wait so long. But maybe it is better this way, since it is nearly the end of the year, and soon you will receive your annual bonus to better support us!

For this crowdfunding round, we need wisdom, social connections, resources and funds. We sincerely hope that Daddy Lab can better serve the public through our concerted efforts and resources and keep our children away from hazards.

There will be a launch event at noon on January 13 presented by www.DreamMove.cn. The roadshow will start at 3 p.m., on January 16. You are welcome to participate! Those present at the event will receive exquisite gifts, and dinner is my treat.

(I would like to thank DY Rice for providing the gifts, which of course, have passed our tests.)

Roadshow date: 3 p.m. – 5 p.m., January 16

Address: Epoch Space, 2nd Floor, Zhejiang University National Science Park, 511 Jianye Road, Binjiang District, Hangzhou

The funding target is ¥1.7 million, with 8.5% of shares offered. The funds will be used for:

- Product testing (est. 45 types of products in 2016)

- Brand promotion (both online and offline)
- Operations (salary and office expenses)

Lead investor for equity-based crowdfunding: Shanghai Niejing Investment Management

Equity-based crowdfunding platform: DreamMove.cn

Note DreamMove was an independent third-party agency specializing in crowdfunding investment management.

Source The article titled "Equity-based Crowdfunding Officially Started," was released on Daddy Lab's WeChat official account on January 13, 2016.

Exhibit 3 Application Form for Testing

Dear parents:

We are currently selecting lamp models for testing, and thank you for your patience. The products now under testing include vacuum flasks, table mats, document wallets and children's modeling clay. While many other products are on the list, it is impossible to meet everyone's needs. Therefore, we have made this simple form to gain a basic understanding of your ideas.

If you are unsure of any products' safety in your house, please click the link to tell us your thoughts.

WeChat ID: ________	Name:
Mobile number: ________	Who am I:
	O a father O a mother O a parent-to-
be Occupation: ________	City:
Products to be tested: ________	Photo of the product
Upload file (less than 500 MB):	
What do you want to say to Daddy Wei?	

Source The article titled "Crowdfunding-based Testing Launched by Parents," was released on Daddy Lab's WeChat official account on October 30, 2015.

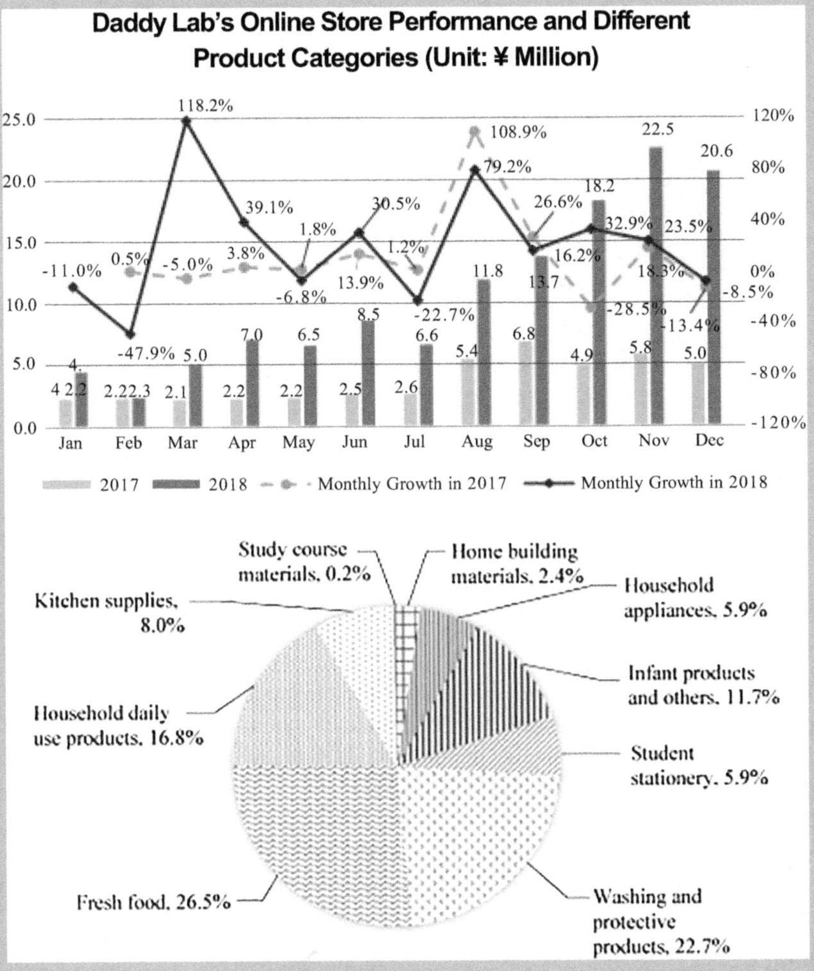

Exhibit 4 Daddy Lab's online store performance and different product categories (Unit: ¥ Million)

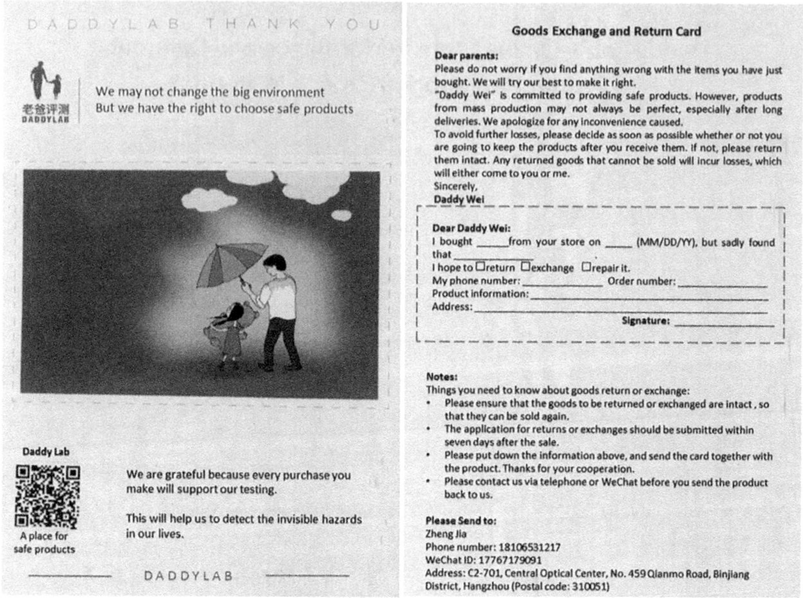

Exhibit 5 Goods return and exchange card. *Source* Daddy Lab

In 2018, Taobao and Youzan contributed about 39% and 60% of the total revenue, respectively. The other 1% came via other media. About 5% of the visitors ordered on Daddy Lab's online stores. By the end of 2018, the total number of customers on Daddy Lab's online stores was close to 400,000, 68% of which were new customers in 2018. There were 155,000 Youzan customers and 242,000 Taobao customers. The repurchasing rate on Youzan was 41%, and the rate on Taobao was 38%. *Note* The numbers shown in the pie chart refered to each category's proportion of the total stock keeping units (SKUs).

Exhibit 6

Platform	Total Number of Fans/ Followers	Total Views/Clicks	Total Posts
WeChat	1.7 million	20.0 million	11,500
Douyin	6.9 million	60.3 million	150
Toutiao	0.2 million	11.1 million	81
Zhihu	233,000	24.5 million	136
Weibo	49,000	NA	308
Daddy Wei Personal Account (Weibo)	151,000	NA	70

Source Provided by Daddy Lab

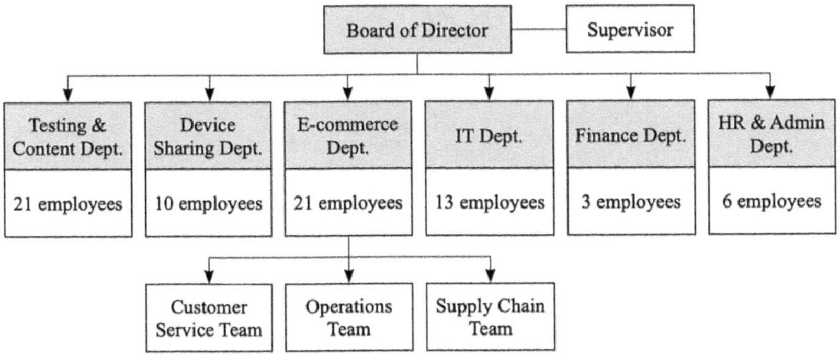

Exhibit 7 Daddy Lab's organizational chart. *Note* This organizational chart was updated on January 1, 2019.*Source* Daddy Lab

Endnotes

1. Yang Shuyuan, Lin Huan, "The fighting of an 'angry' daddy," Jiefang Daily, March 19, 2016, accessed September 18, 2017, http://newspaper.jfdaily.com/jfrb/html/2016-03/19/content_180938.htm.
2. Zhang Wei, "Daddy Wenfeng Wei declares war on 'poisonous' covers and tracks," Beijing News, September 14, 2016, accessed September 18, 2017, https://www.sohu.com/a/114318920_114988.
3. Huang Shulun, Yuan Suwen, Zhou Chen, Quan Ziqing, and Wu Meiwei, "The internet celebrity-Daddy Lab and consumers' rights protection dilemma," caixin.com, May 3, 2017, accessed September 18, 2017, https://www.myzaker.com/article/590983c61bc8e0fa78000000/.
4. Wu Ziru, "Wei Wenfeng, a science geek and angry youth, hopes to build a world without hazards," China Newsweek, November 29, 2016, accessed September 18, 2017, http://news.innewsweek.cn/news/people/235.html.
5. Zhang Wei, "Daddy Wei Wenfeng declares war against 'poisonous' wrapping and track," Beijing News, September 14, 2016, accessed September 18, 2017, https://www.sohu.com/a/114318920_114988.
6. Huang Shulun, Yuan Suwen, Zhou Chen, Quan Ziqing, and Wu Meiwei, "The internet celebrity-Daddy Lab and consumers' rights protection dilemma," caixin.com, May 3, 2017, accessed September 18, 2017, https://www.myzaker.com/article/590983c61bc8e0fa78000000/.

SHEIN: Redefining Global Fast Fashion

In June 2021, China-based online-only retailer SHEIN (Shein) surpassed global giants Zara[1] and H&M[2] to become the largest fast fashion retailer in the US by sales, according to data analytics platform Earnest Research. As of June 16, 2021, Shein comprised 28% of US fast fashion sales, ahead of H&M (20%), Zara (11%), Forever 21[3] (10%), and Fashion Nova[4] (8%) [1] (See Exhibit 1). The platform attributed Shein's sharp growth to the brand's mobile-first strategy, which caught on with consumers in a big way during the COVID–19[5] pandemic that accelerated the adoption of mobile and other forms of digital shopping.

Shein, a global B2C fast fashion brand founded in 2008 by Chris Xu (Chris), mainly focused on women's wear but also offered men's apparel, children's clothes,

[1] Zara is a Spanish clothing retailer based in Galicia, Spain. Founded in 1975, it is the flagship chain store of the Inditex group. Zara is one of the largest international fast fashion companies in the world, operating over 2,259 stores in 96 countries globally as of 2020.

[2] H & M Hennes & Mauritz AB (H&M) is a Swedish multinational retail-clothing company, known for its fast- fashion clothing. The discount retailer, known for its affordable prices, was founded in Sweden in 1947.

[3] Forever 21, Inc., headquartered in Los Angeles, California, is a fashion retailer of women's, men's, and kids clothing and accessories and is known for offering the hottest fashion trends at a great value to consumers. Founded in 1984, Forever 21 operates more than 550 stores in 27 countries around the world.

[4] Fashion Nova is a US based fast fashion retail company. The company operates online and as well has brick-and- mortar stores.

[5] COVID–19 (Coronavirus Disease of 2019) declared as a pandemic by the WHO on March 11, 2020, is caused by the severe acute respiratory syndrome coronavirus. The pandemic caused severe social and economic disruption, affecting travel, industries, academics, sports, and cultural and political events.

Syeda Maseeha Qumer of ICFAI Business School developed this case. The case aims to provide the basis for classroom discussion rather than illustrate effective or ineffective handling of a management situation. This case was the Best Case Award of 2021 Global Contest for the Best China-Focused Cases.

China-Focused Cases, https://doi.org/10.1007/978-981-97-8580-3_3

accessories, shoes, bags, and other fashion items. Its products were available to customers in more than 220 countries, but it did not sell to China. The brand was popular among Gen Z and young millennial shoppers for its fashion-forward trendy designs, affordable prices, and wide assortment of products. The online fast fashion brand undercut rivals on price and used innovative digital marketing strategies to win over young shoppers. Shein pioneered the real-time fast fashion business model which cut design to production from three weeks to as little as seven days and added, on an average, nearly 2,000 new styles to its website every week at significantly lower price points than competitors such as Zara and H&M. The pandemic catapulted Shein to global success as the retailer generated an estimated US$10 billion in revenue in 2020.[2]

Despite its phenomenal success, Shein came under fire for its fast fashion practices that critics alleged encouraged over consumption, generated waste, and impacted the environment negatively. Shein was also subjected to allegations of engaging child labor in its supply chain. Further, the retailer was accused of cultural and design appropriation and creating copycat products of designer wear. Meanwhile, there were numerous complaints on social media over poor product quality that hurt its reputation. Moreover, the firm's lack of transparency and reclusiveness attracted unwanted media attention, with critics questioning whether Shein's low prices would be sustainable if high ethical standards were maintained. Growing competition was also a concern for Shein as several low-priced online retailers such as Blush Mark, Romwe, and Poshmark were flooding the fast fashion market. According to some analysts, Shein's future popularity was at stake in the US, its biggest market, as physical stores reopened and footfall increased post-pandemic. "My takeaway is that the pandemic catapulted Shein to its current position, and the momentum persisted even as the US economy began to open up",[3] commented blogger Yiqin Fu. "It remains to be seen how long the interest in Shein will last post-pandemic and whether the usual seasonality trends apply. As with most things in life", Shein's success is both "being in the right place at the right time" and "working hard to stay prepared."

Going forward, the challenges before Chris were to ensure long-term sustainable growth, enhance the customer base, and maintain a dominant position in the global fast fashion market. Some critics wondered whether Shein could maintain its growth momentum or whether it would succumb to competition. Could it supplant Zara and H&M as the world's largest clothing retailer? Should Shein open brick-and-mortar stores to attract more customers? Would a lack of transparency negatively affect Shein's appeal going forward? Was Shein's growth model sustainable in the long run?

1 Background Note

Shein was launched in 2008 by Chris,[6] a search engine optimization marketing specialist, under the domain name SheInside.com. The online platform initially sold wedding dresses to western customers. Slowly, Shein began to expand its offerings and, alongside wedding dresses, began to sell womenswear. This, over a period of time, became the main staple of its business. Throughout the early 2010s, Shein launched overseas websites in Spain, France, Russia, Italy, and Germany. Back then, Shein was just an online platform and was not involved in any aspect of garment design or manufacturing. It did not have its own supply chain. The retailer preferred to source goods directly from Shisanhang Garment Wholesale Market in Guangzhou.[7] It then uploaded photos of these clothes onto its website and purchased the goods to fulfil each order that came in. There was no factory and no inventory. It operated much like a dropshipping business that sold products from third-party wholesalers directly to overseas shoppers. The dropshippers did not even have to photograph products—the pictures came from the wholesale sellers.

In 2012, Shein expanded its offerings to include cosmetics, shoes, bags, and jewellery, in addition to womenswear. In 2014, it established its own supply chain system, transforming itself into a fully integrated retailer. The same year, Shein launched its mobile shopping app on the App store. In 2015, Chris shortened the domain name from SheInside to Shein and rebranded the company from a website with a focus on fashion to a fully-fledged fast fashion brand with a website. In 2015, Shein shifted its headquarters from Nanjing to Panyu[8] in Guangzhou—China's leading clothes manufacturing hub. Chris began to build up his own clothing and production line. He set up an in-house design team responsible for designs and prototypes for fast production. The team identified designs trending in the West and produced similar items ready for export in just a few days. When Shein moved its supply chain operations center to Panyu, almost all the manufacturers it worked with relocated.

In 2015, Shein acquired LA-based fashion brand MakeMeChic and another Chinese e-commerce retailer Romwe. By 2016, Chris had assembled a team of 800 designers and prototypers, dedicated to rapidly producing Shein-branded clothes. The brand advertised on daytime television shows in the US, and fashion influencers showcased its products and hauls. Shein became a household name overnight. Its annual sales totaled 4 billion yuan in 2016 and exceeded 10 billion yuan in 2017.[4] Despite its popularity, the Shein brand was practically unknown to Chinese consumers as the retailer did not sell directly in China. However, Shein products

[6] Chris was born in 1984 in Shandong Province, China, and graduated from Qingdao University of Science and Technology in 2007 after which he moved to Nanjing. Before founding Shein, Chris was reportedly an employee of Alldao, a Nanjing-headquartered cross-border services consultancy, where he worked in search engine optimization (SEO) operations.

[7] Shein sourced its products from China's wholesale clothing market in Guangzhou, a region where many Chinese garment factories and markets are centralized.

[8] Panyu is a clothes manufacturing hub. It is a district of Guangzhou in China's Guangdong province.

were available on online Chinese stores such as Alibaba. Its business was focused on exporting abroad.

Shein kept a low profile and was reclusive, with little known about its inner workings despite being one of China's most valuable privately-held businesses. According to an investor, the retailer wanted to lay low and protect its business secrets from rivals. Some analysts were of the view that the retailer was deliberately downplaying its Chinese roots amid geopolitical tensions and increased regulatory oversight over China-based companies.

In the midst of rising biases and political controversies, Shein did not disclose who its investors were but Chinese media reports listed JAFCO Asia, Greenwoods Asset Management, IDG Capital, Sequoia Capital China, Tiger Global, and Shunwei Capital among its backers. In January 2019, Shein raised US$500 million from Sequoia China and Tiger Global at a US$5 billion valuation (See Exhibit 2).

Shein did not operate any permanent physical stores; instead, it hosted a series of pop-ups in various cities. Navigation was convenient for buyers on the Shein website. All products were divided into categories: Men, Women, and Children; standard sizes and models, Size +; seasonal collections; promotions and sales; fashion trends and style directions. Shein's had a user-friendly mobile app interface with appealing photos that facilitated the searching and browsing of products based on the specific demands of shoppers. The retailer consistently updated its app with new features like adding videos on its product pages and category pages split into trends versus clothing categories.

Shein did not pay export taxes on any of its products. In 2018, as trade relations between the world's two biggest economies were spiraling downward, China responded to a new round of US tariffs by effectively waiving export taxes for direct-to-consumer companies. Since Shein shipped its orders directly to customers from Chinese warehouses, packages worthless than US$800, or small-value shipments, generally remained duty-free.[5] As a result, Shein managed to avoid paying both export and import taxes, something brick-and-mortar retailers were not able to do. This dramatically reduced costs for the company and its suppliers, allowing them to undercut their global competition.

In 2019, the company launched an average of 10,000 new products a month.[6] Its revenue was US$2.83 billion in 2019.[7] As of June 2021, Shein had a presence in more than 220 countries globally. The online retailer employed more than 10,000 people.

2 Business Model

Experts attributed Shein's success to its aggressive, data-driven, real-time fast-fashion business model that cut the time from design of a new garment to mass production from 2–3 weeks to just 5–7 days. According to Matthew Brennan (Brennan), a tech analyst, "Real-time fashion refers to the model that Shein's developed whereby you're in the Shein app, and you put something in your cart. When they upload a new item, they can actually update the systems that they have in the backend, whereby the action that you take can immediately have an effect on the factory floor. So, everything from the website backend through to the supply chain management system is all linked together."[8]

Shein derived new product ideas from the search and social media behavior within a specific country. It used in-house algorithms and data science to identify new trends. Instead of relying on designers to study and predict fashion trends, Shein relied on Google Trends[9] to identify what was in fashion in different countries and then combined that with in-app and user data to predict popular clothing styles. Shein also studied competitor websites for real-time data analysis of the existing fashion trends in various individual markets. This customer data was used by Shein's design team to develop new designs in as little as three days. The designs were then automatically pushed to suppliers through the central Shein Enterprise Resource Planning (ERP) system to be manufactured and sold at limited volumes. Using real-time data, Shein was able to create a different, relevant offer for different countries and regions around the world without having to understand the cultural nuances between those countries. Through high-volume manufacturing, Shein benefited from economies of scale, according to experts.

Once new items were uploaded to its platform, Shein monitored user behavior, such as clicks and additions to virtual shopping carts, to forecast demand and inventory needs. The company followed an on-demand business model wherein new products were created in small batches of around 100 items, and production was ramped up depending on their popularity. This resulted in less wastage. Shein linked in-app and on-site user behavior to the backend to automatically forecast demand and adjust inventory in real-time. If specific designs seemed popular based on the viewing and buying behavior on the website, the order volume for manufacturing increased in real-time through the ERP. If it did not sell out quickly, Shein sold the remaining pieces and abandoned that particular design. "For fast fashion, speed is really important, and if you're able to quickly spin up when an item is doing well, that gives you a sustainable advantage over your competitors,"[9] said Brennan.

The suppliers were required to use a highly automated supply chain management system that utilized real-time trend data to commission new designs and monitor orders. The supply-chain management software allowed Shein to closely monitor the manufacturing process and share real-time customer search data with suppliers to guide design and production. It generated recommendations for raw materials and where to buy them. An executive from a rival company said, "Every area of their website is tied to the ERP (enterprise resource planning) system and their manufacturing. So they are live-updating their manufacturing capability based on who's looking at what on the website and who's buying what."[10]

---

[9] Google Trends is a free tool that provides data and graphs on the popularity of specific search terms used on Google and YouTube.

3 Affordable Prices

Shein's mission was "everyone can enjoy the beauty of fashion," and it aimed to offer stylish quality clothing at appealing prices to every user in the world. The affordability of clothes on Shein made it an attractive platform for price-conscious teenagers. At Shein, prices were rock-bottom, with T-shirts for US$7, dresses for US$12, jeans for US$17, and coats for US$28.[11] The e-commerce site was popular among millennials and was known for its cheap fashion items, which were similar to those of high-street stores, such as H&M and Zara (See Exhibit 3). A pair of jeans seemingly comparable in appearance and quality to the one Zara sold for US$49.90 was reportedly available for just US$17 on Shein.[12] According to Anushka Sachan, a university student, "It is pretty addictive. I just stopped buying from H&M when I started using Shein. Because I was getting the same things that I saw at H&M, but like, for cheaper."[13]

Shein enticed young price-conscious customers through a barrage of discounts for its low-cost styles. Additionally, the company offered generous shipping deals in return for ordering in bulk or writing feedback on its app or website. Moreover, a battery of promotional codes allowed shoppers to lower the bill or qualify for free shipping. "The brand appeals to young shoppers like myself because of the way they keep up with trends. Not all of us have $200 to spend on a top that will be only trendy for the summer, so Shein gives a solution to that problem that just about every teen faces,"[14] said Tricia Panlaqui, a YouTuber.

4 Wide Assortment

Shein offered an incredibly wide range of clothes in different styles, colors, patterns, and sizes. Each day the selections were different. It uploaded hundreds of new trendy designs on its website and app every week. Reportedly Shein added between 500 and 2000 new items on its website every day. Retail analysts noted that 70% of its products were on the site for less than three months. "We do this because we believe that the clothes we wear reflect our personalities, and we want to empower today's women to explore and express their individuality,"[15] stated the company. While fast fashion retailers such as H&M and Zara introduced new pieces after going through a three-week process to come out with new designs, Shein was able to use real-time data to cut this process to 5–7 days. "They're making fast fashion look slow. They've changed the model,"[16] said Erin Schmidt (Schmidt), a senior analyst at Coresight Research, a global advisory and research firm.

Shein's website featured clothes for women for all occasions and in all sizes, including a huge collection of Plus Size styles that were rare on the market. They offered clothes up to a 5XL size which was far beyond what rivals such as H&M and

Zara offered. Products in the Curve + Plus range made up 16% of the overall assortment at Shein compared to 14% at Boohoo[10] and 9% at Forever 21.[17] In addition, there were categories for men and children, as well. As of June 2021, womenswear made up 81% of products available on Shein's US website, followed by kidswear at 12%, and menswear at 7%. Shein also offered in-house brands in order to attract different customers. These included MOTF, a premium label that used high-quality materials and sustainable fabrics at low prices. Emery Rose was promoted as a lifestyle collection dedicated to Cottage core essentials, while GLOWMODE offered active wear and DAZY provided a streetwear line. Expanding outside of fashion, Shein also stocked petwear, homeware, beauty products, and stationery.

In 2020, Shein launched 150,000 new items through the year, with an average of more than 10,000 new items per month.[18] For instance, in March 2021, Shein's women's wear category alone showcased an average of 2,000 new products per day. While the pandemic caused product arrivals to contract on its competitors' websites, the number of styles available on the Shein US site outpaced 2020 by 153% and 2019 by 370%.[19]

In 2020, in a biannual survey called "Taking Stock with Teens" organized by Piper Sandler, an investment firm, Shein emerged as the second favorite shopping site for teenagers in the US. While Amazon had a large lead, with 54% of teens from upper-income households stating that it was their favorite e-commerce site, Shein with 7% of votes, overtook American companies like Nike, PacSun, and Urban Outfitters[20] (See Exhibit 4). It was also first on the list of brands that upper-income female teens said they were starting to wear, followed by retail clothing brands PacSun and Lululemon.

5 Robust Supply Chain

According to Coresight, Shein added an average of 2,800 new styles to its website each week.[21] This was possible because of its strong supply-chain setup that included material suppliers, manufacturing partners, and finished product vendors. Shein cut out the middlemen and built an advanced cross-border version of the Consumer to Manufacturer (C2M) model. Some analysts felt that Shein was taking advantage of China's manufacturing prowess, which allowed it to cut down on lead times significantly. Researchers estimated that its production schedule was as short as 3–7 days, compared to the average span of three weeks revealed by players like Zara. According to them, Shein's suppliers used the company's backend software, which allowed them to get immediate information on user clicks and orders. "They've integrated their systems with their factory. Based off of what is trending, like, what clicks, what sells, what starts to trend ... the algorithm goes to the factory and says: 'Start ordering material, start producing. ' So they've essentially cut out all of the middlemen,"[22] said Schmidt.

---

[10] Boohoo Group plc is a UK based online fashion retailer.

Shein maintained tight control over its supply chain, working with about 300 loyal suppliers. It required that the manufacturers contracted to make its clothes be located no more than a five-hour drive from its sourcing hub in the southern Chinese city of Guangzhou, according to the company. "Shein doesn't work with very large factories but [with] small to mid-sized workshops that pick up orders daily. It's very much like an Uber system, where new orders are coming into factory owners' phones,and they receive the order. It's very scrappy, but efficient,"[23] said Matthew Brennan, a tech analyst.

The company assessed suppliers based on a stringent set of key performance indicators (KPIs), including timeliness of on-demand procurement, timeliness of stock delivery, and defective rates of products. Suppliers were ranked in five grades, with the weakest 30% being eliminated from the roster. Reportedly, the suppliers were asked to deliver orders in seven to eight days, and sometimes in as little as three days, while the industry average lead time was 15–20 days. "They demand an order turnaround time of eight days (traditional factories take more than half a month), with a piece of clothing having fewer than three stray threads (each being shorter than 3 cm), with a margin for error limited to 2 cm,"[2424] said one supplier.

With all sales happening online, Shein's managers had a real-time view of the performance of each item. Because of its real-time customer feedback mechanism, Shein could order small batches of 100 pieces from its suppliers and adjust the size of the order based on customer feedback. This enabled it to keep a super-lean inventory. "Each new design is basically a bet because Shein can estimate how well a product is going to do, but it doesn't know for sure until it sells," Brennan explained. "Compared to its fast fashion competitors, Shein is able to take more bets, but at a lower risk. It's able to place very small initial orders with these factories, about 100 or even smaller."[25]

Improved demand predictions also allowed Shein to avoid an inventory glut, the most common problem clothing retailers faced. By centralizing inventory in a small number of large warehouses and then shipping directly to customers, Shein was able to push inventory turnover down to just 30 days, compared with an industry average of 150 days, according to a consultant. "If something works, you know about it really quick. If something fails, you only have a couple of hundred units, so how much are you really going to get hurt?"[26] said Michael Horowitz, partner at Retail ROI Ltd., a consulting firm based in Hong Kong. All of this—the demand prediction, fast iteration, small batches, and manufacturing relationships—meant that Shein eliminated waste and was able to deliver low prices on quality, trendy items.

Reportedly, Chris developed a close relationship with his suppliers—paying them on time, within 30–45 days as compared to the industry's normal billing practice of 90 days. He maintained a good rapport with manufacturers who relocated their operations alongside Shein in 2015. The retailer also offered loans to suppliers to help them grow.

6 Aggressive Marketing

Shein's target demographic was Gen Z consumers, mostly young female consumers with a taste for fashion, limited buying power, and extensive mobile usage. To attract young consumers, Shein adopted an aggressive marketing strategy that combined social media, user-generated content, and livestreaming as well as pop-up stores in key places such as Paris and London. Shein attracted young customers mainly through its mobile app, website, and social media networks such as Instagram, TikTok, and Facebook. About 70% of teens in the US shopped on Shein's mobile phone app, which boasted 24 million daily active users.[27] "First off, they focused on building a mobile app that feels more like a social media timeline than a regular shop. It relies on spontaneous discovery by recommendations rather than active search. Through the infinite product scroll with daily additions, tons of discounts, limited inventory, and personalized suggestions, they are successfully generating FOMO with their user base. It's so addictive that the hunt for new, limited items at lower prices than what their friends have access to has in itself become a reason to keep checking back in,"[28] noted Stijn Verhaeghe, a digital strategist.

As early as 2011, Shein began to place ads and promote its website on social platforms. For instance, photos from Shein's online store were used for promotion on Facebook, Instagram, YouTube, Pinterest, etc. Shein encouraged teenagers to upload photos and videos of themselves wearing Shein clothing on these platforms (See Exhibit 5). As of September 2021, Shein had about 22 million followers on its global Instagram account.[29] Shein's Facebook page had about 15 million followers. It also had a presence on Pinterest whose users were mostly female. On TikTok, Shein created armies of fashion bloggers supporting the brand and making posts with the hashtag #Shein. In April 2020 on TikTok alone, the #shein hashtag generated 6.2 billion views[30] (See Exhibit 6). In July 2021, Shein was the leading brand globally on Tiktok based on the number of mentions, with 6,625 for the month.[31] Its official TikTok account was also the third-fastest growing brand on the platform, recording 600% growth in July 2021. "TikTok and Shein is the perfect marriage because Shein offers an attainable price, and it is much more fun to watch people trying on their 'haul' than it is to scroll through pictures of people wearing clothes on Instagram or long videos on YouTube,"[32] said Mae Karwowski, chief executive of Obviously, an influencer agency.

According to analysts, Shein's affordability helped to create a subculture of internet shoppers, mostly teens, who posted Shein "haul" videos on TikTok, YouTube, and Instagram. In Shein's try-on hauls, influencers tried on products they either bought from or were gifted by the brand. According to Mark Greeven (Greeven), a professor of innovation and strategy at the IMD business school, "Looking at Gen Z, the growing cohort of young consumers eager to express themselves and be seen, Shein not only offers them clothes, but also a sense of participation and enjoyable experiences."[33]

Shein activated Key Opinion Consumers (KOCs) to create content, such as try-on haul videos, by giving them free clothes or shop credits. In Shein's affiliate programs, influencers earned a commission on all recommended sales simply by directing customers to Shein.com. These influencers received free clothing every month for their posts and earned 10%–20% commissions on recommended sales if they constantly posted photos and video posts on Instagram, YouTube, or TikTok.[34]

Shein was among the first online clothing retailers to use social media influencers called Key Opinion Leaders (KOLs) and celebrities to sell clothes. In 2020, it collaborated with Western celebrities who were popular among youngsters such as Katy Perry, Nick Jonas, Lil Nas X, Rita Ora, and Hailey Bieber, to promote its collections. In May 2020, Shein launched its very first global streaming event, "SHEIN Together", an online concert featuring special guests such as Katy Perry, Madeleine Petsch, and Little Nas X. According to Shein's website, the event raised US$135,000, which was donated toward supporting the global COVID–19 relief efforts.[35] TikTok's biggest star, Addison Rae, also promoted the company across her channels. In early 2021, Shein launched Shein X, an incubator program that aided independent designers by manufacturing, marketing, and selling their designs under their own name alongside the Shein X label. The program began with seven designers before it was extended indefinitely, widening the pool to work with 50 designers per month. Participants in the scheme received a percentage of the sales of their designs, while a scholarship of US$100,000 was awarded to one of them to launch their own fashion brand.

Shein also offered many kinds of discounts, countdown timers, and free shipping to increase customer retention. Especially during special events like Black Friday or weekends, the company organized livestreams on its website during the golden shopping hours (9pm–11pm) and offered customers special discounts. Shein set up a points system that rewarded users for a wide variety of actions such as verifying their email address, writing a product review, adding a picture of them wearing the item, participating in outfit competitions, watching live events, playing games, and posting pictures within a Show theme. Every 100 points were worth US$1, which could be spent on up to 70% of a total order. Commenting on Shein's success, Rex Pascual, editor at online casino OnlineCasinoMaxi.de, said, "User experience, engagement and retention are also at the forefront of what Shein does so successfully in its journey to prominence. Innovations such as gamification techniques that reward users for each time they login to the app ensures a loyal and active user base. Shein also has an effective ability to mix media and entertainment into the shopping experience, with events such as virtual fashion shows and live streams keeping existing users engaged with the app, while at the same time attracting untapped customers."[36]

7 Global Footprint

Despite being based in Nanjing, Shein did not sell in China and mostly focused on overseas markets. The company shipped to more than 200 countries around the world, including Europe, America, the Middle East, and Australia. The US was Shein's largest market. With websites for the US, Spain, France, Russia, Germany, Italy, Australia, and the Middle East, Shein shipped items from one of its many globally located warehouses. Shein had four R&D centers in Nanjing, Shenzhen, Guangzhou, and Hangzhou, as well as a global distribution network with six logistics centers in Foshan, Nansha, Belgium, India, and on the East and West Coasts of the US. It shipped 95% of its products directly from its central warehouse in Foshan, Guangdong. The retailer operated seven customer service centers, based out of Los Angeles, Liege, Manila, Yiwu, and Nanjing.

Shein entered the Middle East market in 2015. By 2016, some of its key suppliers were receiving orders to the tune of RMB 50 million (USD 7.7 million) annually. Shein's sales revenue in 2016 was RMB 4 billion (USD 617 million).[37] By 2017, it had exceeded RMB 10 billion (USD 1.5 billion). In 2018, 30% of Shein's sales came from the US, 20% from Europe, and another 20% from the Middle East.[38] Following its success in the Middle East, Shein began to expand to other markets and began investing heavily in India and Southeast Asia. It entered India in 2017 and in just a year reported over five million downloads in the country. However, in June 2020, Shein was banned in India along with 58 other Chinese apps due to cross-border tensions between China and India. Shein re-entered the Indian market through Amazon's annual Prime Day sale in July 2021. In September 2020, Shein became the most popular fashion website in Israel. For the first time ever in Israel, purchases on Shein were higher than total purchases on British fashion websites such as Asos and Next with 62% of consumers making purchases on Shein's website, compared to 21% on Next.com,[11] and 17% on ASOS.[12][39]

According to analysts, Shein had more success selling directly to Western consumers than any other Chinese firm in history. In May 2021, it overtook e-commerce giant Amazon for the first time as the most downloaded shopping app on iOS and Android phones in the US, according to App Annie and SensorTower[40][40] (See Exhibit 7). Shein was the top iOS shopping app in 54 countries and ranked top in the category on Android devices across 13 countries. Shein ranked among the top ten shopping apps in the two main markets in the Middle East: the UAE and Saudi Arabia. The Chinese ultra-fast fashion retailer was the third most visited fashion e-commerce site in the UK, behind only Next and ASOS.

In September 2020, the Shein app saw 10.3 million downloads globally from across the App Store and Google Play, according to analytics platform Sensor Tower data. In contrast, H&M's mobile app hit about 2.5 million, and Zara saw 2 million.[41] As of October 2020, Shein had reached 229.4 million downloads, compared to H&M's 123.5 million and Zara's 90.6 million.[42] In the week of September 27-Oct. 3, 2020, Shein was the most downloaded shopping app globally on iPhones. It ranked in the top 10 among the shopping apps in the US, Brazil, Australia, Britain, and Saudi Arabia.[43]

---

[11] Next plc is a British multinational clothing, footwear and home products retailer.

[12] ASOS is UK based global online fashion and beauty retailer.

8 Results

According to analysts, the COVID–19 pandemic boosted sales of online retailers, giving online-only players, such as Shein, an edge over fast fashion giants such as Zara and H&M that had big physical stores. The pandemic proved to be a huge boon for Shein as it spurred annual sales in 2020 to almost three times that of the previous year. Shein's sales rose 250% year-over-year to a staggering US$10 billion, up from US$4.5 billion in 2019.[44] Reportedly, it generated about US$10 billion (RMB63.5 billion) in revenue in 2020, which was reportedly its eighth consecutive year of revenue growth over 100%.[45] Its revenue was US$2.83 billion in 2019. According to Ana Derboven, author at publication Dao Insights, "In a challenging year for retailers, SHEIN has shown how fashion brands can utilize the situation presented by COVID-19 to their advantage with its focus on e-commerce expansion. By investing into its social media strategy, SHEIN has developed a loyal clientele who seem to enjoy influencing others around them to adhere to this 'addictive' brand. Their focus on price and interaction among customers has been key to their success in engaging Gen-Z consumers."[46]

Shein became the biggest web-only fashion brand in the world in 2020, according to data from Euromonitor International. In 2020, Shein's Gross Merchandise Value (GMV) was US$20 billion.[47] By 2022, analysts expected Shein's GMV to overtake Zara's revenues. As of June 2021, Shein became the largest fast fashion retailer in the US, registering 28% of sales, surpassing H&M and Zara. Market share data from Earnest showed that Shein began 2021 with 13% of total fast fashion sales.[48] The total US fast fashion market grew 15% between January 2021 and mid-June 2021, while Shein grew nearly 160% in the same period. Shein reportedly sold US$3.6 billion worth of clothing in the first quarter of 2021[49] (See Exhibits 8 and 9). Its valuation soared ahead each year. In January 2019, it raised US$500 million from Sequoia China and Tiger Global at a US$5 billion company valuation. In August 2020, Shein was valued at US$15 billion. As of September 2021, it was valued at US$46 billion and analysts speculated that the retailer was preparing for an IPO. Commenting on the company's phenomenal rise, George Chiao, head of Shein's operations in the US said, "We didn't come out of nowhere. We spent the past 10 years building the foundations of the company. It has been difficult for Chinese brands to go to the west and make a name for themselves. Chinese people have been very good at manufacturing. Why? Because they lock themselves up in a factory and make products westerners ask them to make. It's a cultural thing. Chinese people don't like to talk about themselves and take away from what the business has built."[50]

9 Challenges

Going forward, one of the biggest challenges for Shein would be to continue selling to a global audience without a physical presence in individual countries and an understanding of the local culture. Moreover, sustaining its position in a crowded fast fashion market where Zara, H&M, and ASOS had a strong presence would be a tough task for it, felt analysts. Also, emerging apparel retailers such as Fashion Nova and Boohoo had begun to target young female shoppers with affordable items, similar to Shein.

Another challenge for Chris would be to continue to evolve and maintain annual growth. According to some analysts, Shein had limited visibility compared to fast fashion heavyweights such as Zara and H&M that also operated brick-and- mortar stores and catered to a wider customer base. With around 7 million monthly active users, Shein's customer base was far less than that of Zara and H&M, which had hundreds of millions of users. Analysts felt that Shein's innovative supply chain model had worked very well at its existing scale, but as its user base increased, the logistical pressures would increase. "Ultimately, Shein will have to make a choice on whether to build a new online ecosystem or join up with an existing one. If it stays with its current model, it will inevitably meet limits in new product categories and then in acquiring new customers. When it reaches its impending crossroads, which way will Shein go?"[51] questioned Greeven.

Over the years, several independent designers had accused Shein of replicating their designs, often claiming that the company had ignored their pleas for copycats to be removed from its website. In August 2021, knitwear designer Bailey Prado (Prado) accused Shein of stealing 45 of her designs and listing them all at under US$20 on its website.[52] Shein declined to comment on Prado's accusations. The company was repeatedly accused of stealing art from smaller artists. According to some artists, Shein created knock-offs of others' work, including prints, pins, and garment patterns. For instance, an artwork on a Shein phone case had been allegedly replicated without permission from a 2014 drawing by French graphic artist Jean Jullien.[53] "Given their growth, [Shein] is probably factoring in that they're going to likely run into these issues. As long as they have the audience that they do, they're going to determine that it's worth their time and energy to move products as quickly as possible—even if some of those products violate intellectual property norms,"[54] said Web Smith, author of 2PM, a leading e-commerce business newsletter.

Shein also faced complaints from apparel brands that claimed it had infringed their intellectual property. UK-based wholesaler of clothing and footwear Airwair International Ltd., maker of the iconic Dr Martens boot, sued Shein over what it described in court filings as a "clear intent to sell counterfeits", pointing to a boot listed as a Martin boot on the Shein website, as well as more than 20 other styles, sold at a fraction of the cost of a genuine Dr Martens shoe.[55] In a complaint filed in California, Airwair accused Shein of not only creating direct copies of its distinctive designs, but also using photographs of genuine Dr Martens footwear to entice customers to its website to buy fakes and copies of the original footwear. In a follow-up filing, Shein denied the claims. Earlier in 2018, American clothing company Levi Strauss & Co sued Shein over allegations it had copied the jeans company's "Arcuate", the stitching pattern usually seen on the back pockets of its trademarked Levi's jeans. The case ended with an undisclosed settlement. Meanwhile, some consumers complained about the poor quality of items sold on Shein's website.

Analysts blamed Shein for lacking cultural sensitivity and understanding of its global audiences. In July 2020, for instance, Shein received a backlash from customers when it sold Muslim prayer rugs as fun home decor. Shein apologized and called it a "highly offensive oversight". A few days later it got into even more trouble for selling a metal Swastika pendant necklace which shoppers felt promoted anti-Semitism. Shein issued an apology and stated that the listing was meant to portray a Buddhist swastika, a symbol that stood for spirituality and good fortune, and not the Nazi swastika which stood for hate.

Shein was also subjected to claims that it used child labor in its supply chain. These accusations usually appeared on comments on videos of Shein hauls, in which users tried to shame the creators for buying from a purportedly unethical company. However, there was no evidence that Shein employed children. While the social responsibility page on its website stated that it "never, ever" engaged in child or forced labor, it did not provide the transparency required. According to some analysts, Shein failed to provide adequate transparency over its supply chain. Unlike Zara and H&M, which provided detailed background on the sourcing of their clothing and the working conditions of employees on their websites and annual reports, Shein provided no details about the manufacture of its products. They felt that it was being deliberately opaque about its supply chain and factory working conditions.

According to an investigation by Sixth Tone, an online publication, Shein used disturbing practices to ensure it could produce clothes quicker and cheaper than its rivals, tactics that left workers vulnerable to exploitation. At a major Shein logistics center in Guangzhou, warehouse staff said they struggled to cope with the intense work, which could involve walking dozens of kilometers during a shift with few rest breaks.[56] Reportedly, Shein recruited many order pickers through dispatch agencies that prevented workers from defending their rights. According to some experts, Shein's aggressive business model and especially its use of an opaque network of subcontractors undermined efforts to improve labor conditions in China's fast-fashion industry. "The worry with what Shein is doing—especially with their target audience of Gen-Zers—is that it is making them think that it's OK to pay next to nothing for an item of clothing, when the only way to have reached that price would mean exploiting people along the supply chain, from the makers to the designers,"[57] commented Rebecca Morter, founder of the sustainable e-commerce site Lone Design Club.

According to some critics, Shein was harming the environment as a "real-time" fashion company and its business model was dependent on overconsumption.[58] Combined with its ultra-low prices, Shein influenced its buyers to buy more frequently, thereby worsening the issue of a global rise in textile waste, they felt.

When experts examined the company's website, they found that 70% of its products in stock were less than three months old, while at other fast-fashion retailers like Zara and H&M, this number was between 40% and 53%. Like every other fast fashion company, Shein used open-loop cycles, wherein waste produced was dumped straight into water and land. Besides, because of its super-speedy supply chain, Shein's products were allegedly mostly of low quality and not made to last, making it even harder for the fast-fashion loop to be closed by recycling, said experts. Jerren Gan, a professional copywriter and web content creator, said, "After all, their clothes are supposed to be trendy. And following the trend means that these clothes do not have to last past their short fashionable lifespan. Yet, being cheap also means that many of their pieces are made with synthetic fabrics like polyester and nylon. Unlike their short lifespans in our closets, clothing made from these materials does not decay. This means that every piece of clothing we buy from Shein will likely spend much more time in a landfill than they will ever spend in our wardrobes."[59]

Chinese media consistently dubbed Shein as China's most mysterious decacorn.[13] Analysts were concerned about the retailer's lack of transparency and questioned whether Shein's low prices would be sustainable if high ethical standards were being maintained. In response to claims that its fashion business was unethical and unsustainable, a spokesperson for Shein said, "Shein is one of the only large retailers that orders 100 pieces or less for new products to help eliminate dead stock-which makes up 10% of the carbon emissions across the entire supply chain for the apparel industry. Shein is fully committed to upholding high labor standards across the entire supply chain and to improving the lives of workers in the global supply chain by supporting national and international efforts to end forced labor."[60]

Despite accusations of supply chain problems, environmental damage, and design plagiarism, Shein continued to woo younger customers through its low aggressive prices, wider product range, and user-friendly app. The global fast fashion industry was expected to reach US$38.21 billion in 2023 at a CAGR of 6.7%.[61] Going forward, the company planned to expand its offerings and develop new businesses in mobile payments, supply chain financing, advertising systems, customer account management, and mobile traffic. It also decided to explore opening brick-and-mortar stores. According to some analysts, though Shein was a hit with global shoppers, its success in the future remained uncertain as the fallin the number of COVID 19 cases was encouraging customers to visit physical stores once again. Whether consumers would continue to be attracted to its cheaper offerings remained to be seen, they said. "The company today remains a jumble of juxtapositions: it's controversial and innovative; it's mysterious and ubiquitous. It's a clothing brand, but also—starting from its SEO roots—a tech outfit. Shein has long hoped to disassociate itself from the low-quality image of 'Made in China' goods. But as Shein becomes better known overseas, the brand's core characteristics—a knack for innovation, propensity for controversy, and unbridled ambition—cannot help but bear the imprint of its home country,"[62] noted

---

[13] The term "Decacorn" refers to a privately held startup with a valuation of over US$10 billion.

Chang Che and Jiayun Feng, a tech reporter and Associate Editor respectively at digital media company SupChina.

Exhibit 1 Fast Fashion Market Share (US) (June, 2021).

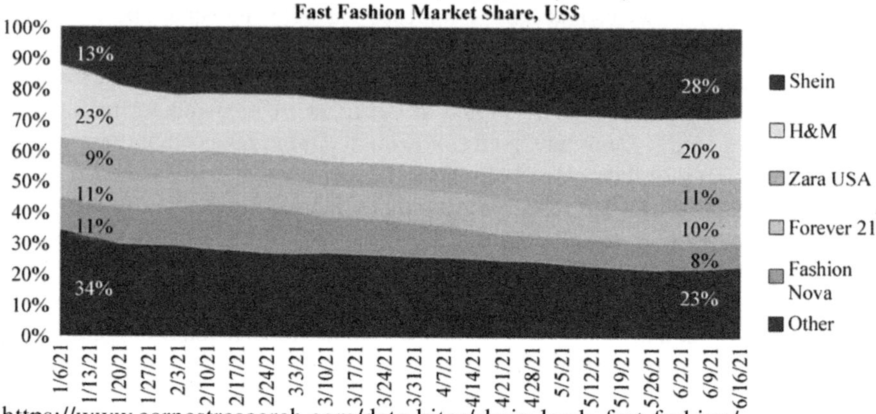

Source https://www.earnestresearch.com/data-bites/shein-leads-fast-fashion/

Exhibit 2 Shein investor funding

Year	Series
2013	Series A : JAFCO Asia US$ 5 million
2015	Series B: Greenwood Investment & IDG US$ 300 million, valued at US$1.5 billion
2018	Series C: Sequoia Capital and others; valued at US$2.5 billion
2019	Series D: Tiger Global & Sequoia US$ 500 million, valued over US$5 billion
2020	Series E : Valued over US%15 billion

Exhibit 3 Shein's prices vis-à-vis competitors'

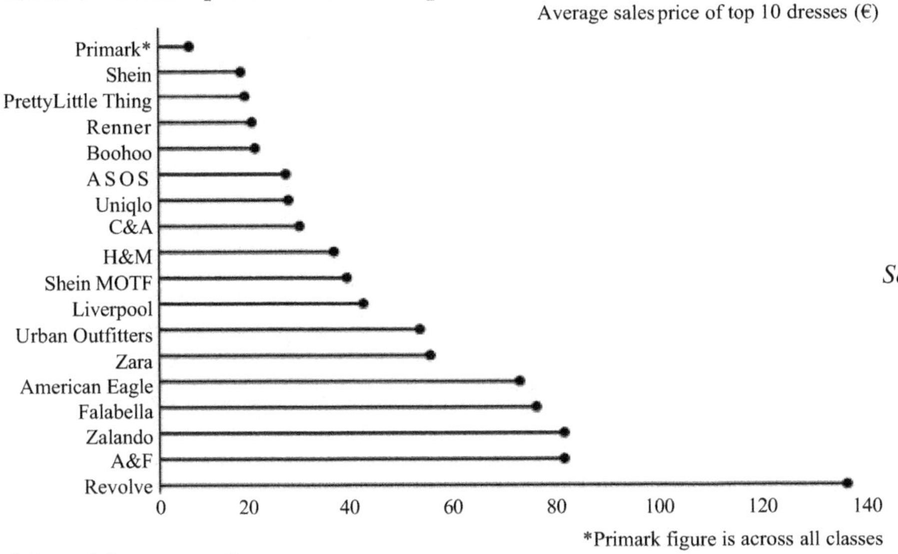

Source Adapted from www.ft.com

Exhibit 4 The favorite shopping websites of upper-income US teens (Fall 2020)

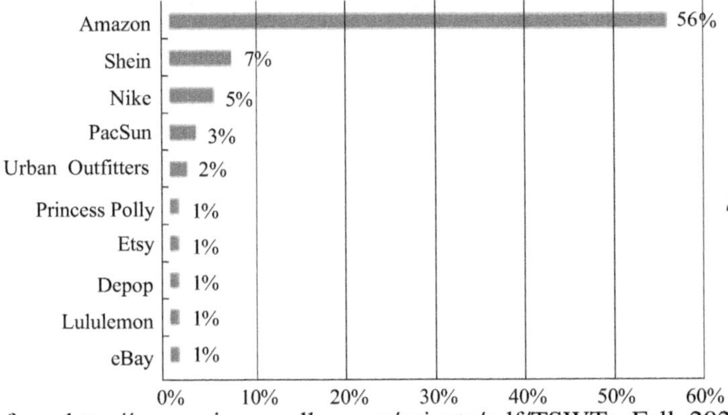

Source Adapted from http://www.pipersandler.com/private/pdf/TSWTs_Fall_2020_Full_Report.pdf

Exhibit 5 The most talked about brand on YouTube (2020)

Rank	Brand Username	YouTube Channels	Mentions	Views
1	shein.com	2K	2.9K	56.13 million
2	sephora.com	1.5K	2.2K	27.78 million
3	epicgames.com	1.3K	2K	188.34 million
4	fashionnova.com	1.2K	1.8K	61.4 million
5	ikea.com	1.2K	1.4K	42.73 million
6	analuisa.com	1.09K	1.3K	17.44 million
7	duvolle.com	1.09K	1.3K	10.8 million
8	rayconglobal.com	1K	1.6K	617 million
9	teamiblends.com	1K	1.5K	22.75 million
10	plarium.com	0.8K	1.1K	230.83 million

Exhibit 6 Leading brands on TikTok worldwide in 2020, by number of influencers (in 1,000 s)

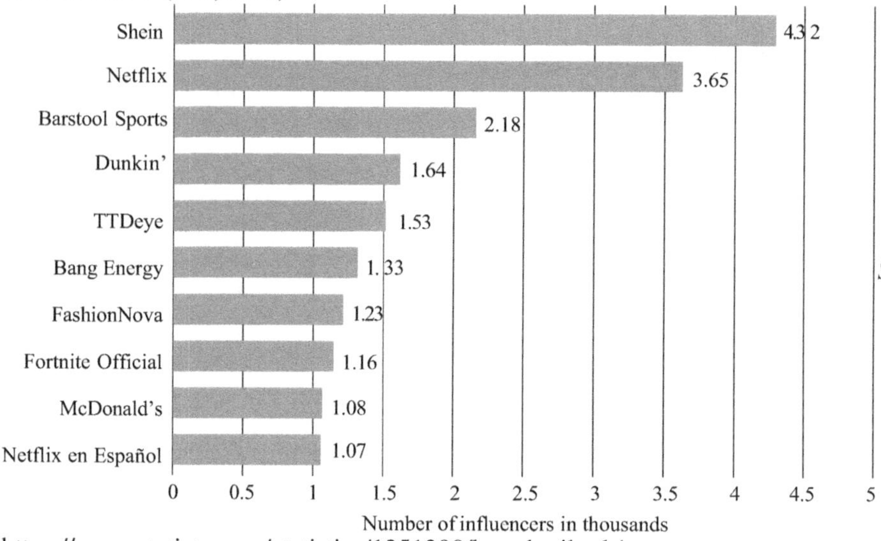

Source https://www.statista.com/statistics/1251300/brands-tiktok/

Exhibit 7 Shein versus Amazon (Estimated downloads App Store + Google Play)

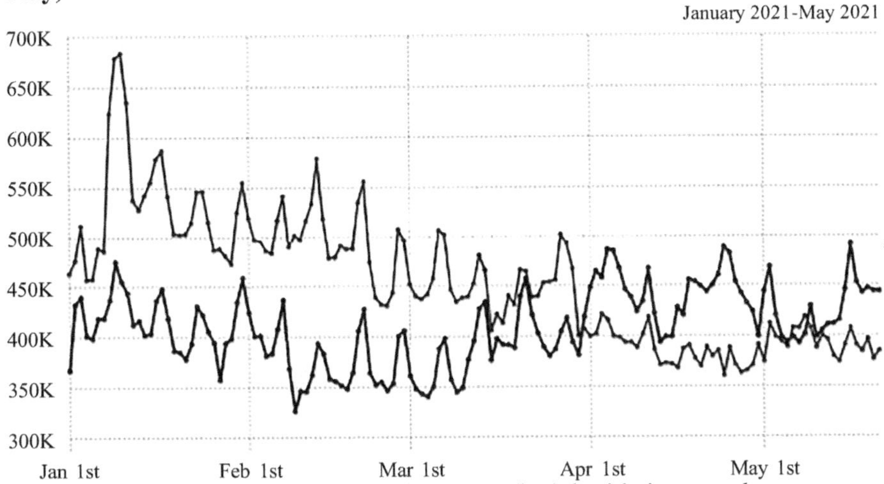

Source Adapted from https://appfigures.com/resources/insights/shein-overtakes-amazon

Exhibit 8 2021 Q1 sales* (worldwide, online and offline)

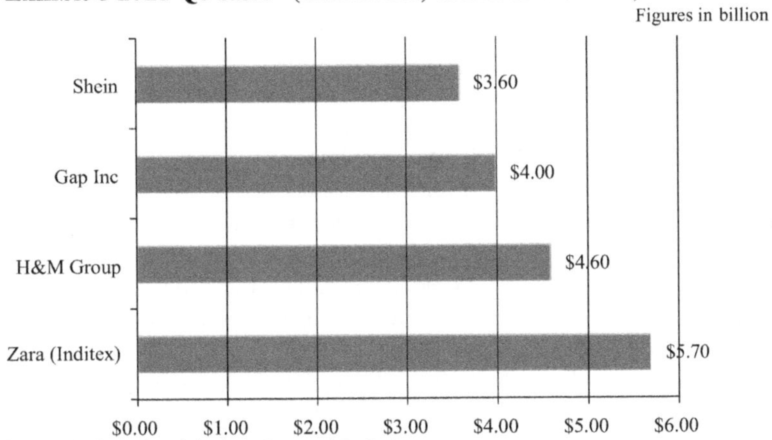

Source https://yiqinfu.github.io/posts/shein/

Exhibit 9 Shein US sales growth (March 2020–April 2021)

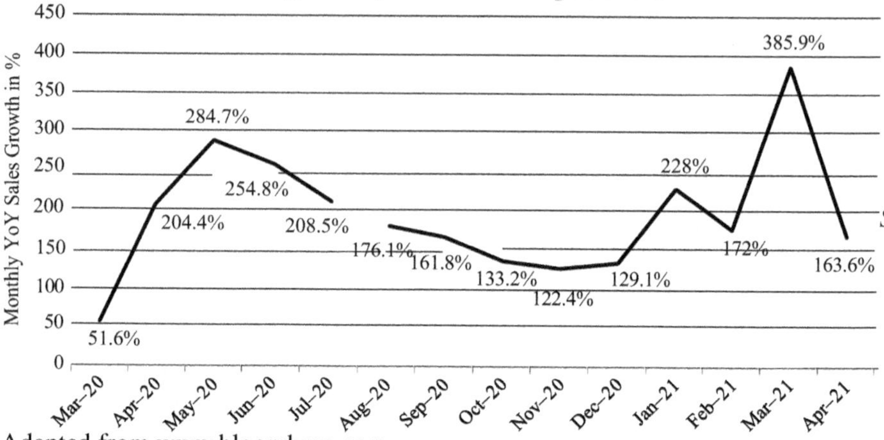

Source:
Adapted from www.bloomberg.com

Endnotes

1. "Shein Now Leads Fast Fashion," www.earnestresearch.com, June 24, 2021.
2. Mary Hanbury, "How China's Most Mysterious Billion-Dollar Company Won Over US teens and Became Tiktok's Most-Hyped Fashion Brand," www.businessinsider.in, August 29, 2021.
3. Yiqin Fu, "SheIn: A Story of Online Segregation and Data as Business Intuition," https:// yiqinfu.github.io, August 29, 2021.
4. Jack Chan, "SheIn Rise-China's Most Mysterious Multibillion Dollar Company," www. firmknow.com, August 12, 2020.
5. How Trump's Trade War Built Shein, China's First Global Fashion Giant," www.bloomberg.com, June 14, 2021.
6. Chang Che and Jiayun Feng, "A Look Inside Shein, the Multibillion Dollar Retail Enigma Upending the Global Fashion Industry," https://supchina.com, June 9, 2021.
7. "Shein: Why American Teens Love the Chinese Fast-Fashion Retailer That's Wildly Popular on Instagram and Sells Clothing at Rock-Bottom Prices," www. scmp.com, October 10, 2020.
8. Kai Ryssdaland Minju Park, "Is Fast Fashion Catching up to Real Time?" www. marketplace.org, July 22, 2021.
9. ibid.
10. Packy McCormick, "Shein: The TikTok of Ecommerce," www.notboring.co, May 17, 2021.
11. https://m.shein.com/ar-en/.
12. Mark Greeven, "China's Shein has Taken the Womenswear World by Storm. Now What?" https://asia.nikkei.com, June 12, 2021.
13. Michelle Toh, "The Mysterious Chinese Fashion App That's As Popular As Amazon," https:// edition.cnn.com, August 16, 2021.

14. Maile McCann, "How Shein Surpassed Amazon As The Most Downloaded Shopping App in the U.S," www.modernretail.co, May 24, 2021.
15. "Shein: Why American Teens Love The Chinese Fast-Fashion Retailer That's Wildly Popular On Instagram And Sells Clothing At Rock-Bottom Prices,".op.cit.
16. Michelle Toh, op.cit.
17. Kayla Marci, "Decoding the Ultra Fast SHEIN Business Model," https://blog.edited.com, July 20, 2021.
18. Daiane Chen, "Shein's Market Strategy: How the Chinese Fashion Brand is Conquering the West," https://daxueconsulting.com, 2021.
19. Kayla Marci, op.cit.
20. http://www.pipersandler.com/private/pdf/TSWTs_Fall_2020_Full_Report.pdf.
21. Mary Hanbury, op.cit.
22. Michelle Toh, op.cit.
23. Terry Nguyen, "Shein is the Future of Fast Fashion. Is that a Good Thing?" www.vox.com, August 10, 2021.
24. "Decoding Shein: Growing Pains and Bitter Splits," https://kr-asia.com, January 27, 2021.
25. Terry Nguyen, op.cit.
26. "How Trump's Trade War Built Shein, China's First Global Fashion Giant". op.cit.
27. "Shein Exemplifies a New Style of Chinese Multinational," www.economist.com, October 9, 2021.
28. "How Shein is Revolutionizing the Fashion Industry," www.dukeandgrace.com, July 1, 2021.
29. https://www.instagram.com/sheinofficial/.
30. Sadie Bargeron, "How China's Shein Conquered Global Social Media," https://jingdaily.com, April 9, 2021.
31. Paul Skeldon, "China's Shein Becomes World's Largest Shopping App with 17.5 m Downloads in July," https://internetretailing.net, September 8, 2021.
32. Margi Murphy, "How Shein Deployed an Army of Tiktok Influencers to Lure British Teens," www.telegraph.co.uk, July 19, 2020.
33. Mark Greeven, op.cit.
34. Tom Ryan, "Has Shein Reinvented Teen E-tailing?" https://retailwire.com, October 19, 2020.
35. Ana Derboven, "SHEIN-China's Mysterious Billion Dollar Company," https://daoinsights.com. com, December 23, 2020.
36. Ben Stevens, "Shein is Now Being Downloaded Twice As Much as Amazon," www. chargedretail.co.uk, September 9, 2021.
37. Mark Faithfull, "Shein: Is China's Mysterious $15 Billion Fast Fashion Retailer Ready for Stores?" www.forbes.com, February 10, 2021.
38. "Decoding Shein: All the World Over (Part 3 of 3)," https://kr-asia.com, January 28, 2021.

39. "China's SHEIN becomes the most popular fashion website in Israel," https://daoinsights.com. com, September 14, 2020.
40. Rita Liao, "Shein Overtakes Amazon s Top Shopping App on US App Stores," https:// techcrunch.com, May 18, 2021.
41. Sonya Dowsett and Sophie Yu, "China's Turbo-Charged Online Fashion Takes on Zara and H&M," www.reuters.com, October 16, 2020.
42. "Chinese Fast Fashion E-Tailer Shein Takes On Zara And H&MAnd It's Winning-With More Downloads, Cheaper Clothes And Better Choice," www.scmp.com, October 27, 2020.
43. Mark Faithfull, "Shein: Is China's Mysterious $15 Billion Fast Fashion Retailer Ready for Stores?" www.forbes.com, February 10, 2021.
44. "How Trump's Trade War Built Shein, China's First Global Fashion Giant,". op.cit.
45. Casey Hall, "Ultra-Fast Fashion Giant Shein Takes Aim at Premium Segment," www. businessoffashion.com, April 15, 2021.
46. Ana Derboven, op.cit..
47. "Shein Exemplifies a New Style of Chinese Multinational,". op.cit..
48. "Shein Now Leads Fast Fashion," op.cit..
49. Yiqin Fu, op.cit..
50. Jonathan Eley and Eleanor Olcott, "Shein: The Chinese Company Storming The World of Fast Fashion," www.ft.com, December 9, 2021.
51. Mark Greeven, op.cit..
52. M.C. Nanda, "Can Shein Clean Up Its Image?" www.businessoffashion.com, August 26, 2021.
53. Terry Nguyen, op.cit..
54. Dave Lee, "Chinese Ecommerce Site Shein Hit With Trademark Disputes," www.ft.com, June 14, 2021.
55. Joan Kennedy, "Shein Accused of Trademark Infringements," www.businesso ffashion.com, June 14, 2021.
56. Wu Peiyu, "The Shady Labor Practices Underpinning Shein's Global Fashion Empire," www. sixthtone.com, September 17, 2021.
57. Marthe de Ferrer, "How are Shein Hauls Making Our Planet Unlivable?" www. euronews. com, September 9, 2021.
58. Rinkesh, "Is Shein Bad for the Environment?" www.conserve-energy-future. com, 2021.
59. Jerren Gan, "Here's Why You Should Never Shop at Shein No Matter What," https://medium.com, July 14, 2021.
60. Priya Elan, 'Worst of the Worst': Why is Fast Fashion Retailer Shein Launching a Reality Show? www.theguardian.com, August 29, 2021.
61. "Fast Fashion Global Market Report 2021: COVID–19 Growth and Change to 2030– COVID–19 Growth and Change," www.researchandmarkets.com, May 2021.
62. Chang Che and Jiayun Feng, op.cit.

A Dispute Over Year-End Bonuses (a)

In the early morning of February 4, 2021, Kingsley James, Chairman of Fairfields, received an email of complaint from Mariah Lee, an architect, leveled at her team director, Eason Choi. Mariah claimed that she had been unfairly treated during her performance evaluation and bonus entitlement without a reasonable explanation from Eason. Kingsley did not take her claim seriously, believing it to be trivial. He asked Hans Lam, Director of Operations, and Michael Fan, Head of HR, to deal with it. Subsequently, a series of unexpected events occurred, one after another.

1 Company Profile

Fairfields Co., Ltd. (Fairfields) was a subsidiary established in Hong Kong Special Administrative Region, China, about 40 years earlier by Equalpath Design Group, an internationally renowned architectural design group, actively providing professional consultancy services in architectural design, interior design, landscape design, as well as urban planning and design. Its mission was to create world-class design solutions for different architectural projects around the world. Over the years, it became a long-term partner for dozens of prominent real estate developers, with more than 600 employees. Its organization chart (see Exhibit 1.1) shows its core business unit was the design department, consisting of about 20 design teams operating independently,

---

Professor HAN Yulan, LEUNG Chi Wai and LI Wenqing of Shanghai University of Finance and Economics developed this case series with the helpful cooperation and support of the case company. The case series aims to provide the basis for classroom discussion rather than illustrate effective or ineffective handling of a management situation. This case was the Best Case Award winner of 2022 Global Contest for the Best China-Focused Cases.

The case series is based on facts, but for the sake of the reputation of the company and individuals, the names of the companies and personnel mentioned in the case have been changed to pseudonyms.

China-Focused Cases, https://doi.org/10.1007/978-981-97-8580-3_4

bringing together over 400 talented designers. Like Eason's team, a typical design team includes one director, one or two associates/senior associates, several architects/senior architects, and a few assistant architects/architectural assistants (see Exhibit 1.2).

Fairfields attached great importance to employee performance management. Performance evaluations were carried out annually in December. The process consisted of three phases (see Exhibit 2). In the first phase, the employee's direct supervisor rated and commented on various aspects of the employee's performance as well as their overall performance for the director's reference. In the second phase, the director made final evaluations based on due consideration of the direct supervisor's evaluation and the employee's performance. The director's overall rating was deemed the employee's final performance score. The evaluation results went to the company's Remuneration Committee in the third phase. Then the Remuneration Committee decided on the employee's bonus award, salary increase, and promotion based primarily on the director's overall rating and recommendations.

The management at Fairfields valued providing performance feedback to employees. Employees and their direct supervisors were encouraged to discuss goals and objectives, strengths, and development opportunities from time to time. They would maintain an open dialogue about job performance. Furthermore, the company encouraged employees to seek feedback from their team leaders and coworkers.

While working hours stipulated in the employment contracts were 9 am to 6 pm, this provision was not strictly enforced in practice. Design team directors were allowed to manage their teams as they wished. In addition, design team members often worked overtime, traveled, and worked or met up outside regular working hours to accommodate the tight schedules and working hours of developers across different time zones. Therefore, flexible working hours were long an unwritten norm in Fairfields.

Fairfields offered employees paid sickness days and maternity leave according to the Employment Ordinance (Cap. 57), nothing above or beyond their statutory entitlements. The provisions for sick leave were enforced under Section 33 of China-Focused Cases: Selected Winners of the CEIBS Global Case Contest II the Employment Ordinance,[1] stipulating that employees were entitled to two paid sickness days every month during the first 12 months of employment. This subsequently increased to four paid sickness days every month, up to a maximum of 120 days. Maternity leave provisions were enforced under Section 12 and Section 12AA of the Employment

[1] Sections 33(1), 33(2) and 33(3A) of the Employment Ordinance stipulate, respectively, as follows: (1) An employee who has been employed by his employer under a continuous contract for a period of 1 month or more immediately preceding a sickness dayshall be paid by his employer sickness allowance in accordance with this section and Sect. 35. (2) Subject to subsection (2A), an entitlement to sickness allowance shall accrue at the rate of — (a) 2 paid sickness days for each completed month of the employee's employment under the continuous contract with his employer during the first 12 months of such employment; and (b) 4 paid sickness days for each such month thereafter, and may be accumulated from time to time up to a maximum of 120 paid sickness days. (3A) Where a female employee who is pregnant or who has given birth to a child and who is required to attend a medical examination in relation to her pregnancy or post confinement medical treatment, any day on which she is absent from work for such examination or treatment shall be a sickness day.

Ordinance,[2] which generally entitled pregnant employees to ten weeks of maternity leave.

Kingsley James: Founder and Chairman of Fairfields and Equalpath Design Group (Equalpath Group), in charge of overall corporate affairs. He focused on Equalpath Group's global strategy, overall operations, and profitability, and handed daily affairs over to directors or department heads. He was not only an internationally renowned architect but also an entrepreneur with outstanding leadership skills.

Mariah Lee: An architect in Eason's team who studied in the United States and has worked in the architectural design industry for more than ten years. In the eyes of her colleagues, she is straightforward and flexible in her work arrangements. She got to the office at irregular times, sometimes around 10 am and sometimes after midday, but she would always work more than eight hours a day. She saw no problem with her attendance because she handled her work properly. She valued equality and respect between people.

Eason Choi: A design director at Fairfields, leading one design team. He possessed over 20 years of experience in architectural design, mainly covering residential and commercial developments in the Chinese Mainland and Hong Kong. He was an outstanding architect and design-oriented but paid less attention to team management and business matters. He valued rules, regularly working from 9 am to 6 pm according to stipulated working hours. He always addressed colleagues in an imperative tone, playing up his authority.

Gorden Chan: A senior associate in Eason's team, reporting directly to Eason and serving as Mariah's direct supervisor. He had about 15 years of experience in architectural design. He mainly assisted Eason in managing projects and the design team so Eason could focus on design work.

Hans Lam: The Director of Operations at Fairfields, in charge of the human resources, administration, and information technology departments. He had about 30 years of management experience. He assigned all daily work to department heads.

---

[2] Before Employment (Amendment) Ordinance 2020 came into force on December 2020, Sects. 12(1), 12(2) and 12AA of the Employment Ordinance stipulate, respectively, as follows: 12. Maternity leave. (1) A female employee employed under a continuous contract immediately before taking any leave under this Part shall be entitled to maternity leave under this Part. (2) Maternity leaveshall be the aggregate of — (a) a continuous period of 10 weeks from and inclusive of —(i) the date of commencement of maternity leave as determined under Sect. 12AA; or (ii) the actual date of confinement,if confinement occurs before the date of commencement mentioned in subparagraph (i); (b) a further period equal to the number of days, if any, beginning on the day after the expected date of confinement up to and including the actual date of confinement; such further period of leave is to be taken immediately following the period of leave under paragraph (a); and (c) a further period, not exceeding 4 weeks, on grounds of illness or disability arising out of the pregnancy or confinement. 12AA. Commencement of maternity leave. (1) With the agreement of her employer, a pregnant employee may decide on the date of commencement of her 10 weeks maternity leave, provided that such date is within a period of not less than 2 weeks before, and not more than 4 weeks before, the expected date of confinement. (2) If the employee does not exercise her option to decide on the date of commencement in subsection (1), or if she fails to secure her employer's agreement to her proposed leave schedule, the date of commencement of maternity leaveshall be 4 weeks immediately before the expected date of confinement.

While a yes-man in front of his fellow directors and superiors, he hardly bothered to address his subordinates.

Michael Fan: The Head of HR at Fairfields, reporting directly to Hans. He had about 30 years of experience in HR management. While busy with routine work, he was used to handling all matters strictly by the book and lacked leadership. He usually had no idea how to deal with emergencies but obeyed orders from his superiors.

Bretton Wong: The Director of Legal and Contracts at Fairfields, in charge of the legal and contracts departments. He was responsible for dealing with all legal issues and matters related to Fairfields and Equalpath Group. He had held this position for more than ten years. He was discreet, goal-oriented, and efficiency-oriented.

2 The Ins and Outs

In November 2019, Mariah joined Fairfields and then passed her three-month probation stipulated in her employment contract. About two months later, she informed the company she was pregnant with an expected delivery date of December 4, 2020. In early November 2020, Mariah applied to the company for four days of paid sick leave, citing complications with her pregnancy. However, Eason was upset with the application. He called Mariah into his office and said seriously, "Mariah, you have often shown up late since you joined the company and usually show up in the office after eleven each morning. I have never seen you work overtime, either. You cannot finish your work on time if you continue to behave like this."

Before Mariah could respond, Eason continued, "You got pregnant shortly after your probation, and you refused to start maternity leave four weeks before delivery as recommended by the Labour Department, instead requesting to start your maternity leave two weeks before giving birth. The company generously approved it. Then you applied for four days of extra leave immediately before your approved maternity leave, meaning you would extend your maternity leave by nearly a week. I do suspect that this was all planned."

Mariah was shocked by Eason's words and argued emotionally, "First of all, regarding punctuality, I gained the impression that the company does not require strict compliance with the contractual working hours. As an employee, I have the right to arrange my working hours flexibly. Moreover, I do work overtime to finish my assignments on time-just because you leave work early, you are not even aware. As for maternity leave, I think it is the best choice to take my leave two weeks before giving birth, which does not violate any employment legislation. I applied for sick leave solely because of health conditions beyond my control. Extending maternity leave in a premeditated way is not something that I would do."

After the argument, Eason eventually approved Mariah's application, but both developed a strong resentment for each other.

On November 27, 2020, the Performance Evaluation System was launched as scheduled. Employees' direct supervisors and the directors evaluated their performance. Then the company's Remuneration Committee decided on each employee's salary increases, promotions, and bonus awards on the basis of the performance score.

In 2020, most employees demonstrating an average performance at Fairfields received bonuses equivalent to one month's salary, while employees with an excellent performance received bonuses of more than one month's salary. Some employees with less satisfactory performance only received bonuses totaling half a month's salary or even none at all.

In this performance evaluation, Mariah's direct supervisor, Gorden Chan, gave her the highest score of "1" because he thought she did an excellent job and could complete tasks assigned promptly. However, Eason, the team director, gave Mariah the lowest score of "3" . Since the team director's rating was decisive and the direct supervisor's rating was only for reference, Mariah's final performance score was "3", deemed to be underperforming. These events took place while Mariah was on maternity leave, leaving her unaware of it all.

Fairfields issued annual bonuses before the Chinese New Year in February 2021. Mariah happily returned to work from maternity leave only to find that she was not awarded any bonus. Only four employees at Fairfields, including Mariah, did not receive year-end bonuses. It felt like a slap in the face; she was shocked, angry, and ashamed, and her happy mood evaporated. She immediately rushed to Eason's office to demand an explanation, but Eason was away. She could only hold back her anger and queries until Eason's return.

Around 2 pm, when Eason was back, Mariah stormed into his office to question him about the bonus.

Mariah considered herself diligent at work. Since her performance was highly regarded by her direct supervisor, Gorden, and she had not received any verbal or written complaints from clients, she felt entitled to a bonus equivalent to one month's salary at least.

After hearing Mariah's arguments, Eason sneered, directly pointing out that Mariah's 2020 performance was not as good as she thought. To Eason, it appeared that Mariah had abused the sick leave policy, as obtaining a doctor's certificate in Hong Kong was relatively straightforward. Eason stated that the projects Mariah participated in were making losses, and the team had to take care of financial concerns rather than just hers alone. Therefore, Eason did not think the team could afford to allot any bonus to Mariah. After speaking his mind, Eason returned to his work, ignoring Mariah as he ordered her out.

Mariah deemed Eason's attitude extremely disrespectful and left his office in a huff. Back at her desk, Mariah could not focus on her work as her anger intensified as she went over Eason's words in her head. Finally, she wrote an email to Kingsley to complain about Eason. She mentioned (see Exhibit 3) that Fairfields, as an international firm, should promote equal opportunity and support women undergoing difficult pregnancies. Nevertheless, when she applied for statutory sick leave for prenatal complications, Eason had attempted to reject her application on the grounds that she had taken "too much" paid sick leave. Moreover, her direct supervisor, who worked closely with her, was quite satisfied with her performance. Although Eason had never made any negative comments on her performance, he gave her the lowest performance score, depriving her of a bonus. She believed Eason's low evaluation score was due to pregnancy discrimination and felt humiliated, thus causing much mental distress and harm. She also believed that Eason's behavior would damage Fairfields's reputation as an internationally renowned firm and hoped Kingsley would deal with this matter fairly.

After reading Mariah's email, Kingsley dismissed the matter as a trivial labor dispute, judging Hans and Michael to be the most suitable persons to deal with it. He forwarded Mariah's email and simply told them, "Please follow up."

Exhibit 1: Organizational Charts

Exhibit 2 The Performance Evaluation System at Fairfields

Fairfields attaches great importance to employee performance management. The Employee Handbook contains the following statement regarding Employee Performance Evaluation.

"The Management is committed to providing real-time feedback on your job performance. In addition, Employees and their supervisors shall discuss goals and objectives, strengths, and development opportunities from time to time. Performance evaluations are held annually in December. Employees and supervisors are jointly responsible for maintaining an open dialogue about job performance. Employees are encouraged to seek feedback from their team

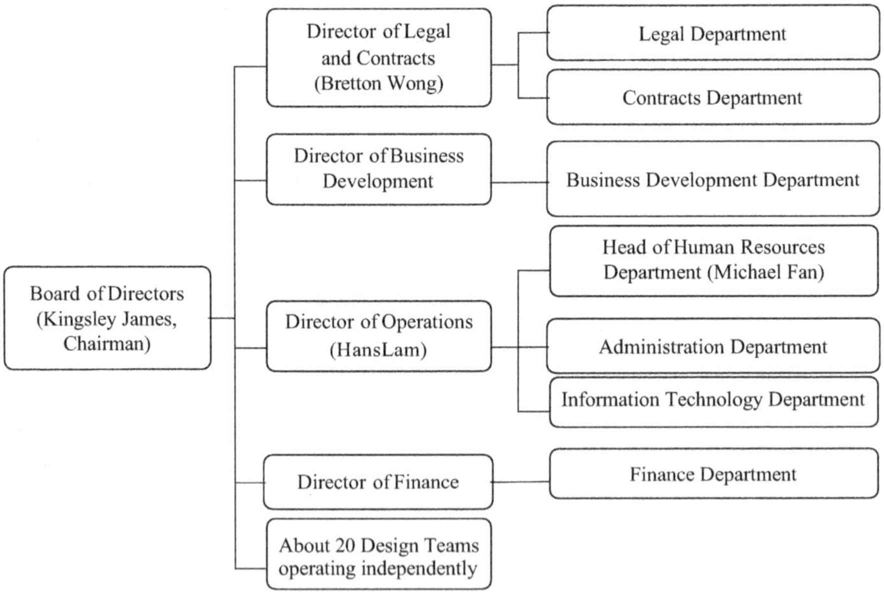

Exhibit 1.1 Organizational chart of Fairfields. *Source* Created by the case authors based on information from Fairfields

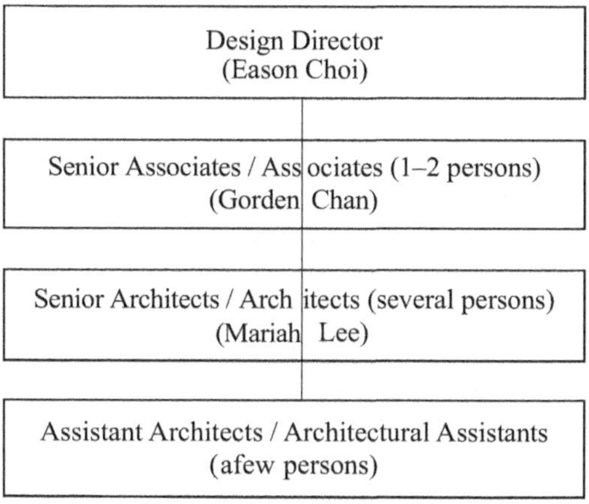

Exhibit 1.2 Organizational chart of Design Team. *Source* Created by the case authors based on information from Fairfields

leaders and coworkers announcement states, "The objective of our Performance Evaluation System is to provide a bilateral communication channel for you and your supervisor to understand each other and provide a fair platform for our Management team to review your performance. Your active and timely input shall be critical to the success of the implementation of this system." It also outlines the performance evaluation schedule. In addition, Kingsley issues another announcement informing all directors of the company's overall performance for the year and the guidelines on bonus allocation, salary increase, and promotion for directors to consider when making performance evaluations and recommendations.

By early December, all employees should have updated their personal information in the Performance Evaluation System, including their design and management expertise, as well as their academic and professional qualifications, for reference by their direct supervisors and directors in the performance evaluations.

The performance evaluation process consists of three phases:

Phase I (Supervisor Evaluation): In early December, all employees in the firm are evaluated by their direct supervisors. There are 13 evaluation criteria, including team player skills, the accuracy of work, efficient and timely completion of tasks, punctuality, extra effort for deadlines, willingness to undertake additional responsibility, initiative and self-starting, quick learner, continuing education and professional development, third-party's satisfaction, knowledge adequacy for tasks undertaken, leadership skills, and consistency and reliability. Supervisors also need to give overall performance ratings to their subordinates. In addition, supervisors could give written comments on each criterion and overall performance in the system. The rating is performed on a five-point scale: Excellent = 1; Good = 1.5; Above average = 2; Average = 2.5; Below average = 3. The overall ratings are deemed the employees' performance scores given by supervisors, while ratings on the 13 criteria are merely used as feedback to the employees. Employees can log in to the Performance Evaluation System to view the ratings and comments given by supervisors.

Phase II (Director Evaluation): In mid-December, the directors evaluate all of their subordinates by three criteria—design creativity, technical skill, and administrative skill. Directors also need to give overall performance ratings to their subordinates. The rating is performed on a five-point scale: Excellent = 1; Good = 1.5; Above average = 2; Average = 2.5; Below average = 3. The overall ratings are deemed the employees' performance scores given by directors, while ratings on the specific criteria are merely for reference in the following evaluations. In addition, directors make recommendations on employees' bonus awards, salary increases, and promotions according to the guidelines from the Board of Directors. When making evaluations, directors may refer to the ratings and comments given by employees' direct supervisors in the first phase but are not bound by such ratings or comments. Directors' ratings and comments are kept confidential to employees.

Phase III (Remuneration Committee Final Evaluation): In late December, the HR department collects all the ratings, comments, and recommendations from the employees' direct supervisors and directors and reports to the company's Remuneration Committee. The Remuneration Committee independently makes the final decisions on employees' bonus awards, salary increases, and promotions by referring to the evaluation results from the employees' direct supervisors and directors. Generally, the Remuneration Committee tends to adopt the overall ratings and recommendations from the directors.

Source Summarized by the case authors based on information from Fairfields.

Exhibit 3 Mariah Lee's Email to Kingsley James on February 4, 2021

Dear Kingsley,

I am writing this letter urging an explanation from the company in regard to the unfair treatment I received.

I believe that I have been unfairly treated, and consequently, my bonus was withheld,which I find unacceptable due to the explanations given by the Director (Eason Choi). I understand bonus is discretionary; however, it is the manner and justification that I find unprofessional and demeaning.

This discussion took place yesterday, February 3, 2021, 2: 30 pm. Eason had explicitly told me the reasons for denying my bonus are:

1. I was involved in "Loss-Making" projects and, therefore, was unable to receive a bonus.

2. My poor performance over the calendar year of 2019/2020. I am writing to refute the reasons mentioned above.

First of all, while it is unfortunate that the projects I was involved in resulted in a deficit, I strongly disagree that I should be punished for it considering other team members were rewarded with bonuses.

Secondly, Eason stated that my performance was "poor". I find it shocking and surprising as I have never received any written records of poor performance, disciplinary letters, verbal warnings from Eason, or any complaints from clients. I have been punctual and conducted my tasks professionally. I have even gone above and beyond and pulled late night still 2–3 am despite being pregnant. More importantly, on my supervisor report, my direct supervisor, who works closely with me, rated me mostly excellent and even commented that I have good leadership skills and was able to complete my tasks efficiently.

Lastly, I was accused of taking too much sick leave during my pregnancy (before I left for maternity leave in November 2020). This is an unjustified and insensitive comment, as I thought the company would be supportive of women who are undergoing a difficult pregnancy. When I informed him that I was experiencing some prenatal complications, Eason attempted to reject my sick leave simply because he did not want to pay for my entitled paid sick leave and stated that I had taken "too much" paid sick leave compared to other teammates and it was "unfair" to others. It was clarified to me that I am entitled to 24 days of sick leave, and I had only taken five days. It was very distressing to hear a senior representative of one of the largest architectural firms in the world insinuated that I am a burden to the team. I truly felt like I had been discriminated against for being pregnant. I am disappointed as I had been given the impression that the company is an equal-opportunity employer. It is unfortunate and disappointing as I was very much looking forward to returning to work after my maternity leave. However, I find myself in an untenable position and would like an opportunity to have a meeting with you to discuss further details in person.

Thank you for your time.

Yours sincerely, [Signed]

Mariah

Source Provided by Fairfields.

Navigating EtonHouse Through Crises: The Paradoxical Leadership of Ng Gim Choo

"So what do you think our next step should be?" asked Ng Gim Choo, the founder and managing director of EtonHouse International Education Group (hereinafter "EtonHouse"), at an executive meeting in March 2020. The executives in attendance fell silent, pondering which strategy to take during the coronavirus (COVID–19)[1] pandemic.

Before the outbreak of COVID–19, EtonHouse had decided to continue expansion in China, where it opened its first international school in 2003. With the radical changes that the pandemic brought, the Singapore-based firm had to reformulate its expansion strategy and thus held this meeting. The key management team, including Chief Financial Officer Ang Poh Seng,[2] Group Director Jimmy Oh[3] and Executive Director Ng Yi Xian, Ng's son and successor, voiced their opinions. Taking different factors and considerations, they came up with three options grounded with valid reasoning.

After listening to their discussions, Ng's mind started to wander. She thought of similar difficulties encountered during EtonHouse's development and the business decisions that had led the firm out of the crises. She knew the most pressing decision, for now, was not to choose from the strategies but instead, decide how

[1] First identified in December 2019, COVID–19 is an infectious disease that transmits through contact among people and quickly spreads all over the world.

[2] Ang joined EtonHouse in 2017 as group CFO. He started overseeing operations in China in 2019.

[3] Oh was responsible for business development in Singapore and overseas, as well as financial and property management for EtonHouse. He is Ng's brother and had more than 40 years' experience in international business.

Professor Jean Lee and Case Researcher Dr. JU Huirong of China Europe International Business School developed this case with the helpful cooperation and support of the case company. The case aims to provide the basis for classroom discussion rather than illustrate effective or ineffective handling of a management situation. This case was the First Prize winner of 2020 Global Contest for the Best China-Focused Cases.

China-Focused Cases, https://doi.org/10.1007/978-981-97-8580-3_5

EtonHouse should cope with the crisis during its leadership transition. Her son and next-generation leader, Yi Xian, had been with the group for five years. Hence, it was an opportunity for Yi Xian and his team to stand on their own feet and test their ability to deal with a crisis. However, COVID–19 posed an unprecedented threat to the education industry, making it especially risky to hand over the reins at this critical time. She pulled her mind back to the meeting as the attendees awaited her response. She had to decide soon whether to lead EtonHouse through this crisis as she had done previously or to delegate responsibilities fully to Yi Xian and let his team learn "on the job".

1 Ng's Entrepreneurial Experience

Ng started her career as an auditor in 1973. She spent eight years at Ernst & Young before becoming partner at a medium-sized certified public accountancy. In retrospect, she believed that accountants were well placed to be entrepreneurs because auditing gave her a sense of what made businesses work. After ten years' auditing experience, she relocated to London as her husband was posted there for work. She prioritized her family over her career, becoming a full-time housewife and taking care of her two young children.

While she put her career on hold, Ng discovered a passion for education, especially early childhood learning. Her daughter, who was reluctant to attend kindergarten in Singapore, was surprisingly enthusiastic about going to school in London and even dressed up for school on the weekends. To find out what led to this change in her daughter, she signed up as a parent volunteer at the school. She realized that education philosophies in the UK were drastically different from those in Singapore. 1980s preschool education in Singapore was very structured. Students had to follow teachers' instructions strictly and risked scolding if they failed to replicate what the teacher wanted. In contrast, UK students learned through inquiry and play. Teachers encouraged them to generate different ideas and solve problems on their own.

When the family returned to Singapore after one-and-a-half years in the UK, they could not find an inquiry-based school for the children. Ng recognized the potential of such a school for children in Singapore. Thus, she decided to open up schools that would allow children to learn through play and exploration in the hope of changing the early education landscape in Singapore.

2 The Development of EtonHouse

When Ng started EtonHouse in her 40 s, the entrepreneurial venture was driven by her passion for education and determination to provide a different approach in Singapore. EtonHouse followed a vision to "shape the future through education" and a mission to "develop confident and capable global citizens" (see Exhibit 1). Ng founded the

Exhibit 1 EtonHouse's education philosophy, vision & mission

Education Philosophy	• *Image of Child*: curious, communicative, capable, confident and respected
	• *Image of Educator*: collaborative, lifelong learner, open-minded, respectful and passionate, also abbreviated as "COLOR with passion"
Vision	• Shaping the future through education
Mission	• Developing confident and capable global citizens

Source Company information

firm on her belief in providing high-quality education to children that would shape their growth and cultivate them into individuals who could positively impact society. Making a profit was never her goal, even though it was vital for sustaining the business. Under her leadership, EtonHouse grew rapidly into a global operation with 120 schools across 12 countries (e.g., China, Indonesia, Japan, Cambodia and Malaysia), providing high-quality education to more than 12,000 children globally. Revenue expanded at a compounded annual growth rate of 27% between 2009 and 2014, and 35% between 2014 and 2019, to exceed SG$100 million[4] in 2019.

3 Setting up the First School

In 1995, Ng set up the first EtonHouse preschool at Broadrick Road, Singapore. However, it was challenging and risky to adopt the UK Early Years Framework and advocate an education philosophy that "learning is fun and joyful" in Singapore, where the system was mainly rote-learning-based. She explained:

> We went against the traditional teaching methods that were instructional and teacher-focused. Instead, we focused on children's interests and competencies. Therefore, we had to spend time convincing parents and advocating for this new approach to education. Meanwhile, we had to invest a lot of time and resources to hire qualified teachers and build their competencies and knowledge to deliver this education approach and develop curriculum content and facilitators at the same time.

Despite all her efforts, Ng admitted EtonHouse had "a terrible start" and lost about SG$1 million in the first year. She knew that if operations continued, additional losses would reach around SG$3 million. After some reflection, she decided to provide prolonged childcare services in her kindergarten. While parents were not pleased with a hike in fees, the concept of a childcare center with longer operating hours catered to the needs of working parents and eventually won them over. "It was a risky move that parents may not have initially appreciated, but fortunately, it worked out and helped us survive the very first years," Ng recalled.

[4] SG$ = SGD = Singapore Dollar; SG$1 = approximately US$0.7436, US$0.5888, US$0.71, as of December 31, 2019, 2003, 1995,respectively.

4 The Gap Between Education Philosophy and Parents' Expectations

By establishing EtonHouse, Ng could transfer the operations and management method she learned in the UK to Singapore. More importantly, she believed that a different education system would cultivate confident and capable global citizens with an inquiring mind, helping them excel and lead in the future. Therefore, she advocated that learning should be fun and enjoyable, denouncing rote learning based on repetition and memorization. For example, when children learned math, teachers would ask each child to bring a teddy bear, sort the toys from small to large and count them. As a result, the learning process was enjoyable, and children could develop cognitive and social competence in a natural and spontaneous way.

EtonHouse was one of the first schools in Singapore to adopt the Reggio Emilia[5] approach in 2007. This philosophy had four key elements: 1. Respect for children; 2. Pedagogy of listening; 3. Documentation of children's learning; 4. Environment as a third teacher. It was a demanding approach that required a rich learning environment and engaged teachers who learned alongside children. Specifically, teachers should respect that children had 100 languages and that learning was informed by observing children's interests and contexts. To achieve the learning objectives, Ng worked hard to recruit and develop educators and came up with "color with passion" as the image of EtonHouse's educators (see Exhibit 1). As educators, they were expected to be creative and move beyond the traditional curriculum to build rich constructs into the environment and interact effectively with children. However, this approach did not work well initially, as parents who were used to rote learning expected to see learning outcomes immediately. Ng said, "We don't have anything like worksheets or textbooks. What we do is learning through inquiry and exploration. What the children get to learn is perhaps not tangible in the beginning, but they develop higher-order thinking, confidence and social competence that lay the foundation for future success. Parents can see their children grow up to be curious, communicative, capable, confident and respected." She explained the challenges of introducing and advocating for her education philosophies. "That's when perseverance comes into play. Istick to the principles I believe in and persevere in pushing them forward,"

she added.

When the challenges surfaced, she realized that communication with parents was crucial. Before enrolment, educators would explain to parents how EtonHouse aimed for a holistic education emphasizing physical development, intellectual ability and social skills that were not merely focused on cognitive development like in rote-learning methods. After students started classes, teachers continuously communicated with parents about their child's daily experiences through documentation. Eventually, their efforts came to fruition, and their teaching philosophy gained parents' trust and approval. Commenting on the adoption of the Reggio Emilia approach,

[5] The Reggio Emilia approach is an educational philosophy and pedagogy that promotes self-directed and experiential learning in relationship-driven environments.

Tina Stephenson-Chin[6], Director of Pedagogy at EtonHouse, said, "Ms. Ng showed her visionary capability by adopting the Reggio Emilia approach even before it was popular. It was not an easy one to implement, but she was able to attract good people and effectively ignite people's passion around it to work it out."

In 2013, EtonHouse was the first organization in Asia to represent Reggio Children. It launched Reggio Emilia in Asia for Children (REACH) to facilitate dialogue and professional development in early childhood. By 2020, most EtonHouse schools followed the "Inquire-Think-Learn" curriculum inspired by the Reggio Emilia philosophy. EtonHouse also implemented a bilingual immersion program that utilized bilingualism and biculturalism to build a strong educational foundation.

5 Local and Global Expansion

5.1 Local Expansion

During EtonHouse's development, Ng carefully crafted expansion strategies and chose school locations. Specifically, EtonHouse started in the eastern part of Singapore and then expanded to the central area. To further build the school brand, she opened schools along main roads, which was a risky decision due to safety concerns and government regulations. EtonHouse set up two safety gates at the schools to address these concerns and gained approval from the local authorities. The move turned out to be an effective marketing strategy and was crucial in creating brand awareness among parents. After the opening of two schools in the city center, EtonHouse became a well-known brand in Singapore.

In terms of programs, EtonHouse started with kindergartens and later expanded to primary, secondary and high schools.[7] "The strategy to extend to K12 education was inspired by our parents," she shared. "In the beginning, even though parents were supportive, we kept losing students. Because at that time, there was an acute shortage of international schools for the primary level, parents would withdraw their children from EtonHouse once they got a place at an international institution. When these children left, their siblings would also leave." At parents' request, EtonHouse started primary, and later secondary and high schools too. She believed that by offering a K12 education, it would be easier for children to transit smoothly between different levels of education. Parents who were familiar with EtonHouse could continue to pick this trusted brand.

[6] Stephenson-Chin joined EtonHouse in 2015. She takes charge of curriculum design and implementation across regions,and professional development initiatives for education practitioners.

[7] Secondary School is equivalent to junior highschool (Grades 7 to 9), whereas highschool is equivalent to senior highschool (Grades 10 to 12).

By 2020, the Group ran 40 schools in Singapore under six school brands, providing both premium and affordable education spanning preschool to K12. They were EtonHouse International Schools and Pre-schools, Middleton International School, E-Bridge Pre-school (one of the Anchor Operators[8] in Singapore), Hampton Pre-school, Islander Pre-school and EIS Japanese International Pre-school.

In 2015, Ng embarked on the EtonHouse Community Fund (ECF) project as the Group celebrated its 20th anniversary. ECF aimed to use the funding to improve the lives of underprivileged children through emotional, cognitive and fitness support. Because Ng felt that it was necessary to cultivate empathy in EtonHouse's children and help them understand that there were many less privileged children out there who might need support.

5.2 *Expansion in China*

As EtonHouse gained recognition and expanded operations in Singapore, the government invited the firm to expand overseas. Realizing that the limited domestic market would hinder her goal of achieving SG$10 million revenue within ten years, Ng decided to enter China, a fast-growing market with huge potential. In 2003, with the support of Enterprise Singapore,[9] she picked the eastern city of Suzhou, China as its first overseas stop. At that time, many expatriates in Suzhou were reluctant to send their children to local schools because classes were in Mandarin with a class size of over 50 students, thus making it hard for their children to keep up. Ng's international school could help the local government address this education issue.

"But still, the decision to step into the education industry as a foreign group in China was a very bold move with high risk, especially to start with a mid-sized school," Ang commented. "To run a school there meant that we had to embrace the culture and the way of doing business in China and understand the Chinese market and education landscape. We needed to comply with the local education bureau's requirements, such as hardware standards, operating hours and teacher/ayi.[10] China is very different from Singapore, and Northern China is different from Southern China. We employed local Chinese staff to manage the school, and it has been helpful."

Since then, China had become EtonHouse's second-largest market after Singapore, contributing 33% of revenue in 2019. Over the years, EtonHouse had grown organically in China, with schools opening in multiple locations. By April 2020, EtonHouse had set up about 50 schools in the country covering different sectors,

[8] Initiated by the Singapore government, the Anchor Operator scheme provided funding to selected preschool operators to scale up the provision of good quality and affordable early childhood care and education services.

[9] A government agency that champions development of small and medium-sized enterprises in Singapore and overseas.

[10] Ayi refers to the helpers that assist in nursing in kindergartens in China.

including international schools with K12 education, affordable preschools and private preschools with relatively higher fees (see Exhibit 2).

The Chinese market was also fast-changing and often brought uncertainties. Over the years, competition among international schools intensified (see Exhibit 3). The country also set out regulations and constraints on licenses to limit growth. Therefore, EtonHouse would find it increasingly difficult to expand naturally and have to consider alternative ways. "But we are confident in Ms. Ng as she always manages to overcome difficulties. Her way is so unique that she can achieve a delicate balance between those seemingly contradictory challenges and find a way out," said Kate Jin, Director of Human Resource in China, as she looked on with optimism.

Exhibit 2 EtonHouse's growth in China

Year	Segments	Number of new campus	Cities in China
2003	International school	1	1
2006	International school	1	2
2007	Local preschool	1	3
2008	Local preschool	1	4
2009	International school	1	5
2010	Local preschool	1	5
2011	Local preschool	2	6
2013	International school	1	7
	Local preschool	2	7
2014	Local preschool	4	10
2015	Local preschool	4	12
2016	International school	1	16
	Local preschool	3	16
2017	Local preschool	10	23
2018	International school	1	24
	Local preschool	4	27
	Local K12 school	1	27
2019	Local preschool	5	29
	Local K12 school	1	29
Until April 2020	Local preschool (To be opened)	5	33
Overall	EtonHouse international schools, local preschools, & local K12 schools	50	33

Source Compiled by authors based on company information

Exhibit 3 Key international education players in China

Segments	Key players	Brief description
International schools	Dulwich College International	Dulwich College International was founded in China in partnership with Dulwich College, an independent school in the UK with a 400-year history. Since its first school in Shanghai in 2003, four Dulwich Colleges have been established in China, with two in Shanghai, and one in Beijing and Suzhou, home to around 9,000 students. They offer early childhood education, English national curriculum, IGCSEs, IB diploma and A-Level programs
	Nord Anglia Education	Nord Anglia Education was founded in 1972 and has grown to be a family of 66 international schools across 29 countries worldwide. In China, the group set up the first international school in Shanghai in 2002 and has expanded to 11 cities, including Beijing, Shanghai, Chengdu and Foshan. The International schools offer both UK and IB programs
	Wellington College	Founded in 1853, Wellington College sought to deliver inspirational education for all of its pupils. Wellington College has been recognized as a leading international school group. Its first international school in China was set up in Tianjin in 2011, and four more schools were set up in Shanghai and Hangzhou, providing world-class British international education that spans early years to high school
	Harrow International School	The Harrow School was founded in 1572 in London. The first Harrow International School in China was founded in Beijing in 2005, followed by Harrow Hong Kong in 2012, Harrow Shanghai in 2016 and Harrow Shenzhen and Haikou in 2020. The international school provides education to pupils aged from 18 months to 18 years. They mainly follow the UK curriculum
	Yew Chung International School	Founded in 1932 in Hong Kong, Yew Chung initially specialized in early childhood education. It now has schools in many cities throughout China, including Shanghai, Beijing, Chongqing and Qingdao. They provide international education to children aged from two to 18 years old. Its curriculums help students develop bilingual abilities in Mandarin and English
Local International Schools	Bright Scholar Education	Founded in 1994, Bright Scholar is one of the oldest international schools in China that offers IB programs. It listed on the New York Stock Exchange in 2017 and runs seven international schools, 15 bilingual schools and 58 kindergartens

(continued)

Exhibit 3 (continued)

Segments	Key players	Brief description
	Maple Leaf Educational System	Established in 1995, Maple Leaf offers high-quality international education for students from preschool to highschool. As of 2020, it ran 28 preschools, 27 primary schools, 16 high schools and three international schools across 23 cities in China
	Ulink College	Founded in 2004 in Guangdong, Ulink College is a boarding school with IGCSE and A-Level programs. It ran six international high schools and one affiliate school across China in Shanghai, Beijing, Suzhou, and Wuhan
	Shanghai Pinghe School	Founded in 1996, Shanghai Pinghe School is a private boarding school. It offers primary to highschool education and has an IB diploma program. The school aims to cultivate well-rounded modern citizens characterized by global mindedness, self- discipline and creativity with Chinese and western cultural experiences under the same roof

Note International Schools only accept children of foreign nationalities, whereas local International Schools provide westernized learning and pedagogy for local Chinese students
Source Hurun Education Top International Schools in China 2020, retrieved from https://www.hurun.net/EN/Article/Details?num=434C6BB30507, accessed in August 2020

6 Paradoxical Leadership

Since its founding, EtonHouse had grown out of adversity to become a renowned high-quality education provider. When dealing with difficulties, Ng came up with the "4Ps", namely, passion, perseverance, people skills and professional development. Because of her passion for education, she did not give up easily when things were not going well and persevered until she found a way through. Her people skills enabled her to deal with business partners, employees, children and parents effectively. She also insisted on the professional development of teachers and built a brand of high-quality education with an inquiry-based curriculum. With these four elements, she could accommodate conflicting demands and respond to paradoxical challenges presented in business operations. When asked about EtonHouse's success factors in China, Stephenson-Chin responded:

China is a graveyard for many education businesses due to its complex context, but EtonHouse has survived and is doing well. I think it's because of her vision and her ability to translate it quite effectively. Education is all about parent appeal. She manages to commit to the education philosophy she believes in yet lives up to parents' expectations and fulfills their requirements. In other words, EtonHouse blends in with the Chinese education system while standing out among schools.

7 The SARS Crisis in China

To establish EtonHouse's presence in China, Ng instilled boldness and caution when making decisions, proposing a holistic and strategized path for development.

The first school opened in 2003 during the severe acute respiratory syndrome (SARS) outbreak,[11] posing multiple challenges for the school. At first, Ng could not visit the school to supervise renovation work, and her Chinese colleagues could not visit Singapore for training due to travel restrictions. When she could eventually go, she was shocked to find that the renovation did not comply with the safety standards specified. As a believer that quality and safety were two things that should never be compromised, Ng pushed back the renovation timeline and incurred additional costs to get them fixed.

As a new brand, it was difficult for EtonHouse to recruit new students, while SARS and deteriorating economic conditions made it even harder. Despite all the efforts, EtonHouse only recruited seven students in the first term while having a team of seven expatriate and 13 local educators and staff. "So we had more staff than students in the beginning," Ng recalled with a laugh.

In the early stages, investors generally hesitated on continuing investments as losses accumulated. Ang explained: "It's a difficult choice because while you need to spend extra money on classroom resources and professional development, you also want to save money to avoid further losses." He continued, "Ms. Ng had the vision to put in extra dollars. When you keep investing in education, the quality will continue to grow, and students will be attracted to your school. So you don't have to worry too much about the end. In contrast, if the quality deteriorates, it will be difficult to attract new parents, and you will eventually fail to make ends meet." When recalling her decisions, Ng said: "I was determined to keep investing to ensure the quality of education. I also believed that when we continued to take in new cohorts, the total number of students would go up, and the cash flow would also pick up quickly."

Her investment bore fruit, as parents soon recognized the quality of EtonHouse education. School places were quickly filled, and there was a long waiting list. After the successful endeavor in Suzhou, EtonHouse actively expanded across China to places such as Chengdu, Nanjing and Jinan. The firm focused on K12 education, and some schools even provided through-train K12 programs.[12]

While EtonHouse showed ambition to open international schools all around China, it took about ten years before opening its first international preschool. As more and more young parents recognized the importance of early childhood development, EtonHouse saw an opportunity and founded international preschools with bilingual courses and an "Inquire-think-learn" curriculum based on the Reggio Emilia approach. Parents warmly welcomed the international preschools.

---

[11] SARS is an infectious disease that spread over the world and caused social and economic disruptions in many countries.

[12] Through-train K12 programs enabled students to get K12 education in one school.

8 Dynamic Balance

As EtonHouse grew, Ng also developed her unique management style that mixed autocracy with autonomy. When entering the China market, Ng was confident of EtonHouse's renowned "Inquire-think-learn" curriculum and implemented it in the same way as in Singapore. Soon, she and her colleagues faced doubts from parents. She found that although parents appreciated the way learning was integrated with play and recognized its value for children's growth, they questioned if it would produce good test scores. Some showed concerns that their children might lag behind their peers from other schools.

In response, she shared with principals and parents that learning was a life- long journey, and it was of paramount importance that they foster an interest in learning. The traditional approach where teachers imparted knowledge to children and assessed them via examinations was not ideal for young children. Instead, they wanted children to be confident, secure individuals with an inquisitive mind. Ng shared her reasoning, "The world is changing so fast, and what they learn today can become obsolete tomorrow. As such, EtonHouse aims to cultivate inquisitive minds to ask questions and seek answers. When children lay good foundation for learning, reading, spelling, and counting will be very easy to pick up." Meanwhile, Ng understood that students would move on to Chinese primary schools. She put in an extra special effort to help the Kindergarten 2 students transit smoothly by introducing a bridging program. In the program, children got exposed to language and mathematical thinking development activities and developed good learning habits, which helped them get ready physiologically and psychologically for the coming primary school life.

At EtonHouse, school principals were given much autonomy in determining the curriculum specifics and managing school operations. However, they had to fulfil one important requirement, that is, to generate a surplus so that the schools could be sustainable. Ng explained, "Surplus tol school is like oxygen to us. We can only support the school and inject capital initially for the first few years. If the school continues to run into a deficit, it is not sustainable." Thus, she encouraged all the principals to understand the economics of running a business and be good leaders.

Moreover, Ng insisted on maintaining decision control but was willing to take her employees' opinions on board. "While it's a family business, we do feel like we are a part of the family," Ang said. When he joined the company two years ago, he wondered if he could push forward some changes to make the business more structured. Ang soon found that Ng was open and receptive and even came up with ideas on implementing the changes. "This gave me a lot of trust and bravery, and I felt I could drive the direction as well," he added. In terms of strategic decisions, he held weekly meetings with the directors and then reported to Ng. If she did not approve, directors would regroup to discuss again.

9 Authority and Benevolence

Ng treated her employees with authority and benevolence by setting high standards and being a role model while maintaining personal connections and showing care and empathy. She believed that talents were indispensable to the success of schools. One of EtonHouse's biggest challenges was hiring new talents, those with not only skills, but also passion and commitment. To ensure the enactment of her educational philosophy, she portrayed the image of educators as "color with passion" and set it as a standard for all employees. Commenting on Ng's requirements, Stephenson-Chin said, "In EtonHouse, every employee gets a ton of autonomy, but also takes clearly-defined responsibility and is held accountable for their jobs, which is very entrepreneurial. It is not easy and often terrifies a lot of educators." Jin said, "All employees are evaluated against 'color with passion.' It is not just a slogan. It is the requirements that we have to meet in everyday work."

To ensure teaching quality, Ng also invested heavily in training and professional development programs for teaching staff and held international forums for educators to share up-to-date research and practices.

Instead of running schools with a methodical approach, Ng gained hands-on experience by working in the classroom. After completing her Advanced Certificate for Preschool Teacher Training and Master in Early Childhood, she spent days as a preschool teacher. She experienced first-hand the pressures and challenges imposed by high standards. That was when she increased teachers' annual leave to 35 days from 21 days to compensate for their demanding work.

Moreover, she went the extra mile to show her thoughtfulness by providing high insurance coverage for expatriates in China, including an SOS service with helicopter rescue in their policy. During the start-up phase, she took charge of team building by interviewing all teachers, conducting training, and spending much time caring for all the employees. She even thought of Chinese names for all the expatriates. Ng worked hard to recruit, develop and retain talents by creating a professional and respected work environment and treating them as families.

More importantly, she connected personally with her employees. Jin shared:

"When participating in school activities, she would try to get familiar with staff and find time to communicate with everyone. She is approachable and appeals emotionally to her employees." Jin had been in EtonHouse for about nine-and-a-half years before she quit in 2012.[13] She left with the curiosity to explore and worked for three international schools in their start-up stages. In September 2019, Ng contacted her to share EtonHouse's recent developments and future plans. In explaining why she decided to rejoin, Jin said, "I could easily tell from our conversation that what drives her now is still her passion for education. She is really dedicated to providing children with quality education instead of purely making money. It reminded me of her respect for everyone, her unique charisma, and the emotional connections between us. So, I was back after seven years' learning and recharging."

[13] Jin first joined EtonHouse in 2003 during the set-up of the first campus in Suzhou.

10 New Stage: Leadership in Transition

Ng's entrepreneurship and leadership qualities were recognized globally. In 2004, she received the Woman of Benevolence award in Suzhou for contributions to the local community. In 2009, she became the first Singaporean woman to receive the Freedom of the City of London for her contributions to international education. In 2011, she received the Jiangsu Friendship Award, the highest honor for foreign experts from the provincial government. In 2019, she won the EY Entrepreneur of The Year Award for education to honor her contributions to the economy and society.

Born in 1952, Ng looked ahead, planning to step back and let her son Yi Xian take over thereins. She remained managing director at EtonHouse and stayed very involved as she hoped for a smooth leadership transition. "While both Ms. Ng and Yi Xian have a passion for education and entrepreneurial spirits, Yi Xian is more open to change and willing to try new things to address the needs of families at EtonHouse," Jin commented on their similarities and differences.

Before joining the family business in 2015, Yi Xian worked as a hedge fund analyst in the US. Talking about why he quit that job, he explained, "I always believe it is necessary to have an innovative business mindset to keep up with changes and innovations. I want to be the new force in introducing changes that help enhance education for families." His joining was a surprise to Ng. "I have never asked him to come back, but I was glad that he was willing to do that. At first, I was a bit worried because running schools was totally different from investment banking. So we had an agreement that if it didn't work, he could go back to his comfort zone," Ng recalled. "I'm glad that it worked out very well. He has earned the authority and respect of others by his commitment and efforts." She added.

When Yi Xian joined the company in 2015, he had no experience related to managing schools. So Ng got him started with managing half of the schools that ran well with few problems to focus on understanding schools' operations and iron out the kinks of working for the family. In his second week of work, Yi Xian promised parents there would be no fee increases. Ng disagreed strongly: "You can't do that. If the government introduces a new education tax, we cannot go with the same fees. What we can promise is that we'll keep our fees increase to a minimum, right?" It was a strong disagreement between them but was resolved quickly. Yi Xian recalled, "It was lucky to have this disagreement early. After we reached an agreement, we managed to work well together with no further disputes." After six months, his work expanded to include the other half of the new or underperforming schools. Because different schools had different problems that needed to be managed case by case, he devoted his time and attention to working closely with each school principal and making tweaks to each school's operations. It took him almost a year to turn the schools around.

After that, he started to divert his attention from operations to strategy and implementation. Recalling his work experience in the US, he found that expatriates in Singapore would find living costs and international education fees too high. So he started an affordable international school called Middleton International School in 2017. Middleton International School borrowed the education foundation and teaching resources from EtonHouse and increased the class size to 28 from 24 to cut expenses to about half without compromising quality. Apart from business diversification, he focused on improving operations to adapt to the firm's growing size. Gradually, he took charge of the Chinese market and worked out the next steps with other executives.

11 Post-COVID–19: Expansion in China

When the COVID–19 pandemic broke out, many countries, including Singapore and China, home to most of EtonHouse's schools, imposed lockdown measures and closed schools. The education industry faced an unprecedented crisis, especially international schools like EtonHouse, as global mobility constraints disrupted the sector. Jin explained how school operations were challenged:

> First, about 15% of our expatriates cannot enter China, so headquarters has to assist each school in recruiting expatriates within China for the coming term. In addition, schools that shifted to online learning have to make extra efforts to guarantee teaching quality. Financially, there is also some pressure due to increased student withdrawals and tuition fee refund requests.
>
> During China's prolonged school suspension, the group faced increased student withdrawals and refund requests. To ensure stable long-term employment for all staff members, management decided on a 30% pay cut for themselves.
>
> In view of a potential downturn in annual end revenue, Ng hosted a meeting with all executives in April 2020 to brainstorm the next steps. After some discussions, three different strategies were brought to the table for further decisions.

Ang emphasized the importance of preserving liquidity during COVID–19 and suggested halting expansion. EtonHouse would be able to hold onto cash just in case the situation continued to worsen. His reasoning was straightforward: "Nobody can foretell how long the situation will last, and there is always a chance that this thing (COVID–19) resurges. On the other hand, schools are susceptible to financial losses due to lockdowns during COVID–19. So it may be a feasible strategy to wait for good opportunities."

Yi Xian suggested that new and incredible opportunities could emerge from crises. Firstly, COVID–19 had imposed radical changes on the whole education landscape, where online learning replaced brick and mortar education. It may thus be imperative to develop a new business model to specialize in digitalized education. Moreover, with a healthy balance sheet, EtonHouse could look for other schools as possible acquisition targets. He explained: "While some schools may fail to weather through this crisis, it may serve as a potential avenue for EtonHouse to grow by enacting strategic acquisitions and increasing our presence in China."

Oh suggested replicating the E-bridge model, an affordable preschool in Singapore, and leveraging E-bridge's resources to start more affordable preschools in

China. "While EtonHouse is one of the key players in affordable preschools in Singapore and has a well-established brand of E-bridge, we have only several affordable preschools in China. We already gained a deep understanding of course structures, school structures, and how to roll out affordable curriculums. Thus, we may take the advantage of this and scale up our affordable preschools in China." This move would also align with China's plans for mass affordable preschools.

It was an important decision that could have a far-reaching impact on EtonHouse. It would also require timely adjustments based on the COVID–19 situation. Ng hesitated, wondering whether she should guide Yi Xian through this crisis or just let go of thereins …

Antigal: Strategy and Succession Challenges in a Family-Owned Vineyard with Global Ambitions

Shanghai, whose skyline boasted a mix of old Shikumens (石库门), the Bund (外滩) with its British-style buildings, and the French Concession area (上海法租界), was a melting pot of past and future, Chinese traditions neighbored by European traits. This was Francesco's first impression of Shanghai, and it continued to enchant him after he moved to China to study and work in February 2016.

Born into a Chilean family with Italian origins, Francesco Cartoni got several job offers after studying engineering. However, an offer to be export manager at Chile's largest producer and exporter of wines intrigued him the most. He felt it would give him a chance to better understand an investment that his father Virgilio Cartoni made back in 2007. Specifically, Virgilio had entered as a minority shareholder in the ownership of an Argentinian winery, Antigal Winery & Estates, with a distribution company in the United States.

In January 2015, Francesco started working for the Chilean wine exporter, and soon realized that the future of the wine business was in China. He also realized that he wished to follow this trend personally. So, in July, Francesco requested to represent the Chilean company in China. In October 2015, Francesco flew to Shanghai for the first time to prepare for his move.

In February 2016, Francesco embarked on the long trip to Shanghai for a second time, but this time to stay. Francesco worked full-time for the Chilean wine exporter for the next two years. His desire to acquire new abilities and enhance his knowledge began to rise.

Moreover, by that time his father, Virgilio, had acquired full control of the Antigal winery, so Francesco felt an even greater sense of responsibility to help him grow

Professor Lucia Pierini of China Europe International Business School, Martin Roll of Martin Roll Company, Professor Gianfranco Siciliano and Case Researcher Dr. CAO Zhijing of China Europe International Business School developed this case with the helpful cooperation and support of the case company. The case aims to provide the basis for classroom discussion rather than illustrate effective or ineffective handling of a management situation. This case was the First Prize winner of 2021 Global Contest for the Best China-Focused Cases.

China-Focused Cases, https://doi.org/10.1007/978-981-97-8580-3_6

and expand the family company internationally. One evening, Francesco opened his laptop, searched for business schools in Asia, and within a few minutes opted for a full MBA program in China. He intended to work for the family winery on his days off.

Francesco's MBA journey started in August 2018. At that time, he also began traveling across Asia on behalf of Antigal, from Japan to Thailand, Mongolia to Indonesia. From his previous working experience, he knew that relationships were everything in the wine business, especially in China. In fact, he found his first B2B customer in the form of an alumnus.

In December 2018, his first MBA term had ended, and Francesco was in the library studying for his exams. He closed his book and began writing an email to his accounting professor to request a meeting. Francesco had begun wondering about the future of Antigal: How could he expand the business and increase the enterprise value of the firm? How much could China contribute? Should Antigal hire an external manager to face the market and new business avenues in China? What about the future of the family business? Francesco asked the professor directly: "What could the potential value of my family company be? Let me first explain Antigal to you ..."

1 The Argentina Winery Industry and the Antigal Group

In 2019, Argentina was the world's fifth-largest wine producer, the tenth-largest wine exporter, and the ninth-largest wine-consuming country. Argentina's total export value in 2018 was US$821 million. Antigal was the second oldest winery in Mendoza still in operation. The property, established in 1897, was considered one of the most productive wineries at that time in terms of capacity (see Exhibit 1).

By 2020, the Antigal Group had an integrated business model in all segments of the wine value chain, encompassing vineyards, wine production, and distribution. The group consisted of three companies: Cork Alliance Inc., a wine wholesaler and importer/distributor based in Miami (the United States) with a 20-year history of importing Antigal wines to the US distributors and with a presence in all 50 states; and high-quality wine producers Bodega Antigal S.A. and Cepas del Sur S.A., both based in Mendoza (Argentina).[1] About 99% of Antigal's total sales were exports, with a strategic focus on premium (81%) and super-premium (6%) wines (see Exhibit 2). By 2020, Antigal's main markets were the US and Canada (62% of total sales), followed by Latin and Central America (21%), Asia (11%), and Europe (7%).

[1] Mendoza, situated at the heart of the Andes Mountain range, is recognized as the "World's Capital of Wine." Seventy percent of all vineyards planted in Argentina are in Mendoza.

Date	Milestone
1897	Facility established. Today it is the second oldest winery in Mendoza that still produces.
2000	Antigal is born as the winery and is completely renovated by the renowned architecture firm Bormida yYanzon. Style ofwine is changed from bulk to high quality.
2003	Bottling equipment imported from Italy.
2005	Antigal creates its first signature wine, ONE Single Vineyard.
2007	The company starts exporting to the United States, with a Florida-based import company managing the distribution network throughout all 50 United States.
2011	"UNO" Malbec receives its first recognition by the prestigious US magazine Wine Enthusiast.
2016	New investors take company control. One single family owner.
2018	HAACP certified/BPM by Bureau Veritas.
2019	ISO 22000: 2005 certified.

Exhibit 1 The antigal winery story *Source* Company information

Exhibit 2 Antigal portfolio *Source* Company information

1.1 The Cartoni Family

Virgilio Cartoni (born in 1959) showed entrepreneurial skills from a very early age. In his teens, he would ask his mother to bake cakes for him that he would later sell to his neighbors for profit. At 17, he enlisted in the Chilean army, eventually becoming a helicopter pilot. But Virgilio never lost his entrepreneurial spirit: in 1981, he started his first real business, manufacturing and distributing baby clothes. In 1986, Virgilio married his soulmate, Ana Maria Castilla, and they soon started working together. Virgilio retired from the army and sold some properties to gather some funds. In 1988, he and Ana Maria bought a gasoline station under the Exxon brand, which they sold in 2000 for a price enabling him to start other businesses. In 1989, Virgilio started a new business with a helicopter pilot friend. It consisted of importing spare parts and lubricants for helicopters and airplanes and engine overhauls. Ana Maria not only helped Virgilio in the management of this business, working as secretary, translator, and accountant, but also developed her own business units within the firm to sell medical supplies to health care companies.

Virgilio and Ana Maria had four kids, Stefano, Francesco, Alessandra, and Antonella, who were exposed to the family business throughout their childhood. "They grew up with that [entrepreneurship] concept, and this was natural for them," Ana Maria recalled.

In 2001, Virgilio and Ana Maria started investing in the winery business with a US$150,000 loan to a family friend, Mr. Horacio P., the original founder of the Antigal winery. Horacio had started the business because he had always dreamed about running a winery and had a suitable piece of land in Argentina. In the next few years, the Cartoni family continued extending loans to Horacio's winery company to sustain its operations. In 2007, the cumulative amount of the loan was about US$2.6 million. Then, Virgilio entered the company as shareholder (see Exhibit 3), but the company lacked a formal board of directors. In this scenario, Horacio, the controlling shareholder, continued managing the company independently. Virgilio was not involved in the company's daily operations. "It was a Pandora's box. My family and I were just visiting the winery, inviting friends, and enjoying wine. I did not get involved because my friend Horacio did not allow me to," Virgilio recalled.

The Cartonis started negotiating with Horacio, requesting access to company information and urging him to repay his loan. In 2016, Virgilio and Ana Maria made a deal with Horacio and his wife Alicia during a roundtable discussion: the Cartoni family would take full control of the company. Owning a winery had been the dream of Virgilio's Italian grandfather. With this deal, Virgilio thought he had at least indirectly realized his grandfather's dream. The reality, however, was different, as Virgilio and Ana Maria soon realized that the business was severely impaired due to large salaries and expenses. The family filed a lawsuit to reach a legal solution. "That certainly broke our friendship with Horacio, in some way," Ana Maria recollected.

	Before 2007	After 2007
Antigal Winery Argentina	• Horacio P.: 85% • Horacio P.'s brother: 10% • Horacio P.'s sister: 5%	• Horacio P.: 90% • Horacio P.'s wife: 10%
USA Cork Alliance	• Horacio P.: 61% • Horacio P.'s brother: 10% • Cartoni: 29%	• Horacio P.: 47.5% • Horacio P.'s wife: 10% • Cartoni: 42.5%

Exhibit 3 Changes in Antigal ownership *Source* Company information

2 The Multigenerational Family Firm

Once Virgilio Cartoni got full control of Antigal in 2016, he wanted the firm to adopt a structure of a multigenerational family firm with a clear ownership structure. In fact, all four of his children joined the Antigal Group, capital ab initio (see Exhibit 4).

Virgilio Cartoni and Ana Maria Castilla each owned 20% of shares in vehicle company, Inversiones ROCKY, while the four members of the second generation of the family each owned 15% of shares. The Inversiones ROCKY vehicle represented the parent company of Bodega Antigal S.A. and Cepas del Sur S.A. with 70% ownership, and the remaining 30% was owned by Virgilio Cartoni.

The vehicle was also the second minority (and unique) shareholder of Cork Alliance Inc., with 42.5% of the shares. The majority shareholder was the BACO company, equally owned (50%) by Virgilio Cartoni and Ana Maria Castilla. Therefore, Virgilio Cartoni and Ana Maria Castilla, via the vehicle and the BACO company, were the controlling shareholders of Cork Alliance Inc. The four children, with their indirect ownership via the vehicle, were the minority shareholders of Cork Alliance Inc.

Between 2018 and 2019, the Antigal Group turned into a multigenerational family firm in terms of managerial structure, as the younger generation of the Cartoni family, specifically Stefano, Alessandra, and Francesco, assumed managerial positions. At this time, the Cartoni family did not consider having a board of directors to be a priority. Unlike Virgilio, who had no higher education background, his children had all attended top universities and business schools, and they all had experience working at multinational companies. The children recognized the importance of having a well-structured business model for operations.

After this change in ownership and management, the Antigal Group witnessed rapid market growth, expanding from one country (US) to more than 50 countries in four years (see Exhibit 5).

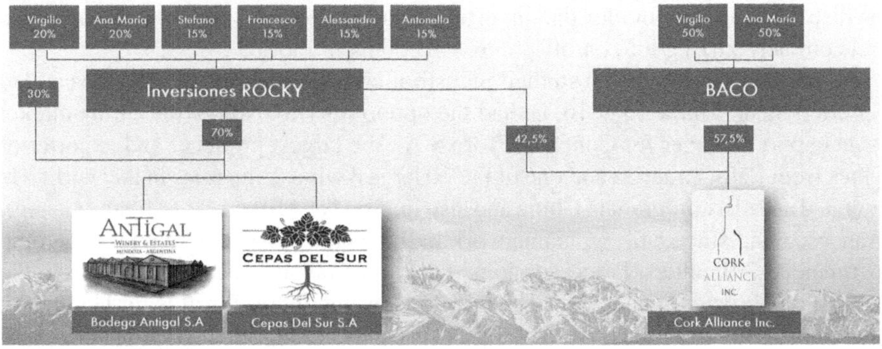

Exhibit 4 Antigal ownership structure. *Source* Company information

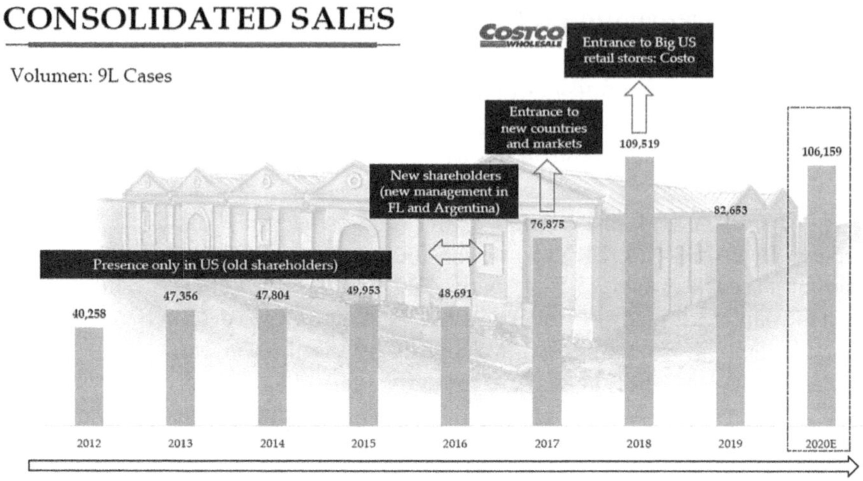

Exhibit 5 Antigal sales growth. *Source* Company information

3 The Younger Cartoni Generation

Stefano (born in 1988) had a bachelor's degree in business administration from the Universidad des los Andes. He was involved in Antigal's financial operations. Before working for Antigal, Stefano worked at Larrain Vial S.A., a family wealth administration company. Several years later, he felt "stuck" in the company because all senior bankers were more than 10 years his senior. Stefano wanted to find another job and applied to a part-time MBA program. However, he said, "One day, my father asked me to move to Miami and work for Cork Alliance." In 2018, he moved to Florida to work for his family company, and at the same time, he attended an MBA program at the University of Miami. In mid-2020, Stefano was in charge of Antigal's US and Canada operations, managing the commercial office in the US and focusing on bringing new business "to the table". In 2020, Cork Alliance also started utilizing his distributor license in Florida, importing wines and spirits from all over the world and commercializing it to on/off-premise accounts in Florida.

Francesco (born in 1990) studied industrial civil engineering at the Universidad Federico Santa Maria. In 2016, he had the opportunity to explore the China market as an export manager for Concha Y Toro S.A., the largest producer and exporter of wines from Latin America and one of the 10 largest wine companies in the world. He attended an MBA program in China and also interned at AliExpress (Alibaba Group). Francesco had since built up his network in the country. To help Antigal overcome its financial difficulties, Francesco joined the company as executive assistant to the US general director in late 2018. The director was mainly responsible for US market operations. "When I joined Antigal, I was very concerned, because I was not able to get a clear financial picture of the company. There was not a clear strategy. It seemed to me that all correct management practices I learned at business school had gone unheeded." Later, Francesco became head of global export markets, except for the US and Canada.

During the first six months of 2019, Francesco's time was fully dedicated to his MBA and the Antigal family business. In September, he moved to Madrid to complete his MBA exchange at the IE Business School. Francesco also considered the move to Europe as an opportunity to find new customers in this geographical area. In December, he came back to Chile to celebrate Christmas with his family. He had planned to return to China at the beginning of 2020 for his MBA graduation celebration and continue developing the Chinese market, but the COVID–19 pandemic led to worldwide travel restrictions.

Alessandra (born in 1992) studied business and economics at the Universidad de Chile and had been working at L'Oréal's marketing department for four years. Later, she quit her job as she did not agree with the company's brand strategy and preferred to do something for her own family. Alessandra joined Antigal to help her father and brother Stefano in June 2019, and she became the general manager of the two Antigal companies in Mendoza. In this role, she had to manage the operations of about 40 people in the production facility and the vineyards, overseeing winemaking, marketing, tourism, human resources, accounting and finance, maintenance, certifications and international standards, as well as COMEX (import/export). "Stefano, in Miami, was involved in Cork Alliance, managing sales and imports, but he did not get involved with daily operations in Argentina. Therefore, there was a lot of room for improvement when I joined Antigal. That is why I was enjoying the family business. I felt responsible for making things happen and professionalizing operations. The first month was very difficult for me, coming from a multinational company, going to a family business without structure, policies, or internal processes," Alessandra said.

Antonella (born in 1998) was the youngest sister. She studied law at the Pontificia Universidad Catolica de Chile. She also worked as a part-time model, represented by Elite Model Chile, styling for many high-end brands and with almost 70,000 followers on social media. With little interest in wine and related business, she showed less passion to run the family business compared with her siblings. However, once she had completed her university studies, she intended to help the family with legal assistance in running the winery business, although she noted that the Chilean law was quite different from those of both Argentina and the US. Antonella also thought she could help the family to manage the family's social networks, such as the Antigal's Instagram profile, leveraging her hefty following. However, her segment and followers were more related to the fashion and beauty industry.

4 New Energy Introduced

After the split between Virgilio and Horacio, the younger Cartonis realized that the company needed new guidelines, processes, and governance. Francesco described the winery business as "a little toy" in the very early stage when they entered the industry. “The business started with my father lending money in a very unprofessional way. When I started to work for the company in late 2018, it was very challenging because I had MBA classes in China, while at the same time, I had to find time to help my family, attract new customers, and grow the business. I was juggling two full-time assignments.”

In the first quarter of 2020, the US general director’s (GD) contract was concluding and subject to possible renewal. At about the same time, Francesco finished his MBA. The Cartoni family decided against renewing the contract with the GD, instead relying fully on family members. “Honestly, from a financial perspective, the GD was very ‘heavy’ in terms of salary. It did not make sense that the GD remained, as it was me who was developing the business for him,” Francesco recalled. The three siblings took over the GD work, according to their experiences.

The organization of the company moved from “one US general director” to a “group of family-directors”. “In terms of governance, we have meetings with our father, and each of us operate his/her own business at the same time. We are also more concerned about having good relationships with our employees now, while before some staff members were scared even to approach and talk with the CEO”, Francesco explained.

The US offices often had internal meetings to discuss the development of the distribution model. Stefano described the North American market as more competitive, “because there were many well-known local and international wineries from Napa Valley to Marlborough, New Zealand”. Besides, the United States had a special alcohol distribution system, the “Three-Tier System”. It was the former founder, Horacio, who had designed the business model of having a US-based company to import alcohol with a special license. This model helped Antigal achieve a wide distribution system in the US market and gain a higher profit margin. To grow the business further, Stefano worked hard to expand the focus of Antigal in the United States. He pushed sales via e-commerce and generated partnerships with specialized wine and spirits retailers like Drizly, Wine.com, Seven-Fifty, and SG Proof, among others. However, he also worked to expand the old channels.

At the beginning, there were five sales district managers all over the United States, each of them working directly with the distributors in their regions. In March 2021, they increased to seven. Yet, Cork Alliance Inc. had various revenue streams, from exporting wine products to distributing third-party wine brands. One of the key successes in the US was its strong sales team, which built a solid relationship with partner distributors like Southern Glazer Wines & Spirits Republic National Distributing Company, MS Walker, Allied Beverage, Johnson Brothers, Vintage Wines, Hayden Beverage, and Intermountain Distributing, among others. This strategy helped Antigal wines establish a tremendous brand reputation in the industry, becoming one of the seven most-sold Malbecs in the United States.

Compared with Francesco, who was more interested in the big picture and building relationships with customers, Alessandra faced different challenges at Antigal. Having previously worked for a multinational company, she had moved from a position with well-defined roles and responsibilities to a business with a rapidly changing working environment. "At L'Oréal I had my goals, which aligned with specific objectives. I had my job description, my boundaries. But at Antigal this is not that clear. The main goal is to keep growing the business in different areas including production, sales, marketing, certifications, and human resources."

Although Alessandra was very excited about working in this new environment, she also felt the pressures involved in internal management. For example, she sometimes had difficulty communicating with senior employees who were older and much more experienced than she was. "It is very challenging because I have to prepare myself. I always tell my team that I am also learning, and I am open to criticism—constructive criticism. Being the owner's daughter helps me because they respect me for that, but what I have tried to do is earn their respect by working hard and being helpful." Alessandra insisted on paying for her own wine rather than just taking it for free if she wanted it. "I work with them, eat with them. I follow the same rules that I ask them to follow. I have to be fair."

5 Relationships Among Different Generations

Virgilio and Ana Maria Cartoni always had great trust in their four children, regardless of whether they worked for the company or pursued other passions in life. Likewise, all the children expressed great respect and gratitude for what their parents had created through hard work. "We know that the creation of our wealth comes from them. Our main job now is to make that wealth grow," Alessandra said. Francesco had a similar opinion: "As a family member, I feel responsible for taking the business to the next level, where it deserves to be because it was very poorly managed, but it has a huge potential."

With this ambition, Antigal's younger generation was eager to ask for more authority and autonomy from their father, Virgilio. "My father is happy to work with us as he relies a lot on us. There is less weight on his shoulders since we joined the company."

However, Alessandra also said that sometimes Virgilio would override his children's decisions. "Then, I will say, please let us talk first and give us more decision power." Alessandra admitted the existence of a generation gap and that it might be detrimental to the company's development. "My father is busy moving forward and has little time to learn. The first generation of a family firm is always very entrepreneurial, opportunistic, pushing for new stuff. However, it does not always take the time to plan for the future because it does not have the experience of being third or fourth generation and has never been through family business succession." She thought it might be a good idea for her father to learn about family governance and succession like she did in business school.

On the other hand, the sons sometimes asked for support from their parents. Successful entrepreneurs like Virgilio Cartoni and Ana Maria had accumulated financial resources and, above all, knowledge and worldwide business connections.

"My father has been working with international companies for 25 years. He has many friends working as managers or CEOs at big companies. I asked him, why do you not call them? They can help us with the wine distribution and the professionalization of our business," Francesco said. Another time, Francesco suggested reducing his father's payroll so that he could hire several experienced industry experts to better explore the market and push sales. Francesco's hardworking style helped him motivate himself. "To be honest, I am not seeking gratification from my father. I gratify myself every morning when I look into the mirror because I like the intensity." He further explained that working for Antigal gave him energy, passion, and a reason to wake up and work hard to build sustainable growth for a company that differentiated from its competitors. "I want to see my father being happy. Besides, building something is always challenging as a personal goal."

As the mother of this Chilean family and a psychology consultant in her own practice, Ana Maria Castilla was worried about whether her children could achieve happiness at Antigal. "I hope my children can pursue what they like, rather than taking the family business as their responsibility." She and Alessandra had a minor complaint about Virgilio's and Francesco's workaholic lifestyle, with no separation between work and personal life. Alessandra commented, "You have to set boundaries. You need a specific schedule and context to conduct a meeting. For example, when I go to the kitchen, my father will come and ask me about some work issues. Sometimes, I get annoyed and suggest that we talk later."

6 Relationships Among Siblings

Although the younger Cartonis had a professional business education, they still had different thinking styles due to their different experiences. On the one hand, they could learn from each other; Francesco and Stefano liked to discuss their ideas about distribution and branding in different markets. On the other hand, their differences could also lead to conflicts. Moreover, while Francesco was working on the company's expansion in new markets and Alessandra was in charge of the administration of the entire Argentina office, Stefano focused on the US operations. Inevitably, different points of view entailed different ideas and perspectives on managing the business.

According to Alessandra, her previous work experience had led to a more structured and organized working style. She spent much time preparing for each meeting and always had clear objectives in mind. Unlike Francesco, a multitasker who was often thinking about multiple projects at once, Alessandra was more conservative,preferring to focus on one project at a time. When communicating with Francesco, who was used to making multiple proposals, she generally behaved more conservatively. "Francesco and I always fight with each other. He sometimes sends a lot of emails about projects from A to Z. But I think we cannot do everything, or I think that we can accomplish them one at a time. My brother likes to contribute his ideas. He is very brilliant, but he is not so organized."

Francesco admitted that this attitude was the result of his negotiation and marketing skills. Francesco knew the most about the wine industry, thanks to his previous working experience, and he tried to learn more about new companies. In 2020, Francesco contacted a big Argentinian wine and spirits group, which asked Antigal to help it distribute products in the US. In exchange, the company offered Antigal logistics service in Argentina. However, the conversation between the two companies cooled because of inefficient communication. "Stefano was very busy with another issue at that moment, and he lost contact with that company. Sometimes, I feel alone in devising new ideas as to how to make Antigal different, adding more value to the brand and achieving sustainable global growth." Francesco said.

Despite these differences, the family worked hard to preserve good relationships. "Our parents have given us good education. This is very important for us. And there has always been communication and transparency about everything. So, we have our discussions, and we may fight about something, but this is normal in business families. Overall, we have managed to work together smoothly", Alessandra said.

7 Family Business Management

> "I worked with a lot of family business management stuff in my previous job. It is sad but also true that the first generation creates the business, the second runs the business, and the third 'screws it up.' We are the second generation. I think so far we are good and there is still hope."
>
> Stefano Cartoni

8 Governance in the Business

At the end of 2020, shares of the Antigal Group were allocated in a way that Virgilio Cartoni owned the majority of the shares, Ana Maria Castilla was the second largest shareholder, and the four siblings were the minority shareholders. In this setting, all family members recognized the importance of having clear responsibilities within the company. However, there was neither a code of conduct for all the family members, nor a defined incentive package for the three children who worked in the company. "We are evolving because this is a process through which we decide how everybody works. Based on this model, you communicate how you feel and how you prefer to work."

However, with so many offices and businesses, it was still difficult to identify boundaries and define clear roles and responsibilities. By 2020, no exact key performance indicators (KPIs) or indexes were defined, and each family member had to deal with multiple tasks or market segments. For instance, Francesco handled the product and strategy, while Alessandra dealt with the Argentinian suppliers who had stock issues and sometimes extended lead times on dry goods. Stefano managed the US team, which was relatively old-fashioned. This unclear and undefined organization would create hurdles if they wanted Antigal to be vertically integrated.

To solve this issue, they organized regular family meetings to ensure well-established communication and transparency. On the first Friday of every month, Alessandra would invite the whole Cartoni family to have a discussion. "We do not have too much overlap in business, but we still try to be informed about everything. I live with my parents, and we can go downstairs to talk. The rest of us use WhatsApp or we conduct weekly meetings to communicate."

9 Board and External Consultants

By 2020, Antigal had not formed a real board of directors; the entire Cartoni family operated the business as joint owners. Meetings would be arranged only if there were important issues to be discussed. Most of the time, Virgilio Cartoni would take the lead. All the family members seemed to behave cautiously and reluctantly to include external people in leading management roles. "For me, the leader is my father, and the rest of us are like directors. It would entail a high cost to introduce external consultants to the company. I do not want to add someone to the inner circle because it will take a lot of time to explain the business," Alessandra said. She thought that the time to include an outsider in the inner circle of the company had not yet come. First, they needed better internal organization to ensure that adding an external leader would add value to the firm.

Stefano also expressed concern due to his previous work experience. "Before entering the company, Antigal had hired both a CEO and a CFO in the Miami office. It was a mess with them. We had a bad experience—for instance, we lacked good management practices, high salaries, a lot of expenses."

However, all the siblings demonstrated an open attitude. An external consultant provided them with advice about shareholding governance and ownership structures. External advisors were hired for specific projects. They organized discussions and had internal reports about different aspects of the business.

Francesco was the most disposed toward hiring external consultants. He thought it could help them professionalize the business and develop a vision. For example, he felt the company needed to be bolder about moving into China and other global growth markets. This was also why he wanted to hire people who had work experience in the industry.

"Inviting an external chairman or board members is more like a global business model, which my family has never understood. I think nobody likes it when there is an external person evaluating your work performance. I believe we may need it because we currently operate in an old-fashioned manner, and adding a new, future-proof vision could be helpful", Francesco said. In 2020, he asked his father about hiring an external consultant to help alleviate internal conflicts about the company's strategy.

10 Succession and Transfer of Power

Virgilio Cartoni had originally entered the winery business to help friends and later to ask for repayment of a loan. Although from the very beginning, all family members were shareholders, it was not until 2018 to 2019 that the second generation started to work for Antigal. Antonella, the youngest of the family, was still in law school. However, Stefano, Francesco, and Alessandra were keen on having her join the company. Alessandra said, "For me, I think it is better with more hands.

Antonella is majoring in law, and she can contribute a lot to the winery business. If she wants to get involved, that would be great. But if she does not want to do so, it is okay as well. She is only 22 and might feel uncomfortable joining an unfamiliar industry."

Another potential issue involved the possibility of opening the company to new family members from the third and later generations in the future. "It would become more difficult because more opinions would also create more confusion. We have to design a clear structure and internal policies at present," Alessandra said. She also mentioned the possibility that conflicts might arise once she or her siblings had domestic partners: "Sometimes people change because their partners behave in a good or in a bad way, and then wealth conflicts between the four of us could start. Thus, we have to have clear rules and make everything clear now." As Stefano asserted, a mutual sense of trust in the family and its entrepreneurial spirit had contributed a great deal to Antigal's rapid growth in the past four years. "Thanks to this family mindset, we have come to the current situation, and we are trying to take the company to the next level. But the most important thing is to achieve a more professional governance structure."

However, the second generation also showed great ambition for entrepreneurship related to other industries. Antonella was involved in modeling. Francesco was always eager to find new opportunities; when he was in China, he developed an import channel to Chile for military equipment like boots, tents, and uniforms. And Alessandra thought winery was a difficult business, "with a lot of stock, a lot of inventory, and immobilized capital". "It's an industry that depends on the weather, something that you cannot control," she said.

Several acquisitions took place in the winery industry in recent years. In June 2019, the second-largest exporting group for Chilean wine, the VSPT Wine Group, agreed to purchase the historic Bodega Graffigana in San Juan, Argentina. In 2020, the mergers and acquisitions market in the wine industry continued to be active despite the COVID–19 pandemic.

11 Entering the Chinese Market

Recent years saw a shift in spending power in the global winery market. The retired generation had an increasing impact on global spending power. However, in China, the situation was slightly different because the younger generation had higher product awareness. According to Wine Intelligence, people aged 15 to 59 in China would contribute about 18% of the global consumption growth from 2015 to 2030 (see Exhibit 6). In 2018, 37% of people aged 40 to 54 consumed wines, compared with 26% in 2011. Furthermore, with the rapid development of mobile internet and market digitalization, many consumers now preferred to buy wine online (see Exhibit 7).

Since the average awareness of the top five wine regions had decreased from 60% to 40% in China, wine brands like Antigal had more opportunities to expand in this

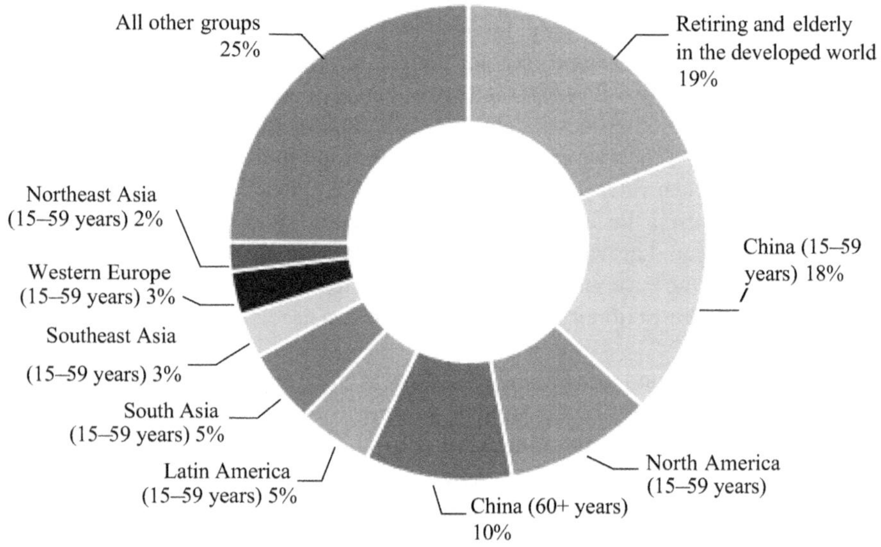

Exhibit 6 Share of global wine consumption growth, 2015–2030. *Source* Company information

Exhibit 7 Shift of wine-buying channel in China

Wine-buying channel	China		
	2011 (%)	2018 (%)	Tacking 11–18
Wine shop/shop specialized in alcohol	78	58	Down
On the internet	36	48	Up
Hypermarkets	84	40	Down
Department store	46	38	Down
Duty free (at airports, etc.)	40	35	Down

Source Company information

market. With his 10 years of learning and working experience in China, Francesco believed China could play an essential role in the future of Antigal. According to the Argentinian Export Department, at the end of 2020 the market size for Argentinian wine in China was US$15–20 million. In contrast, the Chilean wine sector was worth US$250 million. Apart from taxes (trading between Chile and China is tax-free, while the tax rate is 14% with Argentina), Francesco thought that Chilean companies behaved more aggressively.

In this emerging market, Francesco clearly knew that he should conduct deep research and work harder to understand the local business environment. China and North America were different markets in multiple respects, including wine distribution, negotiation, and consumer sentiment. That was why replicating the US business model was not practical for Antigal. "China is a huge country and has a highly fragmented market. It is very hard to sell one brand to different customers. As a result, we are considering doing direct business with big retailers, and we also have other B2B e-commerce partners. Besides, we have built our channel on the Chinese e-commerce platform Taobao because the market is highly digitalized," Francesco said. In 2020, Antigal closed an important deal with Walmart in China. In 2021, sales to Walmart China were expected to be five times greater than in 2020.

12 Taking Antigal to the Next Level

Because of the COVID–19 pandemic and related worldwide travel restrictions, for all of 2020, the Cartoni family managed the Antigal business remotely from Chile. It was only in February 2021 that Francesco, his sister Alessandra, and their father Virgilio could go to Mendoza again. One Friday, the Cartoni family held a regular meeting to discuss weekly business operations and development plans. Francesco prepared a presentation of the company's strategy to explore emerging markets, aiming to create more opportunities for business growth. "We need to build constant innovation and stay close to our customers." He showed the figures for what Argentina exported to foreign countries. One of his proposals was to hire a competent external director for the China market, rather than a sales manager. "We have built good relationships with several companies in large Chinese cities, but the rest of the country is a kind of jungle that we have never explored."

However, Stefano and Alessandra did not have enough information and market knowledge to give any informed opinions about his proposal. They seemed to be cautious when Francesco proposed to quickly build a professional sales team. They were more interested in the daily operations of Antigal: Alessandra had successfully built a human resource department and a marketing department, while Stefano had created KPIs for US salespeople. However, it was still hard for them to see that the only way to grow rapidly, especially in China, was to acquire new customers. According to Francesco, this could take one to two years. Their reluctance frustrated Francesco, who knew that without the support of his family, his plans would go nowhere. At the same time, Virgilio expected the Antigal Group to achieve twice the sales revenue of 2018–2019 and to distribute Antigal products in 80 countries by 2022. This goal put more pressure on his children.

It had been a long day for Francesco. He left the Mendoza office for Santiago with so many issues to consider and several challenges looming ahead. First, the Cartonis needed to reach a consensus on a future focus on the China market and then decide on a feasible, effective long-term strategy. As Francesco would not stay in China for the long term, but wanted to expand Antigal in this increasingly dynamic market, who should take the lead, and how could that leader be integrated within the family? How should global sales and expansion efforts be structured moving forward?

Second, as the company was growing, it was urgent to develop a formal internal structure/organization and focus on strategic governance matters. During the past few years, the Cartoni family had also started businesses parallel to Antigal, exploring alternative industries and making real estate investments. As the business expanded, the Cartoni family was thinking about creating a family office. Who should be the CEO of the Antigal Group? Who and which positions should make up the management team? To what extent should the company engage/hire outside talents and seasoned leaders?

Third, since the family was in its second generation, how should it handle internal tensions and potential conflicts? Why would the Cartonis be a business family? On what grounds could the family members work in the business? Who should take on board and governance roles? Different family members had different career interests and expectations for Antigal. A strategy was thus needed for the business to ensure prosperity and family unity. The Cartonis also had to agree on how to deal with the main management decisions. What about possible acquisition bids or business exits of a family member? Succession plans and a long-term ownership structure also needed to be discussed and agreed upon.

As he arrived back in Santiago, Francesco took a deep breath. With so many issues to ponder, it looked like any decisions about the future of Antigal would not be easy.

Geek+: Challenges and Growth in the World of Autonomous Warehouse Robotics

"What are the key challenges currently encountered by Geek+?" This was the question posed to Yong Zheng, CEO of Beijing Geek+ Science Technology Co., Ltd, in an interview on June 15, 2021, by 21st Century Business Herald, China's largest commercial newspaper. Zheng listened intently to the question. After careful consideration, he answered, "During the six years of its development, Geek+ has faced many challenges. The outbreak of COVID–19 has disrupted the supply chains of many enterprises and made them realize the huge complexity and risks of SCM (supply chain management). The traditional principle of SCM is changing from one that is cost-centered to one that is agility and resilience-centered. For now, the search for ways to better satisfy our customers' diversified needs and to help them create resilient supply chains through robotics and AI [artificial intelligence] technology is the challenge that we are facing. I believe that we can continue to grow with our customers." After the interview, Zheng sat in his office, which had an open layout and was situated close to the installation and debugging workshop. Looking at his employees busy at work, he could not help but reflect on the challenges that Geek+ had encountered along the long and winding road that had led to this moment.

Founded in February 2015, Geek+ started its business operations in automated warehouse robotics. In seven years, Geek+ grew into a leading AMR[1] company globally; it occupied the largest share of the AMR market in consecutive years from

[1] AMR (Autonomous Mobile Robots): Robots that sense the surrounding environment through sensors and that make decisions autonomously. AMRs are different from AGVs (Automated Guided Vehicles). Although AGVs are generally equipped with devices for automatic guidance, such as electromagnetic or optical guidance, they can only travel along prescribed paths based on their sensors and make corresponding decisions autonomously.

Professor XUE Yixi, LONG Zhengqin and Professor YU Xiaoyu of Shanghai University developed this case. The case aims to provide the basis for classroom discussion rather than illustrate effective or ineffective handling of a management situation. This case was the First Prize winner of 2021 Global Contest for the Best China-Focused Cases.

China-Focused Cases, https://doi.org/10.1007/978-981-97-8580-3_7

2019 to 2020, and its contract amount reached ¥2 billion.[2] In 2019 and 2020, Geek+ was featured in the "Top 50 Global Robots List" of Robotics Business Review, an authoritative international publication on robotics; this was the first and only time that a Chinese AMR company had featured on the list. In March 2021, Geek+ was included in the "World's Top 10 Most Innovative Robot Companies" list by Fast Company.[1] In July 2021, Geek+ featured in the "Top 50 China's New Economic Unicorns List", and its valuation reached US$5 billion.[2]

"Technology and product, not profit, are what we have cared most about since the foundation of Geek+", Zheng said during the Geek+ 2021 Smart Logistics Summit. He felt lucky and confident in his entrepreneurial choices. He believed that intellectualization constitutes a strategic direction in traditional logistics and that robotics could revolutionize a wide range of industries. However, he was also deeply aware of the many barriers that Geek+ had overcome along the way, such as innovating a diverse array of robot products to solve different warehousing problems, selling products at high prices, and balancing large-scale production with customized demand. He was also concerned about the critical challenges that Geek+ would face in the post-COVID–19 era. In particular, he needed to ensure that Geek+ could continue to empower its customers and be an industry leader in the future.

1 Starting Geek+ Founder: Yong Zheng

Zheng received a bachelor's degree from Tsinghua University and a master's degree from RWTH Aachen University; both degrees were in the field of industrial engineering. After completing his tertiary education, Zheng pursued a decade-long career with ABB (Asea Brown Boveri), the Saint-Gobain Group, and New Horizon Capital. At ABB, Zheng was responsible for SCM and was thus exposed to the application of robotics and automation in industrial scenes. Within the Saint-Gobain Group, Zheng accumulated all-around experience in the operation of logistics, quality control, sales, marketing, and management. At New Horizon Capital, Zheng had the opportunity to be directly engaged in a variety of entrepreneurial projects in the robot industry.

"I like making products and want to produce some 'cool' things. After entering New Horizon Capital and seeing so many start-ups, I realized that I missed my dreams and I want to change," Zheng said. In 2012, Amazon, the e-commerce giant, acquired KIVA for US$775 million to obtain its warehouse robotic technology. In 2014, Zheng investigated Amazon's automated warehouse logistics project. He was shocked by the sight of thousands of robots working in the warehouses. Sensing a business opportunity, he said at the time, "I believe in the great value and potential of robotics in the field of logistics and warehousing.[3]"

---

[2] ¥ = CNY = Chinese Yuan Renminbi, ¥1 = approximately US$0.1611, US$1539 as of December 31, 2014 and 2015, ¥1 = approximately US$0.1520, US$0.1439 as of January 31 and December 31, 2016, ¥1 = approximately US$0.1453 as of December 31, 2018.

2 Pain Points of China's Warehousing Industry

Unlike Amazon's automated warehouses, China's warehousing and logistics enterprises are plagued with pain points. China's logistics industry began expanding rapidly in 1999 owing to the explosive growth of e-commerce. In 2013, the total value of social logistics goods was ¥197.8 trillion, a figure that was 3.1 times that of 2005.[4] However, despite its tremendous growth, China's logistics industry still faced many problems at the time that prevented its further transformation and upgrading. For instance, many companies relied on an extensive growth model and high operation costs, and had low levels of efficiency. Problems in warehousing, a critical component of logistics, were widely regarded as the main contributors to these challenges.

Rising land costs. Industrial land is typically used for warehousing in China. This type of land is acquired primarily through the transfer of state-owned land or through the leasing of collective-owned land. Since 2013, however, the amount of state-owned land suitable for warehousing has begun to decline sharply (see Exhibit 1). An increasing demand for land amid this shrinking supply of state-owned land has led to a significant increase in warehouse rental prices and land costs (see Exhibit 2).

Single service mode. Most traditional warehousing enterprises in China relied too heavily on revenue from leasing warehouses and overlooked the potential to benefit from other value-added services. Consequently, intense market competition accompanied by rising land costs significantly lowered the revenues and profit margins of such asset-heavy and large-scale enterprises. The annual growth rate in the primary

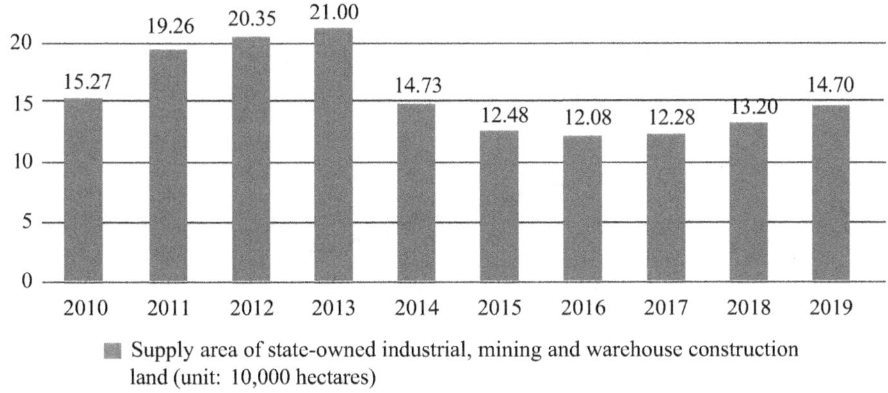

Exhibit 1 China's supply area of construction land supply area for state-owned industrial, mining, and warehousing construction land. *Source* "Supply area and growth of state-owned industrial, mining and storage construction land in China from 2010 to 2019," Qianzhan Logistics Industry Research Institute, December 30, 2020, accessed March 3, 2022, https://bg.qianzhan.com/wuliu/detail/616/201230-fe4c32f6.html

	Beijing	Shanghai	Guangzhou	Shenzhen
Land price in 2014 (unit: ¥10,000 per mu)	160–200	100–180	60–170	130–150
Land price in 2015	180–200	100–200	80–150	100–200
Average warehouse rent in 2014 (unit: ¥ per m2 per day)	1.45	1–1.6	1–1.4	1.1–1.7
Average warehouse rent in 2015	1.5	1–1.7	1–1.5	1.1–1.8

Exhibit 2 Logistics land prices and average warehouse rent prices in major Chinese cities from 2014 to 2015. *Note* Mu is a municipal land area unit in China; 1 mu is equal to approximately 666.667 m^2. *Source* Compiled by the author based on public information

business revenues of China's large-scale warehousing enterprises decreased every year from 2010 to 2014, even with –28% in 2014 (see Exhibit 3).

Low operational efficiency. By the end of 2014, the total area for warehousing in China was 5.5 million m^2, but only 20% of this met the high standards required for automated warehouses. Consequently, most warehousing jobs were held by workers, and problems such as low levels of efficiency and accuracy plagued the development of enterprises. At the same time, labor wages continued to rise, thereby increasing the operating costs of warehouses. In 2014, warehousing constituted approximately 47% of China's total logistics costs and accounted for 5.8% of its national GDP. In contrast, warehousing only amounted to 2.8% of GDP in developed countries.

More challenging customer demand. At the time when e-commerce sales were on the rise, warehousing jobs were becoming increasingly difficult to fill due to the extensive and increasing variability of items and the need to fulfill orders rapidly.

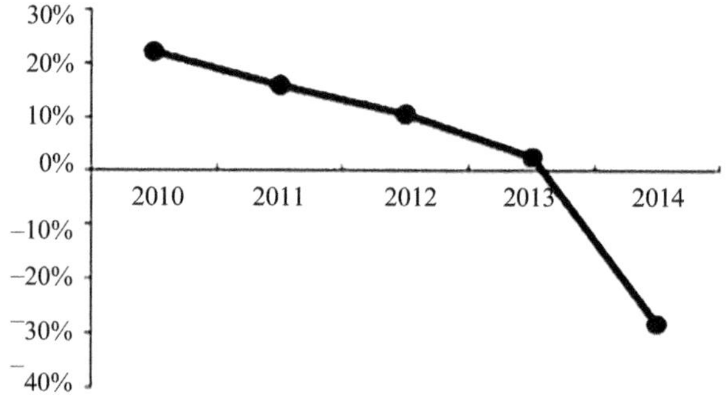

Exhibit 3 Annual growth rate of primary business income of large-scale warehousing enterprises in China. *Source* "Warehouse management—a critical core of the development of express industry in the future Changjiang Securities," baogaozhan.com, May 20, 2016, accessed March 3, 2022, https://www.baogaozhan.com/413197.html

In 2014, online retail sales in China reached ¥2,789.8 billion; this represented an increase of 49.7% over the previous year.[5] As customers purchased a growing range of products online, the variety of SKUs[3] expanded, and orders became increasingly large and scattered. Such rapidly expanding customer demand for logistics and warehousing was a major challenge for the logistics industry.

These internal and external problems highlighted the need for an urgent transformation and upgrading of China's logistics industry. In October 2014, the Chinese government promulgated the "Medium and Long Term Development Plan for the Logistics Industry (2014–2020)." This document clearly stated that vigorous efforts had to be made to reduce logistics costs. It also emphasized that developments in the strategic areas of mechanization, automation, and intelligence were required to advance China's logistics and warehousing.[6]

3 Setting Up the Entrepreneurial Team

Zheng commented, " The logistics industry in China is still labor-intensive, but as the 'post-90s' and 'post-00s' generations enter the labor market, these young people are unwilling to work in a warehouse, as these jobs are often menial, not value-added, low-paying, and provide little by way of career development. Therefore, logistics must be the first important area for the application of AI and robotics, and automation must be the future trend of warehousing."[7] After making up his mind, Zheng, who only possessed a background in engineering, decided to visit his alma mater, Tsinghua University, to search for like-minded people. "I am a CEO often 'despised' by our company's technical team due to my engineering background", Zheng once mocked himself.

Following an introduction from a mutual friend, Zheng became acquainted with Dr. Hongbo Li, who earned a doctoral degree in computer science and technology from Tsinghua University and had become an associate professor in the same institution upon his graduation, working at the Institute of Artificial Intelligence in the Department of Computer Science. He possesses a solid theoretical foundation and extensive practical experience in the navigation, perception, and scheduling of AI algorithms and large-scale advanced robotics. Dr. Li said, "My group has been researching cutting-edge robotics for the past 30 years. The most exciting thing for me is to conduct research relating to robotics with my fellow apprentices and to participate in various robot competitions. When Zheng contacted me and told me about his idea. I thought it was great."[8]

Dr. Li then connected Zheng with two of his friends, Dr. Kai Liu (the current System R&D Director of Geek+), who excels in robot design, including mobile robots, vision services, control systems, multi-agent AI algorithms, and software systems; and Dr. Xi Chen (the current Robot R&D Director of Geek+), who has over

---

[3] Stock Keeping Unit (Inventory unit).

10 years of experience in research on applied robotics and expertise in industrial automation and intelligent manufacturing.

In February 2015, Zheng co-founded Geek+ with Li, Liu, and Chen. The outstanding research and work experience of the four founders is a key resource and core component of Geek+. As Zheng explained, "We choose logistics, especially warehousing, as the application field of our dreams. What Geek+ provides to customers is intelligent robotic logistics rather than logistics robots, as our product is a whole intelligent logistics system with hardware and software, not just robots."[9]

4 What Warehouse Robots Should Be Produced? Birth of the First Robot Prototype

"Although we decided to produce automated warehouse robots, when we actually started, we did not even have a clear idea of what the first product would be," Dr. Li explained. The warehousing process involves many tasks, such as loading and unloading, picking and carrying, docking, packing and checking inventory, replenishing stocks, and handling returns. Zheng and his team had to decide which problems encountered by warehousing enterprises their first robot product would solve, and what this product would look like. After several rounds of discussion and investigation, they chose the task of picking.

In traditional warehouses, picking is performed by workers. This process first involves the warehouse management system sending an order to a worker's handheld PDA (Personal Digital Assistant), a device used to scan barcodes or electronic labels when obtaining specific information about orders in the warehouse. Then, the worker wheels a trolley to the location of the target commodity in a large warehouse. Finally, the worker retrieves the commodity, scans it, and carries it to the designated position. The whole process is time-consuming and labor-intensive. As Zheng said, "Our investigation revealed that warehouse workers typically spend about 60% of their working hours picking. The total distance that a worker walks in a warehouse per day can reach 20 km, sometimes even 40 km. Besides, this traditional picking method requires workers to be familiar with the location of the commodities, and this sometimes inevitably results in low efficiency and accuracy in picking."[10] This often leads to a high turnover rate—usually around 7% to 10%—even in companies that boast high levels of employee welfare, such as Alibaba and JD.

Zheng thus decided that the first project of Geek+ would be to automate the picking process in warehouses. This would be done by transforming the process from "person to commodity" to "commodity to person." Four months after the founding of Geek+, the prototype of its first robot passed the stability test and was formally born.[11]

Unlike AGVs, Geek+'s robot is an AMR. This warehouse robot looks like a robot vacuum cleaner. Using information about an order and existing inventory, it can automatically plan the optimal route to the target shelf and head in its direction. The robot then lifts the entire shelf and transports it to the workers, who simply have to

Exhibit 4 First robot product of Geek+ and its application in a warehouse. *Source* "Customer case," Geekplus.com, https://blog.geekplus.com/cn/casestudychinese. China-Focused Cases: Selected Winners of the CEIBS Global Case Contest II

stand in a fixed position (see Exhibit 4). When the shelf arrives, the workers pick up the target commodities according to the prompts displayed on the robot's display screen and the electronic labels, and put these commodities into the box for the given order.

Geek+'s robot has the potential to revolutionize the traditional picking process. Unlike the traditional "person-to-goods" picking method, Geek+'s robot system features a "goods-to-person" picking method, which can double, if not triple, the average level of picking efficiency and reduce the required workforce by 50–70%. Its picking accuracy rate exceeds 99.99%, while the proportion of damaged goods is also greatly reduced. These improvements allow for a significant increase in the picking accuracy rate and density of items stored on warehouse shelves while significantly reducing the operating cost of warehousing.[12]

Geek+'s robot outperforms other products that have a similar function. QR codes are installed at one-meter intervals on the ground to facilitate the robot's navigation and perception of the warehouse environment. With these, Geek+ effectively shortens the time and costs required to construct intelligent warehouses for its customers. The robot is only 30 cm tall, 10 cm shorter than that produced by Kiva, making it comparatively stable when carrying shelves and quicker and more accurate when processing QR codes located on the ground. The use of QR codes greatly increases the flexibility of this robotics solution. It also allows the robot to achieve higher positioning accuracy and a faster movement speed, which peaks at 1.5 meters per second. The robot is also conveniently charged; it only needs to be charged for 5 to 10 minutes every hour during a 24-hour operating period.[1313]

5 From Laboratory to Commercialization

Acquiring angel financing. Zheng initially thought that it would be difficult to commercialize what was essentially a laboratory prototype of the product. To seek venture capital financing, he visited Alog Company, the warehousing service provider for Tmall supermarkets, which at the time was searching for solutions to enhance the efficiency of its logistics. Wei Xing, chairman of Alog, was impressed by Geek+'s prototype and technical system, declaring, "We will definitely invest in Geek+, and valuation is not a problem."[14] In September 2015, Geek+ obtained its angel financing of ¥10 million from Alog.

Overcoming the first challenge of scale production from Alibaba. Soon after providing financing, Wei informed Zheng and Dr. Li that Alibaba's "November 11 Shopping Festival" was approaching and that the identification of solutions to speed up logistics processes was a key objective of that year's festival. Alibaba had even issued a ¥100 million incentive plan for solutions of this nature. "This is a great opportunity. If you can do it, Alog can try it out in our warehouse in Tianjin this year. It is up to you, and I won't force you to do it," Weitold them. Both Zheng and Dr. Li recognized that this was an amazing opportunity but also one that presented considerable challenges. They estimated that at least 20 robots would need to be produced within two months if they were to fulfill orders from the November 11 Shopping Festival. However, at the time, Geek+ only had one prototype, and its supply chain was imperfect. "It was a task that was hardly possible, but we decided to accept it without much hesitation," said Zheng.

After assuring Wei, Zheng and his team began to work frantically. First, they focused on optimizing the design of the prototype, for example, by improving the stability of its visual navigation and making its driving control technology more flexible. These adjustments were meant to help the robot to adapt specifically to the characteristics of orders from the November 11 Shopping Festival. Once the new version of the prototype was finalized, they immediately placed an order for its parts from suppliers, stipulating that delivery should arrive before the end of October. However, it was not until November 5 that all of the parts were delivered. In the next three days, the team assembled one robot in the laboratory to test the product. On November 8, the team rushed to Alog's warehouse in Tianjin, where they spent two days and nights finishing the assembly of the remaining 19 robots.

At last, the team completed this impossible task and succeeded.[15] Tmall's transaction volume reached ¥91.2 billion during the 2015 November 11 Shopping Festival. The warehouse robot, which sported the respective logos of Geek+ and Alog, featured in many media reports. Members of the public began to refer to Geek+ as the "Chinese version of Kiva".[16] Through this cooperation, Geek+ also achieved its own breakthroughs in commercialization, large-scale multi-agent scheduling technology, data intelligence, and quality control management.

6 Overcoming the second challenge of product reliability from Vipshop

Geek+'s first success gave Zheng and his team great confidence. Nonetheless, another challenge and opportunity soon arrived. In May 2016, Vipshop, another Chinese e-commerce company listed on the New York Stock Exchange since 2012, signed a cooperation agreement with Geek+ for the construction of intelligent warehouses. After four months of work, Geek+'s robots could stably handle 200–300 orders per day. However, with the November 11 Shopping Festival and the December 12 Shopping Festival approaching, Vipshop proposed that Geek+'s robots would have to reach a handling capacity of between 10,000 and 20,000 orders per day.

Instead of throwing in the towel, Zheng and his team chose to rise to the challenge. In the following two months, the team continuously conducted pressure tests and prepared various remedial measures. "At last, our robots can handle 50,000–70,000 orders a day under test conditions. However, no one knew whether there would be a problem in practice. In fact, we were particularly worried,"[17] Li Hongbo said at the time. Fortunately, the reliability of Geek+'s robots withstood the test of two shopping festivals.

By the end of 2016, Geek+'s robot picking system had been successfully commercialized in Tmall, Vipshop, and Suning Tesco. Across these businesses, more than 200 robots served in warehouses of 30,000 m^2, with a maximum daily handling capacity of over 60,000 orders.[18] The successful cooperation between these leading enterprises helped Geek+ to gain popularity in the domestic market. From 2016 to 2017, Geek+ completed its A, A+, pre-B funding rounds.

7 Continuous Product Development

Extending product lines from picking to full warehouse scenarios. Although Geek+ achieved success with its "goods-to-person" robot, picking is only one part of warehousing; customers urgently needed automated solutions for other parts of warehousing. From 2017, Geek+ began its continuous development of new robots to solve different warehousing pain points. To date, Geek+ has produced six customer solutions that use robotic systems: the "goods-to-person" system, "bin-to-person" system, "order-to-person" system, "smart moving" system, "smart forklift" system, "smart sorting" system, and the "integrated smart warehouse" system (see Exhibit 5). These robots are equipped with the most advanced AI algorithms, allowing them to build a comprehensive intelligent order fulfillment system that covers the entire process of shelving, picking, carrying, replenishing, returning, and inventory.[19]

Upgrading the robot scheduling system. While continuously improving the robot product matrix, Geek+ is constantly upgrading its robot scheduling system. Geek+'s iterative robots are able to achieve flexible scheduling through intelligent path planning and AI algorithms for congestion control. According to Geek+'s order

Exhibit 5 Robot products of Geek+. *Source* Xiong Chunyi, "At the beginning of the year, Geek+ completed the C2 round of financing, and the total amount of C1 + C2 round of financing exceeded the US $200 million,"36kr, June 18, 2020, accessed March 3, 2022, https://www.36kr.com/p/757023773806724

frequency and SKU correlation analysis, its robots can adjust the layout of shelves dynamically to achieve optimal shelf combination matching. Connected seamlessly with the warehouse management system, Geek+'s robots can standardize the operating process and enhance storage density and picking efficiency. They are also poised to meet the challenges of oversized shipments and massive SKUs.

8 Resolving the Sales Dilemma

As a result of its dependency on superior automated warehousing solutions, Geek+ had to aggressively expand its scale of sales. However, an unexpected problem appeared during this expansion: very few new customers were acquired, and most of them did not return. Many of these customers expressed their intention to cooperate but had delayed their final cooperation agreement with Geek+, despite the commercial value of Geek+'s robots, demonstrated by Geek+'s cooperation with Tmall, Vipshop, and Suning Tesco. By May 2017, only 500 "goods-to-person" robots had been sold, most of them bought by a few customers.[20] Geek+ urgently needed to acquire more customers and expand its market.

9 Discovering the Reasons

For several months, Zheng led his team in conducting several rounds of research, interviews, and discussions. This allowed them to grasp their customers' concerns: the huge sunk investment associated with the installation of robotic systems. First, the process of upgrading a traditional warehouse typically requires dozens or even hundreds of automated robots. "The price of a Geek+ robot, such as the 'goods-to-person' robot, is equivalent to the full year's salary of a warehouse worker," Zheng said, representing a large expense for Geek+ customers. Furthermore, following any upgrading of their logistics systems, customers would need to invest in employee training. Second, as Zheng said, "Our customers' businesses fluctuate greatly." E-commerce industries typically display fluctuations in their demand for warehousing. The utilization patterns of warehouses differ greatly between off-season and peak season. Flexible warehouse robot systems are preferred over fixed amounts, and there are not enough of them during peak season when many upgrades to intelligent warehousing are underway. Therefore, Geek+'s one-time purchase business model was ill-suited to the needs of its customers.

Meanwhile, Zheng's ideas shifted throughout the investigation and discussions.

He realized that one-time purchases only bring revenue for hardware sales, while "hardware+ service" could extend Geek+'s value chain. Furthermore, the massive amount of data acquired in real application scenarios is a fundamental resource for Geek+, as these robots are controlled by systems and AI algorithms. By working in actual customer warehouses, the robots can capture and accumulate massive data on practical scenarios. These data are then used to enhance the training and optimization of Geek+'s AI algorithms and robotic systems, such that they are better prepared to handle various practical scenarios. Upgrading Geek+'s AI algorithms and systems could further enhance the operations scheduling of its robots. With increasingly intense market competition, the differences between Geek+'s hardware and technology and those of its competitors were becoming increasingly smaller. To address this, Geek+'s core and differentiated competitiveness would come from data and AI algorithms.[21]

10 Innovating Business Models

Based on the results of the investigation, Zheng decided to innovate Geek+'s business model. At the start of 2018, after carefully designing the new model, Geek+ proposed an innovative robotic solution, which he dubbed "Robot-as-a-Service (RaaS)". This service was entirely new to the logistics industry. Specifically, in addition to one-time robot sales, Geek+ would provide its customers with three choices: to rent a robot, to serve as an operations agent in entire warehouses, and to integrate the provision of warehousing and distribution services.[22]

Under robot rental, Geek+'s customers could choose to rent rather than purchase a robot, thereby effectively reducing their initial investment and purchase threshold. Moreover, being able to rent a robot on a temporary basis would help customers become more flexible in their responses to business fluctuations.

In its role as an operations agent in entire warehouses, in addition to robots, Geek+ would provide its customers with professional operators and automated warehouse management services. This would help customers reduce their learning costs and improve their warehouse efficiency.

By adopting an integrated model of warehousing and distribution, Geek+ has established its own smart warehouses and nationwide distribution network. Its customers can rent smart warehouses and access its distribution network, allowing them to significantly reduce their financial burden and increase their flexibility. To realize the full intelligent warehousing process, Geek+'s six types of robots are deployed in its self-built warehouses. This service model allows Geek+ customers to triple their warehouse efficiency and increase their picking accuracy rate by as much as 99.99%. By implementing standardized operating solutions, Geek+ helps its customers optimize their warehousing, save on storage space, and minimize breakage. Using real-time information, their robotic systems can also provide recommendations for intelligent warehousing management related to optimal packaging, use of appropriate bin types, product replenishment, product selection, and promotion strategies. Furthermore, Geek+'s nationwide distribution network enables its customers to expand the coverage area of their logistics operations, flexibly respond to market demand, and penetrate lower-tier cities or markets.[23]

11 Remarkable Success

Since its launch, the RaaS model has been well received by the market. With the help of RaaS, the cumulative shipment of warehouse robots exceeded 3,500 in August 2018. In fact, Geek+ only took a few months to increase its shipment of robots from 500 to 3,500. Its self-built intelligent warehouses are distributed across North China, East China, South China, Central China, and Southwest China, occupying a total of 330,000 m^2. By cooperating with other express delivery partners, Geek+'s distribution network can deliver goods to 32 provinces and cities (including 2,752 counties) within 48 hours via a fleet of more than 5,000 vehicles operating over 500 transportation routes.[24]

Geek+'s exposure to numerous complex logistics scenarios provides extensive training for its robots' software systems and AI algorithms, allowing them to become increasingly sophisticated. During the November 11 Shopping Festival of 2018, over 5 million orders were handled by Geek+'s robotic system, breaking the global record.[25] In particular, up to 850 orders were imported into Geek+'s intelligent system every second. The average picking efficiency was 1,000 pieces per hour per workstation; that for scattered orders and batch orders peaked at 900 and 7,000 pieces per hour per workstation, respectively. The system only takes 2 minutes to move a product from the order import to the delivery stage. The capacity of the full system (i.e., receiving orders and undertaking parallel processing, single-point feedback, preprocessing, and interface feedback processing) peaks at 60,000 pieces per minute.

12 Balancing Customization and Scale Production

12.1 The Bottleneck in Project Implementation

With the continuous penetration of intelligence in the logistics industry, an increasing number of companies have started to transform and upgrade their logistics management. Meanwhile, several companies that had already piloted intelligent logistics, such as Decathlon and Bosideng, accelerated the overall and comprehensive transformation of entire logistics parks into smart ones. Dr. Li once said, "If the first stage of industrialization is to cultivate market, and the second stage is to explore the development trend, then the third stage is large- scale application. Today, the warehousing robotics is between the second and third stage[26]." From the end of 2018, Geek+'s number of products sold and the number of projects increased. However, new problems occurred with this sharp rise.

Intelligent warehousing involves developing a systematic solution for a specific scenario. Industries differ in their characteristics and their diverse warehousing needs. One example is the differences between the e-commerce, pharmaceutical, and manufacturing industries. The e-commerce industry is characterized by abundant long-tail commodities, massive SKUs, large business fluctuations, and high requirements for timeliness. In comparison, the pharmaceutical industry needs management solutions for products with expiration dates and requiring low-temperature/partitioned storage. The manufacturing industry requires warehousing solutions for the entire logistics process from material storage, stacking, picking, replenishment and packaging, to delivery; the continuity of production must also be guaranteed. In addition, the design of intelligent warehousing solutions must consider the physical features of each warehouse (e.g., its size, shelving conditions, types of goods) and changes in business operations. Faced with these customer needs, it is nearly impossible for Geek+ to provide a standard warehousing solution to its customers, even those within the same industries.

Initially, Geek+ had difficulty meeting the pressing demands of its customers owing to its slow progress in project implementation. How to find a balance between scale and customization? "The problem of responding quickly and agilely to our customers' needs has become our pain point. There are so many projects; how can we finish? Project implementation has become the bottleneck for the further advancement of Geek+," Zheng said during an interview in 2019.[27]

In order to solve this problem, Zheng held several rounds of discussions, research, and experiments with R&D, production, and marketing departments. Finally, a feasible solution was developed: Standardized and modularized hardware + modularized and customized system + innovation ecosystem. Standardization and modularization of hardware robots can meet personalized demand to a certain extent while ensuring large-scale production and improving production efficiency. Modularization and customization of software systems keep the simple operation of systems and maintain a flexible customization capability, shortening the project implementation time. At the same time, by building tech and industrial ecosystems, Geek+ can better meet the customized needs of customers with the help of partners. "Use standardized robots equipped with modular systems to form customized schemes to adapt to the ever-changing scenes, and form scale advantages with the help of partners."[28]

12.2 *Standardized and Modularized Hardware*

In the face of complex application scenarios, Zheng admitted, "More customized software will not increase much more burden on Geek+, but a lot of customization of robots will definitely lead to the soar of production costs and much more difficulty in quality control."[29] In consideration of such a conflict between costs, scale, and customization, Geek+ finally decided to tackle it through robots standardization and some parts modularization.

As for the standardization, Geek+ stipulates unified technical standards for product quality, varieties, and specifications, parts of robots during the production process to achieve the consistency of product quality and product specifications improve production efficiency and project implementation speed. In addition, Geek+ uses a fully automatic and intelligent smart factory to produce robot products, reduce manual intervention, ensure more accurate process control and higher accuracy, and further improve the standardization of robot products.[30] Besides, according to industry pain points and customers' needs, Geek+ has created several combination schemes suitable for different industries and operating scenarios, such as "shelf-to-person + tote-to-person" picking, "shelf-to-person + intelligent sorting," "shelf/tote-to-person + order case caching," and "shelf/tote-to-person + robotic arm" picking. Geek+ customers can quickly deploy standardized solutions according to business characteristics.

To solve the customization problem, Geek+ has designed a variety of modular components that can be integrated into the robot, and customers can freely integrate them according to the actual situation of warehouse operations. For example, a variety of standardized components can be incorporated into the top of Geek+'s "M series" handling robot. These include jacks, single-layer rollers, double-layer rollers, box holders and traction, complete rack/pallet handlers, conveyor line docks, and material truck handlers, among others. Further, Geek+ also provides a variety of models for the same module. For instance, the height of the gantry of the jacking module can be flexibly customized according to the height of warehouses and shelves to meet the needs of different scenarios (see Exhibit 6).[31] Modular components meet the personalized needs of customers and make installation and deployment more convenient, as well

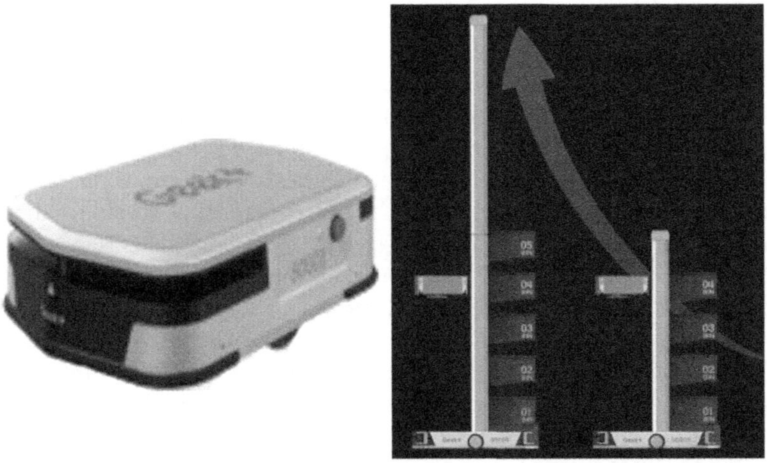

Exhibit 6 Geek+ intelligent handling robot and its jacking module. *Source* "Break through the single-layer storage limit of the robot warehouse! Geek + 's innovative AMR solution is launched!" It era network, May 8, 2020, accessed March 3, 2022, https://tech.sina.cn/2020-05-08/detail-iirczymk0465201.d.html

as more accessible transportation and loading. In addition, Geek+ provides a wealth of standard docking interfaces for 100+ robot bodies to take into account the existing automation equipment of customers to better meet the unique needs of customers. For example, Geek+'s "shelf-to-person" picking robot can realize "shelf-to-person" space storage and picking by integrating with traditional automation equipment such as steel platforms, conveyor lines, and elevators.[32]

12.3 Modularized and Customized System

A complete solution of warehousing robotics includes not only robot hardware but also software systems behind each robot. Therefore, to solve the conflict between scale and customization, Geek+ can not only rely on the standardization and modularization of hardware. In fact, for a long time, the powerful intelligent storage system of Geek+ has had problems such as "complex operation interface and difficult to debug." Each project implementation requires face-to-face communication between Geek+'s engineers and customers to obtain an in-depth understanding of customers' needs, combined with project expertise and continuous debugging to complete the construction of the system. In addition, customers must adjust and maintain the system to accommodate changes in business operations. However, this complex operation interface makes system construction and adjustment time-consuming and labor-intensive. Such problems have been a constant source of stress for Geek+ customers and Zheng's team.

The rapidly increasing number of projects makes the system problem even worse, and it is time for Zheng's team to solve it. After exploring different solutions, Geek+ launched its "application platform as a service (APaaS)" system to complement its intelligent logistics system "Geek+ cloud brain." In the APaas system, the application layer is highly modularized knowledge map related to the service and system is generated, and the APaas template is finally formed, which can support customers for secondary development. This allows customers to quickly develop and integrate various functions through a simple and user-friendly operation interface and a "zero code/low code module drag and drop" function. In this way, customers using the APaaS system can realize the adjustment and even reconstruction of logistics solutions themselves and respond quickly to changes in their business operations. For instance, customers using the APaaS system can easily schedule different types of robots according to their specific business needs by selecting the operating system characteristics of their devices and using the command transmission function of the Geek+ cloud brain to realize solution automation and intelligence. The simplification of the operation interface has also greatly reduced the time taken to train warehouse operators. In the past, it would have taken customers up to a week to train their employees to master operations of the system. With APaaS, training only takes 2 h.[33]

In addition, the APaaS system provides Geek+ customers with the ability to deploy logistics solutions on the cloud. This feature makes the APaaS system easy to deploy and maintain while also ensuring that it is scalable. Research by the consulting company Garter indicated that the use of the Geek+ cloud brain platform could help companies save significant development costs, greatly enhance development efficiency, and rapidly meet customers' specific requirements.[34] To address the diverse needs of its customers on-site, Geek+'s robotic solution allows customers to configure over 200 operating rules and strategies on their own. These rules and strategies cover more than 50 business scenarios such as warehousing, logistics, and flexible distribution, thereby significantly enhancing the APaaS system's level of customization and allowing customers to flexibly adapt to varying operating processes.[35]

12.4 Constructing an Innovative Ecosystem

To realize the leap from a project-by-project approach to a large-scale approach to production and reap competitive scale advantages, Zheng argues that it is not enough to upgrade Geek+'s hardware and software on its own. In order to occupy a leading position in the market, Geek+ also needs to seek help from external networks and actively promote the development of Geek+'s innovation ecosystem.[36]

On one hand, Geek+ builds a tech ecosystem by establishing R&D alliances with leading enterprises in cloud computing, the Internet of Things, mechanical arm, and other fields. Through the empowerment of technology ecological partners, Geek+ absorbs the technical advantages of partners to improve the performance of AMR and the service ability of intelligent logistics solutions, so as to better realize the large-scale application of intelligent logistics solutions. For example, in October 2020, Geek+ reached strategic cooperation with Poweramp Technology, a lithium- ion battery enterprise. Geek+ realized the improvement of the performance and safety of the AMR power battery system by using several patented lithium battery technologies of Poweramp Technology, such as low-temperature charging and fast charging. By March 2022, Geek+ has reached strategic cooperation with Intel, transmission and control technology provider Bosch Rexroth, mobile robot company Zhejiang Guozi Robotics, etc.

On the other hand, Geek+ has built an industrial ecosystem through cooperation with automation integrators, equipment agents, third-party logistics enterprises, express transportation companies, and other enterprises. Geek+ absorbs industrial ecological partners' experience, integration, and maintenance ability in different industries to provide customers with better customized intelligent logistics service solutions. At the same time, Geek+ can also focus more energy and resources on improving robot products and technologies[37]. For example, in December 2021, in the project of Shenzhen Comix Group, Geek+'s storage robot and AI algorithms combined with the robot cluster scheme in the enterprise service field provided by Guangzhou HENGYAN Technology, customized an AMR intensive storage scheme for Shenzhen Comix Group. And with Guangzhou HENGYAN Technology's efficient and professional customer service capability and operation service capability, the project took only two months to complete successfully. In January 2022, in the project of American shoe and clothing brand Ariat company, with the help of Körber's mature end-to-end supply chain solutions and rich experience in the shoe and clothing retail industry, Geek+ provides customized solutions for Ariat warehouse. As of March 2022, Geek+ had reached strategic cooperation with Conveyco Technologies, a North American material handling system integrator, FDL group, a European supply chain solution integrator, SF supply chain, a Chinese logistics service provider, CJ logistics, a Korean third-party logistics provider, and many other industry partners.

13 The End

In the AI era, the global mobile robot industry is going through a crucial period filled with strategic opportunities. In recent years, China has paid close attention to the construction of intelligent logistics systems, issued relevant plans and policies, advocated for and encouraged the combination of logistics with science and technology, and promoted the intelligent development of all logistics components through the combination of software and hardware (see Exhibit 7).

With its stable and reliable products, rich global project experience, and efficient and high-quality after-sales service, Geek+ has become an intelligent logistics partner for many well-known brands both at home and abroad, such as Nike, Decathlon, WalMart, Dell, Suning, and Yonghui. Geek+ has sales, operation, and

Exhibit 7 Policy support for China's smart warehousing industry from 2014 to 2021 (in partial)

Policy name	Date	Policy aims
"Medium and long-term development plan of the logistics industry (2014–2020)"	2014.10	By 2020, China will establish a modern logistics service system, focus on reducing logistics costs, and promote the expansion of logistics enterprises
"13th Five-Year Plan for the Development of Integrated Transportation Services"	2016.07	Meet the needs of intelligent manufacturing, promote innovative logistics services, and guide logistics enterprises to improve intellectual freight and logistics systems
"13th Five-Year Plan for the Development of Commerce and Logistics"	2017.02	Promote the application of advanced technologies such as the Internet of Things, cloud computing, big data, AI, and robots; and explore the development of an intelligent logistics ecosystem
"New Generation Artificial Intelligence Development Plan"	2017.07	Strengthen R&D of intelligent logistics equipment such as smart loading and unloading, sorting and packaging, processing and distribution; and build a depth-sensing intelligent warehouse system and other technologies
"Opinions on Further Promoting Logistics Cost Reduction and Efficiency Improvement to Promote the Development of the Real Economy"	2017.08	Vigorously develop new forms of business and business models—such as "Internet+" warehousing transactions—that rely on the Internet, big data, cloud computing, and other advanced information technologies
"Opinions on Promoting the Coordinated Development of E-commerce and Express Logistics"	2018.01	Encourage warehousing, express delivery, and third-party technical service companies to develop intelligent warehousing, extend service chains, and optimize their supply chain management to meet the demand of e-commerce companies
"Opinions on Promoting the High-Quality Development of Logistics and Promoting the Formation of a Strong Domestic Market"	2019.02	Support the application of the Internet of Things in logistics parks and large-scale warehousing facilities to realize the standardization of information collection and electronic processing in logistics
"Implementation Notice on Further Reducing Logistics Costs"	2020.05	Promote the construction of unmanned warehousing and develop an unmanned distribution express network. Build cold chain infrastructure such as intelligent cold storage, intelligent transportation, and express delivery
"Guiding Opinion on Promoting the Construction of New Infrastructure in the Field of Transportation"	2020.08	Promote the application of new technologies and intelligent equipment, and improve the level of intelligence in logistics chains such as warehousing, transportation, and distribution

(continued)

Exhibit 7 (continued)

Policy name	Date	Policy aims
"Implementation Plan to Promote the Deep Integration and Innovative Development of the Logistics Industry and the Manufacturing Industry"	2020.09	Encourage manufacturing enterprises to adapt to the developmental needs of intelligent manufacturing, carry out intelligent logistics transformation, and promote the application of new technologies for logistics and equipment, such as robots, intelligent warehousing, and automatic sorting. Improve the level of automation, digitization, and intelligence in production logistics
"14th Five-Year Plan for the Development of Intelligent Manufacturing"	2021.12	Promote R&D of intelligent logistics equipment, such as intelligent multi-layer and multi-directional shuttle vehicles and large-scale intelligent three-dimensional warehouses. Build intelligent distribution systems for logistics and optimize the production and operation of decision-making systems

Source Compiled by the author based on public information

service capabilities in more than 30 countries and regions worldwide. It has served more than 300 customers and deployed more than 20,000 AMRs globally. Geek+ has completed projects for customers in many industries, such as retail, footwear and clothing, medicine, third-party logistics, automobile, lithium batteries, photovoltaics, and electronics.[38]

Nonetheless, Geek+ faced a seemingly endless number of problems during its development. The COVID–19 outbreak in 2020 increased business demand for supply chain solutions. Accordingly, the next challenges and opportunities that Zheng's team will face involve the development of agile and resilient supply chains for Geek+ customers and the transformation and development of intelligent global logistics.

Endnotes

1. "The only award-winning Chinese AMR company! Geek+ won the Fast Company 2021 World's Most Innovative Company," Financial headlines, March 12,2021, accessed March 3, 2022, https://t.cj.sina.com.cn/articles/view/5752614292/156e1ed9402000wq5o.
2. "2021 China's top 200 new economic unicorns released: 14 companies are valued at over 10 billion US dollars, and e-commerce growth is extremely high," iiMedia Research, July 26, 2021,accessed March 3, 2022, https://www.iimedia.cn/c460/79870.html.

3. Wang Leisheng, "Tmall and JD.com used his products. Jack Ma and Liu Qiangdong wanted to invest in him," China Entrepreneur Magazine, August 16,2017, accessed March 3, 2022, https://www.sohu.com/a/165036013_355015.
4. "Notice of the State Council on Printing and Distributing the Medium and Long Term Plan for the Development of the Logistics Industry (2014–2020)," The Central People's Government of the People's Republic of China, September 14, 2014, accessed March 3, 2022, http://www.gov.cn/zhengce/content/2014-10/04/content_9120.html.
5. "In 2014, online retail sales reached ? 2.7898 trillion, an increase of 49.7% over the previous year," People's Daily Online, February 16, 2015, accessed March 3, 2022, http://politicspeople.com.cn/n/2015/0226/c70731-26,599,876.html.
6. "Notice of the State Council on Printing and Distributing the Medium and Long Term Plan for the Development of the Logistics Industry (2014–2020)."
7. "Future enterprises | Interview with Zheng Yong, founder of Jizhijia: The logistics field is more worthy of companies to use technology to subvert," Sino-Singapore Jingwei, November 3, 2021,accessed March 3, 2022, https://www.sohu.com/a/498970922_561670.
8. Ma Cheng, "Tsinghua help AI to make wealth: from landing to hand-to-hand combat, to decision and robbing people," All-weather Technology, December 8,2018, accessed March 3, 2022, https://www.cnbeta.com/articles/tech/796131.html.
9. AI walker, "Let the logistics industry" fallin love "with robots," Weike.com, November 9, 2017, https://robot.ofweek.com/2017-11/ART-8321202-8500-30175044.html.
10. "Zheng Yong | Founder & CEO of Geek+ Technology: Robotic Intelligent Logistics: Transforming Technology, Going Agile," Grape Ventures, July 20, 2017, accessed March 3, 2022, https://www.sohu.com/a/158707619_355046.
11. AI walker.,"Let the logistics industry" fallin love "with robots."
12. Stone Jin, "Geek+ , a logistics robot company, plans to be listed on the scientific innovation board: the global AMR market share ranks first, with GGV and Gao Rong as investors," Financial headlines, June 15,2021, accessed March 3, 2022, https://cj.sina.com.cn/articles/view/6589734409/188c75e0901900ydv4.
13. ICEBIN, "Geek+ completed 50 million round of A financing, co-led by Gaurong Capital and Volcanic Rock Investment," Move point Technology, October 12,2016, accessed March 3, 2022, https://cn.technode.com/post/2016-10-12/geek-plus-series-a/.
14. Wang Leisheng, "Tmall and JD.com used his products. Jack Ma and Liu Qiangdong wanted to invest in him."
15. Du Muyu. "The goods-to-person warehouse robot" Geek+ "wants to be China's Kiva," 36Kr, March 26,2016,accessed March 3, 2022, https://www.36kr.com/p/1721054806017.
16. AI walker. "Let the logistics industry" fallin love "with robots."
17. "From robot warehousing and logistics to flexible supply chain, what is Geek+ 's game of chess?" Entrepreneurship State, October 17, 2019, accessed March 3, 2022, https://robot. ofweek.com/2019-10/ART-8321202-8500-30412075.html.

18. New strategic robot, "New cutting-edge intelligent logistics robot: Geek+ 's new round of financing valuation may exceed 1 billion," Sohu Technology, October 13, 2016, accessed March 3, 2022, https://m.sohu.com/n/470144471/?wscrid=95360_5.
19. "Pursuing the ultimate smart future | Geek+ series robots made a stunning appearance at the International Logistics Equipment Exhibition and received wide attention and praise," Geek+ Technology, June 2, 2017, accessed March 3, 2022, https://mp.weixin.qq.com/s/XkfiDTCvFMtdPzymYmYbEg.
20. Pan Minyao, "Geek+ CEO Zheng Yong: We are a 'madman' who is exploring the integration of 'robots, intelligence, and logistics'," High-tech robots, June 23, 2017, accessed March 3, 2022, https://www.leiphone.com/category/robot/bUnWF2XxgeqxhdFo.html.
21. Guo Jiaying, "After five years of entrepreneurship, it has occupied more than 80% of the Asia Pacific market. What is the secret of this Chinese robot company's overseas goldrush | Robot Company," Sina Finance, October 31, 2019, accessed March 3, 2022-, https://finance.sina.com.cn/roll/2019-10-31/doc-iicezuev6126760.shtml.
22. "Robot as a Service RaaS," Geekplus.com, https://www.geekplus.com/cn/raas.
23. "Geek's RaaS model helps e-commerce logistics efficiently reach multi-level markets," AGV Network, September 12, 2020, accessed March 3, 2022, https://mp.weixin.qq.com/s/EL1_6ZXnUEjGHDX0hzgo8w.
24. "Geek+ RaaS smart warehouse helps brand owners achieve new track leadership," Geek+ Technology, February 4, 2021, accessed March 3, 2022, https://mp.weixin.qq.com/s/xYoIAT3H-GkPHrCBGKJGog.
25. "2018 'Double 11' Geek+ robot picking orders exceeded 5 million," Ebang Power Network, November 20, 2018, accessed March 3, 2022, https://www.ebrun.com/20181120/308485.shtml.
26. Wei Pang, "Orders are soaring, mobile robots are gaining momentum," The Paper, July 23, 2021, accessed March 3, 2022, https://m.thepaper.cn/baijiahao_13,830,894.
27. Yu Huiru, "After the sales volume exceeded 20,000 units, how does Geek+ bridge the gap between robot products and intelligent logistics?" All-Weather TMT, July 23, 2021, accessed March 3, 2022, https://awtmt.com/articles/3636156.
28. Pan Minyao, "After 10,000 units, Gek + 's new product wisdom and new ecological cooperation."
29. Wei Pang, "Orders are soaring, mobile robots are gaining momentum."
30. "News," Geekplus.com, https://blog.geekplus.com/cn/news-center.
31. "Break through the single-layer storage limit of the robot warehouse! Geek's innovative AMR solution is launched!" It era network, May 8, 2020, accessed March 3, 2022, https://tech.sina.cn/2020-05-08/detail-iirczymk0465201.d.html.
32. Pan Minyao, "After 10,000 units, Gek+'s new product wisdom and new ecological cooperation."
33. Wei Pang, "Orders are soaring, mobile robots are gaining momentum."

34. "Geek+ successfully held the Global Smart Logistics Summit and announced the" CARE "strategy for the first time," Geek+ Technology, October 15,2019, accessed March 3, 2022-, https://mp.weixin.qq.com/s/neMVWp0oUK3IzuOHAjTU-Q.
35. "Geek+ helps flexible manufacturing, and the four keys make AMR maximize its value," Geek+ Technology, June 23,2020, accessed March 3, 2022, https://mp.weixin.qq.com/s/sg_6g1H_50OX3t8MIurHwg.
36. Pan Minyao, "After 10,000 units, Geek+'s new product wisdom and new ecological cooperation."
37. Ibid.
38. "Who are we?" Geekplus.com, https://www.geekplus.com/cn/company.

AstraZeneca (China): Promoting Social Innovation with Holistic Disease Management Solutions Throughout the Patient Journey

On February 10, 2022, AstraZeneca ("AZ"), a global pharmaceutical giant, announced its FY2021 results. Total revenue for 2021 was up 41% to US$ 37.41 billion, of which AstraZeneca China ("AZ-China") contributed some US$ 6 billion as it continued to outperform other pharmaceutical multinationals in China.[1]

Back in 2014, Leon Wang, as newly promoted president, had set a challenging goal for AZ-China: to grow its share in AZ's global revenue from 4%–5% to 20% or US$ 1 billion to US$ 5 billion within five years, thereby adding weight to AZ-China's voice at global headquarters.

From 2015 to 2020, AZ-China's contribution to the company's total global revenue reached 10%, 12%, 17.2%, 20.7%, and 20.2%, respectively, going up year on year. AZ-China's increasing influence earned Wang greater autonomy to innovate. As early as 2014, Wang began promoting cross-sector collaboration to overhaul its business ecosystem. Joining hands, AZ-China and its partners were committed to building **a patient-centric, integrated disease diagnosis and treatment platform that provided patients with holistic disease management services throughout their illness**. This platform significantly improved disease screening rates and made it easier for patients to access standardized and comprehensive therapies, winning wide acclaim from the government and the community. This new health management ecosystem benefited every participant across the industry chain.

At AZ-China, social innovation aimed to serve the public interest and was never allowed to be pegged to sales or performance targets. However, many years into building the integrated disease diagnosis and treatment platform, some employees

---

Professor CHEN Weiru and Case Researcher Dr. LIU Geng of China Europe International Business School developed this case with the helpful cooperation and support of the case company. For the sake of confidentiality, the author may have revised financial indicators and key figures relating to the case company. They do not affect case discussions or decisions. The case aims to provide the basis for classroom discussion rather than illustrate effective or ineffective handling of a management situation.

This case was the First Prize winner of 2022 Global Contest for the Best China-Focused Cases.

China-Focused Cases, https://doi.org/10.1007/978-981-97-8580-3_8

wondered much the company needed to invest in sustaining this social innovation program despite its virtuous nature. At the time of writing, pharmaceutical companies, local and global alike, faced an uphill battle in China, especially when selling brand-name drugs. This was because the National Healthcare Security Administration began implementing a volume- based drug procurement policy, cutting the prices of drugs on its National Reimbursement Drug List ("NRDL"), and AZ-China was no exception. It had stepped up in-house R&D of brand-name drugs and pursued more non-hospital partners, even trying out programs like its internet hospital project, and revenue was inevitably affected. It wasn't easy to recover in the short term. Since AZ-China's innovation autonomy was primarily backed by its impressive operating performance in China, if revenue growth slowed, could the company continue its eight years of social innovation?

1 About AZ and China's Pharmaceutical Market

AZ was a global, innovation-driven biopharmaceutical company operating in over 100 countries and regions, developing, manufacturing, and selling prescription medicines. AZ entered the Chinese market in 1993 and based its headquarters in Shanghai,[1] employing approximately 15,000 people nationwide by 2021. AZ-China focused on the most unmet medical needs of Chinese patients suffering from cardiovascular disease, diabetes, cancer, respiratory, digestive, and kidney disease. After acquiring Alexion in 2021, AZ set up a division for infection and vaccines, marking its entry into rare diseases, vaccines, neutralizing antibodies, and autoimmune diseases.

Since 2006, AZ had exhibited robust performance, with sales reaching a record high of US$ 33.59 billion in 2011, ranking seventh among global pharmaceutical companies. However, things didn't last long, as 2012 saw a slow decline in AZ's financial results, with patents expiring for some of its blockbuster drugs. At the same time, AZ-China delivered a lackluster performance, reporting US$ 710 million in sales in 2009 and an even lower US$ 500 million in 2013.

In October 2012, AZ appointed Frenchman Pascal Soriot as the new CEO to lead the company out of an ocean of red. Under his leadership, AZ boosted innovation through the massive adoption of digital tools: AI in pharma R&D reduced costs and accelerated time-to-market; digital team management tools streamlined internal management processes; digital tools enhanced patient engagement and compliance;[2] digital marketing methods delivered academic and drug-related information to patients and physicians, and helped build the brand.

---

[1] Shanghai, located on the eastern coast of China, is the largest city in China.

[2] Patient compliance or treatment compliance describes the degree to which a patient correctly follows medical advice. Compliance can be divided into three groups, namely complete compliance, partial compliance (over or under dosing, increasing or reducing dose frequency, etc.) and complete noncompliance, each of which accounts for one-third of actual treatment compliance.

2 China's Pharmaceutical Market

2.1 *Accelerated Digitalization of Medical Care*

Digitalization of medical care (primarily regional medical information systems) in China lagged far behind the United States and other developed countries. Hospital information systems built in the 1990s consisted mainly of stand-alone software for queuing. The proliferation of digital technologies like AI and cloud computing after 2011 triggered and accelerated explosive growth in smart medical care: China's 12th Five-Year Plan (2011–2015) clearly emphasized the need to build healthcare information systems and develop telemedicine networks. The 13th Five-Year Plan (2016–2020) called for constructing a clinical information system centered around electronic health records, accelerating the consolidation of medical information systems, and promoting collaboration among hospitals at various levels. The 2020 COVID–19 outbreak catalyzed the integration and standardization of medical care platforms. In the 14th Five-Year Plan period (2021–2025), China would increase efforts to digitize its healthcare system, promote inclusive, patient-centric medical services and establish a smart healthcare ecosystem.

2.2 *Medical Resource Shortcomings*

Medical resources were unequally distributed across China, with varying quality of services and a widening gap between supply and demand for services. The eastern region was home to significantly more medical resources than the central and western areas in terms of the number of hospitals (especially tertiary hospitals), medical professionals, and licensed physicians. Developed eastern cities attracted the best medical resources, while many more densely populated towns, rural and remote areas faced severe shortages of doctors and drugs. Once affected by serious diseases, people in these areas would turn to big cities for medical treatment, adding to the cost of medical treatment, further straining resources, and putting additional pressure on medical staff, leading to more doctor-patient conflicts. Leveraging digital technologies was essential for developing and upgrading an innovative medical service system to resolve such a predicament. The digital transformation of China's healthcare system involved multiple stakeholders such as national and local health commissions, hospitals, medical insurance companies, and pharmaceutical companies, each playing different roles and taking on different functions, influencing and interacting with each other. In 2009, China started a new round of healthcare system reforms, launching the National Essential Medicine System to improve affordable and equitable access to medical services. All essential drugs would come from designated manufacturers or via a centralized bidding system. In addition, most essential drugs used for China's high-prevalence diseases as well as high-end and newly developed drugs, were unlikely to be included in the list. Therefore, if pharmaceutical multinationals were to gain access to this vast mass market, they would have to provide quality drugs at lower prices.

2.3 Pharmaceutical Multinationals in China

In 1980, the first pharmaceutical multinationals arrived in China. As the country embarked on market-oriented economic reform in the early 1990s and joined the WTO at the turn of the twenty-first century, more multinationals flooded in. They brought more money, sophisticated technology, new concepts, and management systems, as well as more new drugs. In addition, they introduced a mainstream sales model—"academic marketing" and a new profession—"medical representative (MR)" to the local market. MRs played an instrumental role in opening up China's healthcare industry by facilitating training and knowledge updates within the medical system. In the late 1990s, thousands of private pharmaceutical companies popped up around the country. Increased market competition led many MRs to offer hospitals and individual physicians rebates in exchange for larger drug procurement orders. In 2013, a corruption scandal related to a global pharmaceutical giant in China shook the entire industry and led to stricter regulations.

3 Leon Wang

Wang had no educational background in medical sciences. After graduating from Shanghai International Studies University as an English major, he became a tour guide for foreign tourists. Before joining AZ, he had held positions of increasing responsibility in administration, marketing, and business development at Roche for 16 years, where he was a Business Unit Vice-President. In March 2013, he joined AZ-China as Vice President of the Gastroenterology, Respiratory & Anesthesia ("GRA") division.

At that time, the GRA business constituted an important revenue source for AZ-China. But the patent expirations of Nexium™, Symbicort Turbuhaler™, Seroquel™, and Pulmicort Respules™, coupled with fierce competition, hindered business growth and posed significant challenges for the then-newly appointed VP.

At that point in time, families with asthmatic children had difficulties accessing medical treatment. Wang had personally experienced this during childhood and witnessed the painful experience of families traveling to Shanghai for medical treatment. In his mind, asthma patients in lower-tier cities and smaller hospitals should also have easy access to nebulizers. After several rounds of discussion within the company, AZ-China decided to sponsor the establishment of pediatric nebulization centers in hospitals across China so children with asthma could get treatment more

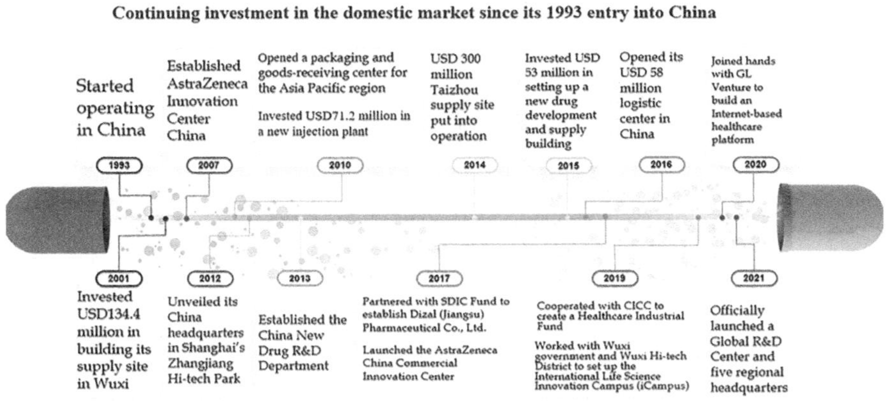

Exhibit 1 Milestones of AstraZeneca in China. *Source* AZ-China

easily. It was a completely new venture for the company, and some of its people questioned the decision. They asked, "Why not focus on drug sales instead of building treatment rooms?"

Nevertheless, Wang carried the project forward. AZ collaborated with partners, including Omron Healthcare, a global leader in medical equipment manufacturing, to set up the nebulization centers. They also worked with academic institutes, medical institutions, and regulatory authorities to set standards for the centers.

Wang was promoted to President of AZ-China in late 2014, making him one of only five Chinese professional managers to hold a top position in a multinational pharmaceutical company. The media attributed his success to leading the GRA division by moving products into entry-tier markets.[2] After assuming his new role, Wang outlined three goals for AZ-China:

First, increase supply: bring new drugs to the Chinese market more quickly while stepping up local R&D efforts (Exhibit 1).

Second, equitable access: China's medical resources had long been disproportionately located in large cities and large hospitals, and these locations had therefore been the target of most multinational pharmaceutical sale strategies. AZ-China chose to go the other way by incorporating counties, towns, and villages into its sales network. It also vigorously expanded its county-level salesforce, setting up dedicated teams to serve customers at retail and community levels (see Exhibit 2), and established an omnichannel business unit in 2021. Its products were sold to 1,850 counties in 28 provinces nationwide.

Third, communicate proactively: pursue proactive and constructive communication with government agencies. Regular communication between AZ Global CEO and Board Chairman with Chinese government officials on policy-related issues about market access, national medical insurance negotiation, and volume-based procurement, just a few examples, would help AZ-China expand its business in China.

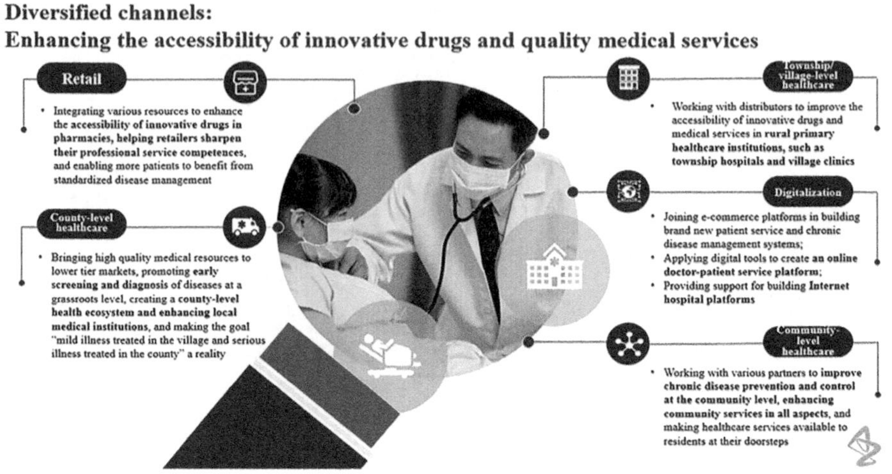

Exhibit 2 AZ-China's channel diversification. *Source* AZ-China

Departing from the two former non-Chinese presidents, Wang brought a unique work culture to AZ-China. He was committed to cultivating a mentality of ownership and innovation. He emphasized, "How much influence you have depends on how much you contribute." He wanted to build AZ-China into an organization strong on execution, underlining that each corporate goal should be broken down into actionable tasks specific to each product and each province, city, county, and village.

4 Innovating AtAZ-China

With his clear goals and action plans in place, Wang had another task on his agenda: innovation.

4.1 Building and Iterating the Innovation Model (2014–2017)

4.1.1 Interest Group: A Spearhead for Innovation

Wang started exploring innovation possibilities outside the company's main business of pharmaceutical sales. He and several core IT staff formed an "interest group" to study innovations in digital technology and other industries on weekends. He wanted to address patients' needs and pain points to create more value for them by exploring new treatment solutions enabled by emerging technology.

The interest group was tasked with "going out" to dialogue with the outside world and "bringing in" innovation insights from external experts. Most companies they approached were from the **diagnostics**, **device**, and **digital** industries (subsequently, many of AZ-China's innovation partners would come from these fields). In 2015, AZ-China officially announced its "3D innovation" strategy.

As more creatively inclined employees joined, the interest group grew into a "weekend group," dissolving departmental silos and hierarchies within the organization. All activities were held on weekends to avoid disrupting normal business activities.

Wang exercised quantitative control over the intensity and speed of in-house innovation, stressing that "our approach to innovation is disciplined… it is not realistic to have every member of the company engaged in innovation. Instead, only a few people will be assigned to innovation projects when necessary."

4.1.2 Medicine + Nebulizer + Internet of Things: Beating Down the Door of Innovation

The interest group acted as an essential interface for innovation at AZ-China. They tried to think outside the box, using new perspectives brought by external partners, all the while relying on external help to action new ideas in a short time.

The success of the "medicine + nebulizer" model earned AZ-China general buy-in from its workforce to continue exploring new possibilities, attracting international partners like Omron. Thanks to these partnerships, over 10,000 nebulization centers were launched, with more than 100,000 nebulizer pumps used nationwide.

Omron played a significant part in the commercialization and mass production of nebulizers. To make these nebulizers smarter, Omron added a built-in Internet of Things (IoT) module to each one, making its geographical location and working status traceable. By constantly exploring solutions for patient pain points, AZ-China and its partners kept their intelligent nebulizers in incremental and iterative development.

To alleviate pediatric patients' fear of nebulizer treatment, a small screen was installed in front of each treatment seat to play educational videos and cartoons. Interactive games developed for children addressed procrastination and low compliance. For example, in the "balloon blow-up" game: an on-screen balloon would grow bigger the more the patient inhaled. These methods significantly improved treatment efficacy and the equipment turnover rate.

After each treatment, the patient's parent could scan a QR code on the nebulizer to learn the number of treatments remaining and fill in an online questionnaire covering topics about controlling asthma in children. This enabled medical institutions to record and trace back testing reports for pediatric patients' pulmonary function and updated doctors on their patients' condition, allowing for greater speed and flexibility to modify treatment plans. The nebulization centers also regularly invited pulmonologists to deliver talks on patient education, helping pediatric patients and their parents improve disease awareness and management skills.

More and more companies joined AZ-China's collaborative innovation ecosystem, including Future,[3] Homed,[4] and Gentec.[5] They volunteered to provide hospitals with nebulization equipment for free, reducing construction hospitals' costs and benefiting more patients. Inspired by AZ-China's "10,000 nebulization-center plan," Qingdao Future Medical Technology Company was founded in 2014 with the mission of "safeguarding children's respiratory health in China".

As these nebulization centers sponsored by AZ-China and other pharmaceutical companies expanded further into local communities, "nebulization bars" occupying only two square meters popped up across community-level medical institutions. This all-in-one nebulization bar, like a karaoke pod on the street or in a shopping mall, offered greater accessibility to asthma patients.

4.1.3 Putting Patients at the Core of Innovation

In 2016, the interest group met in Hangzhou[6] to review the nebulization center project. A group member recalled:

> At that meeting, we, for the first time, decided not only to focus on innovative ways to sell drugs but on patients' pain points and needs throughout the disease management process. We had to determine whether these pain points were essential or optional and how to give patients access to high-quality disease management services. After that, we mapped a patient journey to explore and address their essential needs at each stage of disease management. That meeting set the tone for our subsequent innovation initiatives.[3]

In a keynote speech, Wang emphasized the "awakening of aspiration"[7] for innovation, outlining the objectives and features of AZ-China's initiatives: innovations were for the patients, not just for sales targets.

> In many cases, what I have done does not necessarily relate directly to sales, but it has always paid off. Just do what is best for the patient. Accumulation of good intentions delivers better results.

---

[3] Since its inception in 2014, Qingdao Future Medical Technology Co., Ltd. had been committed to providing digital solutions for chronic respiratory diseases.

[4] Homed was a high-end brand of Shenzhen Homed Medical Device Co., Ltd. which was founded in 2003, specializing in the R&D of home oxygen therapy, home nebulization solutions, smart nebulizer systems, etc. Their smart nebulizer system was the first of its kind in China, and featured a "smart" big data model.

[5] Gentec (Shanghai) Corporation developed and manufactured medical air supply systems, oxygen and negative pressure therapy devices, respiratory care products, etc.

[6] Hangzhou, the capital of Zhejiang, a developed province in eastern China, is known as the Internet capital of China, with the headquarters of large Internet companies such as Alibaba and NetEase.

[7] In Buddhism, the "awakening of aspiration" can be achieved by cultivating the direct mind, the deep mind, and the compassionate mind.

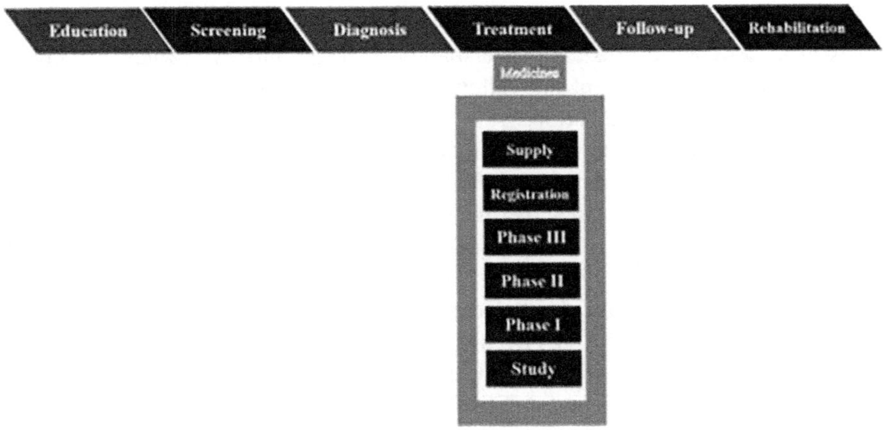

Exhibit 3 T-shaped innovation model. *Source* Authors

4.1.4 T-shaped Innovation Roadmap

Traditionally, drugmakers followed a business development process going from pharmaceutical R&D and commercialization to doctor education and medication. Under the new "patient-centric" disease management concept, a drugmaker could, ideally, become further involved inpatient education, disease screening, diagnosis, treatment, follow-up, and rehabilitation throughout the patient journey.

Drugmakers conventionally had a deep vertical involvement during the treatment stage, which could serve as an anchor point for expanding into all stages of a patient journey, thus forming a T-shaped business model (see Exhibit 3). For AZ-China, the vertical part of the "T" meant further tapping drug development pipelines. In contrast, the horizontal position meant delving into the entire disease management cycle, focusing on treatment areas where its expertise, experience, and insights lay.

With patient-centricity as its guiding principle and based on the success of the nebulization center project, AZ-China encouraged all business units to explore integrated treatment solutions from 2015 to 2016 in collaboration with academic institutions, medical institutions, regulatory authorities, and enterprise partners. As the focus of business units varied by type of disease, they worked out corresponding plans based on specific disease characteristics, treatment features, as well as available resources and expertise.

4.1.5 A Holistic Solution to Prostate Cancer with Win–Win Results

As their first attempt at holistic disease management, the nebulization center project set a model for subsequent shots. However, the "prostate cancer integrated diagnosis and treatment (PiDT)" project calibrated this model by devising a new benchmark, ensuring clear benefits for all participants.

As requested by AZ's Oncology Business Unit, several external urologic oncologists broke down the prostate cancer patient journey into five stages: screening, puncture, diagnosis, treatment, and follow-up care, leaving much room for expansion, optimization, and standardization.

Specifically, the prostate cancer screening rate was meager in China, resulting in 58% of patients being diagnosed at an advanced stage.[4] A patient would have 6–12 needles inserted into their perineum for a prostate biopsy. Due to a lack of standard procedures, some doctors performed biopsies using ultrasound guidance, while others performed only a "blind" operation. Most hospitals failed to provide patients with follow-up care checks after discharge. Unlike female patients' active involvement in breast cancer survivors' clubs, China's male patients were unwilling to organize or participate inpatient education organizations.

To address these problems, AZ-China and its partners worked with China's leading urologists to discuss and develop treatment standards for prostate cancer. In December 2018, the Chinese Prostate Cancer Consortium (CPCC), AZ-China, Yidu Cloud,[8] and other organizations launched the PiDT project. Hospitals that met eligibility requirements were certified as PiDT cooperative institutions and contributed to implementing a new integrated solution.

As medical infrastructure varied by city and hospital size, PiDT centers took various forms, including screening centers, puncture centers, pathology centers, standardized treatment centers, and model centers of excellence (ranked from lowest to highest). An upper center encompassed all the functions of lower centers, with a lower center enabling seamless referrals to upper centers.

The PiDT project aimed to provide low-cost PSA[9] tests for early detection and treatment, making prostate cancer screening as common in men as cervical and breast cancer screening in women, along with a supportive policy environment.

Hospitals could use PSA testing to diagnose prostate cancer as early as possible. With the support of CPCC and other partners, the construction of PiDT centers enabled hospitals to obtain advanced testing reagents and medical equipment at lower or zero cost. The introduction of standardized medical procedures also optimized hospital management.

Early detection, diagnosis, and treatment served to uphold the central government's disease management principles of "prevention before disease occurs, treatment before disease develops, and relapse prevention after recovery". This, in turn, helped improve people's health, saved public medical expenditure, and turned the Healthy China 2030 action plan into reality.

---

[8] Yidu Tech Inc. (Yidu Cloud) was a healthcare AI company, offering healthcare solutions built on big data and AI technologies. With the mission to "make value-based precision healthcare accessible to everyone," the company leveraged its AI strength to promote technology integration and business integration, remove information barriers, and collaborate with government agencies, hospitals, and the whole healthcare industry, to exploit smart healthcare solutions.

[9] The prostate specific antigen (PSA), which is normally found in very small amounts in serum, is the main diagnostic tool when it comes to prostate cancer. A higher PSA level means a higher risk of prostate cancer.

AZ-China intended to provide patients with better, more standardized treatment through innovative solutions. The incidence of prostate cancer in China was below the worldwide average, while Chinese patients with abnormal PSA values showed a lower puncture-positive rate. Data from the Institute of Urology at Peking University indicated that from January 2000 to June 2005, among patients with PSA values of 10–20 ng/ml and PSA values > 20 ng/ml, positive puncture rates were 24.9% and 56.7%, respectively.[5] In practice, for every 100 people screened, one or two patients were confirmed cases, with only one likely to take medicine. Obviously, PiDT was not an innovation model designed to boost drug sales.

AZ-China hoped more partners would join and pledge ample resources to the PiDT project to build a more extensive vertical ecosystem.

4.1.6 Slow and Steady not Only Wins the Race but Keeps the Goal in Sight: How Management Balanced Innovation and Financial Performance

As the chief architect of AZ-China's innovation strategy, Wang had to strike a balance between financial performance and innovative activities, often at odds with each other.

Wang balanced them with a subtle mix of incentives and pressures, personally involving himself at key points during their respective processes to ensure both financial performance growth and the successful completion of innovation projects. Even before 2018, he often communicated in-depth with key members of the innovation group. Personally, he oversaw the critical stages of innovation projects to ensure they were relevant and patient-centric.

He firmly believed that sincere "patient-centricity" could create a just and profitable business. He even criticized employees who rushed to profit from their innovation efforts:

> Please hold your horses. Patients are our customers, and we should put them first. Our purpose is to serve patients, not to profit from them. You can't force customers to buy your products just to make more money.

As a patient-centric company, AZ-China sold medicines developed in-house and by third parties. It would not mind being the largest CSO[10] in China if it could bring high-quality, innovative drugs from around the world to the Chinese market and still drive local R&D drug efforts. However, the company did act as a conventional CSO. It set high standards for selecting collaborative products and innovation projects based on its academic expertise.

[10] Contract Sales Organization.

4.1.7 Patient-Centric Model and Social Co-Innovation

The integrated centers co-built by AZ-China combined characteristics of patient-centricity with a commitment to the public interest and de-prioritized sales.

The Chest Pain Center ("CPC") project was headed by Ge Junbo, an academic from the Chinese Academy of Sciences. It defined standard practices against German quality control standards. In pre-hospital emergency responses, a CPC project collaborated with medical institutions at all levels and relevant departments within the hospital for real-time synchronous data transmission. Doctors could make a remote diagnosis in the shortest possible time, while patients could be transported to a hospital that provided the most efficient treatment. Before the establishment of CPCs, clinicians treated patients inline with their clinical practice guidelines.

In contrast, a CPC strictly followed D2B[11] time rules and other indicators for emergency treatment. The in-hospital treatment started once the patient was admitted to the ambulance, shortening the D2B time from 112 to 69 min (shorter than the international standard of 90 min). In addition, the ambulance was equipped with a "first-aid kit", greatly simplifying the routine admission process of "diagnosis-prescription-payment-dispensation-medication-Cath lab", thereby delivering an average of 20 min of valuable treatment time for acute heart attack patients.

A national metabolic management center (MMC) provided a one-stop patient-centric metabolic disease management service, integrating various functional areas like an information desk, patient education area, waiting area, metabolic panel area, and treatment area. Each MMC was equipped with patented all-in-one screening equipment: patients need only to take off their shoes and lie flat to undergo screening for six possible complications in just 20 min. Before, a patient needed to spend three or four days visiting various departments for a complete examination, but the MMC addressed this pain point.

For diabetic patients, self-care behavior is more important than medication. That was why MMC physicians focused on patients' diet, exercise, medications, blood sugar monitoring, and health education while developing follow-up schedules accordingly. Among the diabetic patients managed by MMC, the HbA1c (glycosylated hemoglobin A1c) compliance rate increased significantly from 21.07% at baseline to 47.05%. The overall metabolic compliance rate increased from 7.18% at baseline to 18.97%, hitting the internationally accepted advanced level.[6]

By 2021, the MMC project had attracted the participation of almost 1,000 hospitals across China, with an awareness rate exceeding 90% in the endocrinology world. Building on this successful case, AZ-China would collaborate with its partners to further bolster academic research and invest in constructing metabolic disease industrial parks centered on developing metabolic therapies.

---

[11] The door to balloon (D2B) time is an important cardiovascular measurement. On a patient level, the D2B time directly correlates the amount of time the myocardium undergoes ischemic damage. Reducing such time reduces the degree of ischemic damage and ultimately improve patient outcomes.

4.2 *Replicating and Expanding Innovation Models (2018–2021)*

Three years after the "interest group" for innovation was formed, AZ-China embarked on a new chapter of its innovation journey. It had reached a stage where it could make case-based reflections, redefine its focus, and expand its initiatives.[12]

4.2.1 Innovation Showroom: China Healthcare IoT Innovation Center in Wuxi

On June 28, 2017, the China Healthcare IoT Innovation Center ("CHIIC") officially launched in Wuxi's Hi-tech District. Here, AZ-China presented its vision of ideal healthcare models illustrated through eight solutions.[13]

In over four years of operations, the CHIIC received visiting medical professionals from across the country and demonstrated the possibilities of better healthcare.

By mid-2021, AZ-China had worked with a wide range of partners on launching 14 integrated diagnosis and treatment solutions, one of which was patented, and seven others were patent-pending. These solutions were implemented in hospitals nationwide, benefiting nearly 10 million patients.

The CHIIC served as an incubator, showroom, and relay station for AZ-China to polish, showcase, and popularize innovative solutions. The company organized an innovation competition every year, selecting and awarding outstanding innovators. They would then fund the winning ideas, provide opportunities for the most outstanding competitors to undergo training, and receive personal guidance from senior executives.

4.2.2 Establishing an Ecosystem of Innovation

The integrated diagnosis and treatment platform was not an isolated idea but originated from AZ-China's grand vision to build an innovation ecosystem. Wang was determined to lead AZ-China's transformation from a traditional drugmaker to an innovative platform company. This required the synchronized development of business innovation, R&D innovation, and operational innovation.

In terms of **R&D innovation**, AZ significantly stepped-up R&D efforts in China after Wang took office. In 2013, the China New Drug R&D Department was established to boost the clinical development and commercialization of innovative drugs

---

[12] Wuxi, the third largest city in Jiangsu, a developed province in eastern China, has a well-developed IoT industry.

[13] Namely, China Chest Pain Center, National Metabolic Management Center, Pulmonary and Critical Care Medicines, Smart Nebulization Center, Gastrointestinal Cancer Center, Community Center for Chronic Disease Management, Integrated Center for Lung Cancer Diagnosis and Treatment, and Integrated Center for Prostate Cancer Diagnosis and Treatment.

in China. In 2017, AZ cooperated with the SDIC Fund to establish Dizal Pharmaceutical[14] to accelerate the local development of medicines in the therapy areas of respiratory, oncology, and chronic kidney disease, which were prevalent in China. In 2018, China became the first country to approve AZ's first-in-class anemia drug Roxadustat, and then in 2019, marketing authorization followed. In 2020, AZ-China upgraded its Shanghai R&D platform to a global R&D center, shifting the focus away from confirmatory studies in the pre-launch phase to earlier stage R&D. In late 2021, Dizal Pharmaceutical, specializing in drugs for cancer and immunological diseases, listed on the SSE STAR Market. At the time of writing, AZ's China R&D pipeline comprised over 150 projects, with nearly 90% international. Over the next five years, 55 new drugs and new indications were expected to receive approvals in China. Through Wang's efforts, the Global R&D China Center not only engaged in developing new drugs in China but also handled drug regulatory affairs globally, accelerating the delivery of drugs from China to the world and vice versa.

In terms of **operational innovation**, AZ increased investments in Chinese production and supply networks, introducing state-of-the-art facilities and technologies. At the same time, it leveraged its 28 global production and supply bases in 16 countries and regions to build a lean and efficient global supply network, including two new supply sites in Wuxi and Taizhou. Internally, the company used technology to improve efficiency and externally by fostering a culture of open dialogue with its partners. In addition, IoT technologies enabled the collection of first-hand information from equipment during the diagnosis process, making it conducive to medical decision-making.

In terms of **business innovation**, AZ continued working with government, industry, university, research, hospital, and investment partners to create an innovative healthcare ecosystem with mutually beneficial results. Backed by their social innovation centers and with the concerted efforts of business and innovation teams, the company kept developing end-to-end holistic disease management solutions for patients in their respective therapeutic areas to meet patients' needs in disease education, screening, diagnosis, treatment, follow-up, and rehabilitation, among many others. It also cooperated with local governments to build the International Life Science Innovation Campus (i-Campus), a one-stop innovation and collaboration platform for Chinese and international companies to incubate and undertake healthcare projects, as well as to accelerate project commercialization and replication. Furthermore, AZ cooperated with the China International Capital Corporation (CICC) to create a Healthcare Industrial Fund to provide full lifecycle support to its investees' innovation efforts.

With a three-pronged innovation strategy, Wang hoped to further improve China's position in AZ's global R&D and innovation network and spearhead the creation of

[14] According to publicly available data, in October 2017, AZ and SDIC Fund established Dizal Pharmaceutical to support a new venture lead by Dr. Zhang Xiaolin. Backed by AZ's R&D strength in Asia and emerging markets, the joint venture was devoted to the discovery, R&D, and commercialization of small molecule drugs.

an innovation ecosystem emphasizing cross-border cooperation and industry-finance integration to support the development of China's healthcare industry.

4.2.3 Building an Innovation Organization and Nurturing an Innovation Culture

Over the last few years, AZ-China developed an innovation system with dedicated innovation personnel and a corporate-level business innovation team (Central). The company also formulated a set of procedures to manage and showcase innovation projects. At the same time, it assisted each business unit's marketing team in incubating new projects and upgrading existing ones. Functional departments also had designated staff to provide professional support for such tasks.

In terms of regulation, the company introduced standards and requirements specific to each innovation stage, developed checklists with measurable criteria, plotted an innovation roadmap applicable to most cases, and formulated rules for allocating and coordinating internal and external resources.

In terms of innovation philosophy, the company developed innovative models and theoretical frameworks to make innovation practices more relevant, powerful, and popular. For example, it created the T-shaped innovation model and consolidated its core concept of patientcentricity.[15]

In terms of communication, the company kept adding new words to its "innovation glossary," such as "innovation 0–1", "innovation 1–10", and "innovation 10–100", coined to indicate different stages of innovation. These terms made internal communication on projects more concise, efficient, and persuasive.

Regarding the atmosphere, about one-third of the sales staff no longer held innovation activities at arm's length. Instead, they began actively exploring using innovation platforms to serve their customers better. With the buy-in of many more employees, innovation itself would become an element of company culture.

In addition, a full-fledged innovation talent rotation program took shape, encouraging marketing and sales professionals to try innovation jobs. This rotation program assigned employees to AZ's partners while some government officials joined AZ's innovation team. The company's supply site in Wuxi also housed a team to facilitate proof of innovation concepts and help build smart digital factories with "lean thinking" concepts and tools.

The "going out" and "bringing in" activities of the interest group, the company's impetus for innovation, became a tradition, but now in more diversified forms. Looking back, AZ had come a long way, and its culture of innovation was thriving.

---

[15] In April 2017, AZ published a research paper in a BMJ journal, probing into the impact of patient-centricity on the biopharmaceutical industry. Based on a survey of 470 U.S. patients and 703 European patients, AZ redefined patient-centricity as "putting the patient first by an open and sustained engagement of the patient's needs, in order to achieve the best outcome for the patient and their family.".

4.3 *Keeping Innovation Alive: The Road Ahead (2022—)*

AZ-China's seed which had begun from its idea of an integrated diagnosis and treatment platform was growing.

In 2021, AZ-China exported its "Wuxi model" to regional innovation centers in Shanghai, Beijing, Guangzhou, Hangzhou, and Chengdu,[16] focusing on healthcare AI, community-level smart healthcare, precision diagnosis, digital healthcare, and the integration and modernization of traditional Chinese medicine (TCM) and Western medicine. These innovation centers were expected to fully tap advantageous local resources, integrate all aspects of local economic development, and promote a more profound integration of the entire healthcare industry chain. The centers would be tasked with exploring digital disease management products and digital therapeutics while driving continuous improvements for integrated diagnosis and treatment solutions.

Wang also made a variety of innovation forays beyond the area of medicine. The "i-Campus" co-built with the Wuxi government was successfully replicated in several other cities, providing one-stop innovation services for local and international companies to incubate and undertake innovation projects. At the time of writing, 60 enterprises had joined the "i-Campus companies" list. With a target funding size of US$ 1 billion, the AZ-CICC Healthcare Industrial Fund was committed to supporting innovation initiatives throughout the industry chain, including global R&D, manufacturing, operations, and the commercialization of new drugs. It also planned to invest in 100 out of 1,000 candidate startups. As of March 2021, the fund had completed first-round fundraising of US$ 338.46 million while investing in eight innovation firms. With emerging digital technologies such as 5G and AI, the fund looked to vigorously explore the internet hospital model.

Between creating regional headquarters, innovation centers, i-Campuses, the healthcare industrial fund, and a robust digital network, AZ-China appears committed to establishing itself as a powerhouse of innovation.

"I hope that by 2025, AZ-China will grow into a patient-centric, service-oriented, platform-based organization and that our patient-centric business innovation model will lead the way at AZ globally,"[7] Wang said.

However, to make strides in innovation, Wang had to show unwavering grit from the very start.

On one hand, AZ's headquarters (AZ-Global) was still wary of large-scale business innovation trials conducted by the Chinese division since innovation in Europe and the US was more concerned with developing effective drugs than with inventing platforms that addressed complete disease lifecycles. However, AZ-Global also kept an open mind to Chinese innovation models and anticipated more from them. Over the years, AZ-China had become synonymous with innovation at AZ-Global,

---

[16] Beijing, the capital of China, is the second largest city in the country. Guangzhou, located on the southern coast of China, is the third largest city in China. Chengdu is the largest provincial capital city in western China.

encouraging more localized innovation centers to spring up in other developing countries.

Within AZ-China, ongoing debates took place over how much resources to invest in developing these integrated platforms. With an unwavering commitment to serving patients, Wang kept emphasizing that all innovation initiatives were made on behalf of the public, not for sales or performance appraisals. "It is the right thing, and we should stick with it", he said. "AZ-China will continue upholding our strategy of building an ecosystem—an open and cooperative ecosystem that can grow with the addition of firms, promote the advancement of medicine, and ultimately meet the needs of patients, delivering win–win results to all stakeholders."

In November 2018, China's National Healthcare Security Administration piloted a volume-based procurement ("VBP") program,[17] throwing pharmaceutical companies into turmoil, including AZ-China. On June 23, 2021, AstraZeneca's blockbuster asthma drug Pulmicort[18] failed to win a bidin the fifth round of the VBP, and only its Gefitinib[19] was included in the previous round. Under such circumstances, how was the company still willing and able to continue its path of innovation?

To achieve its new growth targets in a challenging environment, should AZ-China continue developing patient-centric integrated healthcare services to spur social innovation already eight years in the making? If so, how should it strike a balance between social innovation and its pharmaceutical businesses for integrated and synergistic development? How should it make social innovation serve its vision of becoming a patient-centric, service-oriented, and platform-based company? Would Wang and AZ-China stand these tests of fortitude? (Exhibit 4 and 5)

Endnotes

1. https://www.astrazeneca.com/investor-relations/annual-reports.html.
2. Hao Han, AstraZeneca to build an Internet hospital? Data insights into pharma multinational's innovation in China. 2020–03–31[2021–02–25]. http://www.innomd.org/article/5e82a75507bace052148ecc2.
3. TMTPost, AstraZeneca's Xu Jing on pharmaceutical platform innovation: Demand has changed and so has the traditional business model |Global Digital Value Summit 2019. 2019–08–08[2021–02–25]. https://baijiahao.baidu.com/s?id=1641310716777376546&wfr=spider&for=pc.

[17] VBP is a pooled bulk purchase of drugs by the government at the lowest possible prices, allowing pharmaceutical companies to gain more market share by dramatically lowering their drug prices. For the first wave of drugs that were selected for the pilot program, the overall price dropped 52% with the highest drop at 96%. The procurement volume should account for 60–70% of the total annual drug consumption of all public medical institutions in the pilot cities. For most MNCs and other large pharmaceutical companies, if they could not lower the price of their brand-name drugs to generic levels, they would only have to compete for the remaining 30–40% of the market.

[18] Pulmicort (budesonide) is an inhaled anti-inflammatory glucocorticosteroid for initiation and maintenance treatment of bronchial asthma.

[19] Gefitinib (Iressa) is an orally administered, small-molecule inhibitor of epidermal growth factor receptor tyrosine kinase (EGFR-TK), which results in inhibition of proliferation and angiogenesis, and induction of apoptosis.

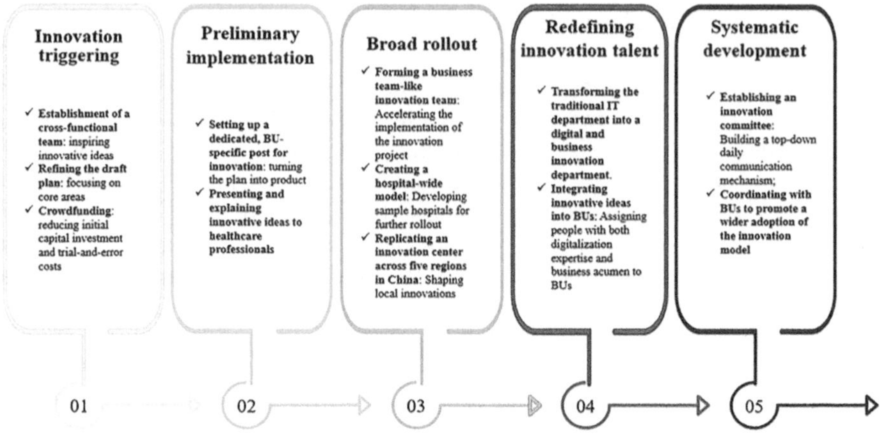

Exhibit 4 The development stage of an innovation project. *Source* Authors

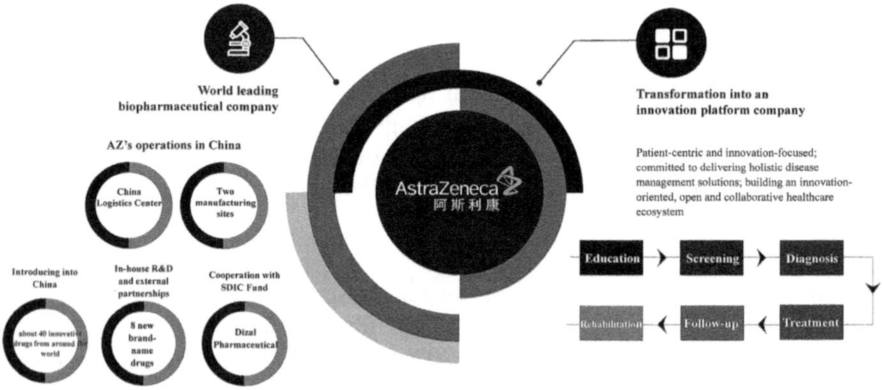

Exhibit 5 AZ-China's transformation from a traditional drugmaker to an innovation platform company. *Source* Authors

4. Chen R, et al. Asian Journal of Urol.2014;1(1);15–29.
5. Dxy.cn, Data on the positive rate of prostate puncture biopsies 2019–01–03[2021–08–18]. http://urol.dxy.cn/article/593868.
6. Association of metabolic management centers along the Yangtze River Delta established with international leading overall metabolic compliance rate.2019–11–14[2021–09–30]. https://www.cn-healthcare.com/articlewm/20191114/wap-content-1075694.html.
7. Eyjlr.zazhi.com.cn, AstraZeneca Leon Wang: Setting a new life record.2019–10–21[2021–02–25]. https://med.sina.com/article_detail_1001_25,121.html.

Midea in India

On a Friday afternoon in June 2018, Mr. Krishan Sachdev, Managing Director of the Indian joint venture company created by Midea Electric and Carrier (hereafter called "the joint venture company"), and Mr. Wei Li, Vice President responsible for marketing and operations of the joint venture company, were standing on a fan-shaped lawn in the air conditioner production base in Haryana State, engaged in warm conversation. Taking a look around, they noted that the whole production base covered a huge area and that the layout was well organized. The base was only 60 kilometers away from the joint venture company's headquarters. Since commencing operations in 2012, it had become the largest air conditioner production plant in India, with the highest capacity. Despite the huge capacity of this production plant, the joint venture company's revenue in 2017 was only a fraction of that of Midea Electric in China.[1]

In addition to the Haryana air conditioner production base, a technology park located in Pune, a city in southwestern India, was being constructed. This technology park covered an area of about 270,000 square meters, and its construction was expected to be completed in 2020. The plan was for the technology park to serve as a production base for household appliances, HVAC (heating, ventilation, and air conditioning), and air conditioner compressors in five years.[2] Looking at the expansion of the joint venture company, Krishan and Li, both ambitious managers, had mixed feelings; On one hand, they were delighted about the expansion. On the other hand, they were worried because the competition in the Indian market was intensifying even as the joint venture company was increasing its production capacity. Despite the joint venture company's rapid development, there was still a large gap between its market performance and Midea's expectations. The joint venture company was

---

X. U. Yuehua, CHEN Honghui, L. A. I. Hongyu, HUANG Xinyi of Sun Yat-sen University developed this case. The case aims to provide the basis for classroom discussion rather than illustrate effective or ineffective handling of a management situation.

This case was the Nominated Case Award winner of 2018 Global Contest for the Best China-Focused Cases.

China-Focused Cases, https://doi.org/10.1007/978-981-97-8580-3_9

facing several challenges at present. If those challenges were not overcome, they would greatly hinder the future development of the joint venture company. As they contemplated the future, Krishan and Li were both excited and somewhat bemused. A hot and humid monsoon mixed with the peculiar smell of dust storms interrupted their thoughts. Without them realizing it, their foreheads and backs were soaked with sweat.

1 Introduction of Midea Group

Midea Group was a Chinese technology group specializing in consumer electronics, HVAC (heating, ventilation, and air conditioning), robotics and industrial automation systems, and intelligent supply chains. The company offered highly diversified products and services. Its products included household kitchen appliances, refrigerators, washing machines, all kinds of small home appliances, consumer electronics, and household air conditioners. Its HVAC business produced central air conditioning, heating, and ventilation systems. Its robotics and industrial automation system business was based on the core techniques of KUKA AG from Germany and YASKAWA Electric Corporation from Japan. It also had an intelligent supply chain business called Annto, which was the integrated solution service platform. Midea Group adhered to the principle of creating value for customers, and was committed to creating a better life for consumers, by focusing on innovation and improving the quality of its products and services.[3]

Midea was founded in 1968 in Foshan, Guangdong, China, and was headquartered in Beijiao New Town, Shunde. Xiangjian He, the founder of the company, started his career working in a small plastic bottle cap company. He overcame many hardships and made Midea the star-studded enterprise it was today. From a small workshop to a township enterprise and then becoming a listed company ranked among the world's top 500 companies in 2016 (481th), Midea Group had witnessed the miracle of a Chinese enterprise's development. In 2017, Midea Group ranked 450thin the world's top 500. In 2018, it climbed 127 places to 323th, achieving sales revenue of US$35.794 billion and a profit of 2.557 billion US$.[3]

After 50 years of development, Midea Group had transformed from a company focusing on home appliance manufacturing to a technology giant involved in consumer electronics, HVAC, robotics and automation systems, and intelligent supply chains. It had a presence all over the world. By 2018, Midea Group had about 200 subsidiaries, more than 60 overseas branches, and 10 strategic business units around the world, and was the most important shareholder (about 95%) of the German KUKA Group.

2 International Expansion of Midea

2.1 Entering the Global Market

In the late 1980s, Midea Group entered the international market as an OEM (original equipment manufacturer). In order to make full use of low-cost domestic and foreign resources and labor, and to avoid trade barrier risks, Midea Group established its production bases in Shunde and Vietnam as OEM factories. To attract more international orders, Midea Group had to retain its own corporate brand image. This mode of operation enabled Midea Group to expand rapidly, with an annual growth rate of 40%, to receive OEM orders from 18 global retail giants and 10 globally renowned brands.[4]

2.2 Broadening the Market

"The OEM production helped earn money through hard toil. Our equipment roared every day, and the workers were busy on the production line, but they were all working for other brands." Thinking about this situation, Wei could not help but give a wry smile. Ten years before 2018, Weiserved as Director of Air Conditioner Production and Operations for the company, and was busy managing the company's production scheduling and operations every day. In the process, Midea Group accumulated a certain amount of capital, technology, and management expertise, and thus began to establish its reputation in the international market. Since 2005, Midea Group had started to explore new markets through acquisitions, joint ventures, equity participation, and holdings. It expected to continue enhancing its image and to further expand in the international market.

In 2011, Midea Group selected the American company Carrier as a partner and established a joint venture with the aim of developing the Latin American market.4 Entering through a joint venture successfully reduced the risks and uncertainties of Midea Group in the Latin American market, making it the largest household air conditioner manufacturer in that market.

In 2012, Midea Group acquired a 32.5% stake in Egypt's Miraco for US$57.48 million.4 Egypt's Miraco had mature sales channels in the country's air conditioning market and was highly recognized internationally. By acquiring Miraco, Midea Group obtained the company's brand, market, and channel advantages, greatly reducing the overall risk of entering the Egyptian market.

In 2016, Midea Group acquired 80.1% of the shares of Toshiba Life Electric Co., Ltd., the main body of Japan's Toshiba appliance business, and obtained the rights to use Toshiba's global license for 40 years and access to more than 5,000 patented technologies. In the same year, Midea Group acquired an 80% stake in Italy's Clivet.4 Clivet was a central air conditioning company in Italy with a strong reputation and abundant resources. The acquisition enabled Midea Group to obtain advanced production technology and management experience, improve its central air conditioner production line, and enhance its share of the European central air conditioning market.

In 2017, Midea Group acquired KUKA and Servotronix in the field of robotics and automation, and entered the commercial field of robots through Swisslog,[5] which belonged to Servotronix. In this way, Midea built its presence in the field of home robots.

2.3 Establishing Overseas Branches and Production Bases

"By the end of 2017, Midea Group has established more than 60 overseas branches in the United States, Italy, the United Kingdom, Germany, France, etc. It has established six overseas production bases in Belarus, Egypt, Vietnam, Brazil, and so on." Wei talked about the status quo of the international operations of Midea Group in a tone that was full of pride and joy.

Midea Group expected to change its internationalization strategy from "exporting" to "foreign direct investment", by continuously expanding the number of overseas production bases, increasing the types and production capacity of localized products, promoting supply chain localization strategies, and improving the quality of products from its overseas factories. At the same time, Midea Group had established Midea E-Commerce Co., Ltd., which was responsible for operating e-commerce platforms such as an online mall, accelerating the development of e-commerce, and making it easier for consumers in overseas markets to buy Midea products.[6]

3 Entering the Indian Market

3.1 Indian Society

India was the seventh-largest country in the world by land area, with a population of 1.36 billion, which was similar to that of China. According to the International Monetary Fund, India's Gross Domestic Product in 2017 was US$ 2,597.4 billion, ranking sixth in the world.[7] India had one of the fastest economic growth rates in the world. The average age of an Indian was 27 years old. Its huge consumer market and labor supply had attracted the world's attention.[8]

The customs of India were deeply influenced by religious beliefs. These customs attached great importance to traditions and were rather conservative. Generally, Indians were mild mannered, not prone to conflict, and had a higher tolerance of different races and religious beliefs than people from other races. Except for the occasional terrorist and violent sabotage of political affairs in Kashmir and the northeastern provinces, Indian society was generally stable.[9]

Due to the shortage and uneven distribution of educational resources, the overall educational level of Indians was not high. In many parts of India, illiteracy was widespread, which led to unpunctuality, untrustworthiness, and a lack of civic awareness among Indians. Littering and spitting were commonplace. Food markets were generally messy, and sanitation was poor in residential areas. Even in high- end commercial and residential areas, the roads were often in a state of disrepair, and the drainage systems were problematic, resulting in sewage stagnation. There were indeed individuals who were fluent in English and had an international perspective. However, they were vastly outnumbered by unrefined people. People cutting in line in public places and women being harassed were not uncommon. The traffic conditions in India made it difficult for foreigners to adapt. Car drivers generally lacked awareness of rules and driving ethics, and they rarely gave way to pedestrians. Animals, people, and cars jostled for space on the roads.[9]

3.2 *India's Human Capital*

There were about 500 million people working in India, 60% of whom were employed in rural areas. The number of factory workers was only one-third of that in China, and there was not enough technical or semi-skilled labor. Those who were illiterate were mainly concentrated in places where the infrastructure and governance were poor.[9] The labor quality was not high, which did little to help the supply of labor to the manufacturing and semi-manufacturing industries.

According to the Annual Survey of Industries conducted by the Central Statistical Organization of India, the annual growth rate of Indian industrial workers was 7.5% from 1998 to 2004. Since 2005, salaries had risen markedly. The average labor wage increase between 2005 and 2010 was about 15%–20%. The wage level of Indian workers was no longer as low as it used to be. By November 2018, the monthly salary of technical workers in India had risen to approximately US$ 601 to US$658, and the monthly salary of unskilled workers had reached approximately US$ 151 to US$ 188.[10]

3.3 *Overview of Household Appliance Market in India*

According to India China Economic and Cultural Council, 40% of all households in India had TV sets, 29% had refrigerators, 11% had washing machines, and only 6% had computers or laptops. Households with air conditioning accounted for less than 4% of the whole population. In 2017, the Indian durable consumer goods market was aboutUS$ 15.5 billion.[11]

The products in the Indian market had regional characteristics. Both window- type air conditioners and variable-frequency split-type air conditioners were sold in India's home appliance chain stores. Single-door refrigerators, side-by-side luxury refrigerators, two-cylinder washing machines, and large-capacity-drum washing machines could also be found. In the case of a refrigerator, the price ranged widely from about US$ 99.50 to US$ 4,174. One of the reasons for this large price range was that the wealth gap between the rich and the poor was enormous. Most households were low income. About 80% of households earned less than US$ 4,000 a year, and the mid-to-low-end products had the largest market share, accounting for about 70% of the home appliance market.

According to data collected by Carrier Midea India, the penetration rate of white goods in India was much lower than that in China. The penetration rate of refrigerators was about 20%, while that of washing machines was only 9%. That of air conditioners was not high, either.[12] Such low penetration rates indicated that there was still significant room for white goods. In addition to the Haryana air conditioner production base, Midea Group was gradually expanding its production scale of white goods in countries along the "Belt and Road." Aside from that, in the city of Pune in the state of Maharashtra, construction of an Indian industrial park was in full swing.

China Household Electrical Appliances Association organized a survey of the Indian market in 2018. The results of the survey showed that although the Indian market had great potential, it was less efficient than mature markets. When it came to culture, economic level, and consumption habits, significant differences existed between India and China. Laws and regulations were complex in India. Companies from other countries could unintentionally break rules. Chinese companies had to be fully prepared before investing in India.[13]

4 Choosing a Partner: Carrier

Midea Electric, a subsidiary of Midea Group, announced on January 7, 2012, that it would expand to the Indian air conditioning market through a joint venture with the American company Carrier. Midea Electric invested around US$20 million, accounting for about 60% of the joint venture's shares. Carrier invested aboutUS$13 million, accounting for about 40% of the shares.[14] The joint venture integrated the production and sales operations of both parties in India, including the production and sales of household air conditioners and several types of light commercial air conditioners from Midea, with an initial invested capacity of approximately one million units.[14] Once established, the joint venture company developed rapidly and eventually gained a foothold in the Indian market. From 2012 to 2017, Midea Group's sales revenue in India achieved a compound annual growth rate of approximately 30%, and sales in 2016 reached US$140 million.

Carrier was a member of United Technologies Corporation, which was headquartered in Farmington, Connecticut, United States, with production and sales in more than 180 countries worldwide. It was one of the world's largest suppliers of HVAC and refrigeration equipment, as well as energy management and sustainable building services. Willis Carrier, the founder of Carrier, invented the first modern air conditioning system in 1902. Thus, he gained a reputation as a global air conditioning expert in the industry. By 2012, Carrier was one of the leaders in the development of the air conditioning industry and had thousands of patents on air conditioner technology and 11 research and development centers around the world. It had its own production lines across six continents, the most famous of which were the production lines for commercial and domestic air conditioners, refrigeration equipment, transport refrigeration equipment, and automotive air conditioners.[15]

This was not the first time that Midea Group and Carrier were cooperating. In 2009 and 2010, Midea Group acquired a portion of equity in Carrier's air conditioning business in Egypt and South America, and the ownership continued to increase today. It held 32.5% of the shares in Egypt in 2009, 51% of the shares in South America in 2010, and 60% of the shares in India in 2012.[14] Compared with the way that Gree entered the Brazilian market, which was through setting up a wholly owned subsidiary, cooperating closely with Carrier and exploiting its sales channels and international experience enabled Midea to enter the markets quickly without taking too many detours. Moreover, cooperating with a single company could shorten the period for them to build trust and thus accelerate business development.

5 Challenges Facing Midea in the Indian Market

The Indian market had great potential and had attracted the world's attention. Chinese companies were eager to enter the Indian market. However, Chinese home appliance companies were late to the game in general. Further, Chinese companies lacked experience in adapting their operations to local conditions, so many of them faced very tough times when they first entered the Indian market.

The biggest challenge facing Chinese home appliance companies when entering the Indian market was usually that their products did not suit local conditions or local consumer habits. Midea Electric's joint venture with Carrier was established in February 2012, upon which it began its local operations in India. The joint venture company first entered the Indian market with air conditioners. But the company quickly realized in the first year of its actual operations that it had underestimated the difficulties. Due to differences in customs, habits, environments, and cultures between China and India, the products that sold well in China could not be simply sold in India, and had to be modified to meet local needs. Wei recalled that in 2012, Midea Electric tried to directly introduce the domestic inverter platform to the Indian market. However, due to the large voltage fluctuations in India and the high temperatures in some areas, the air conditioners directly imported from China failed to generate enough cool air. Midea had to modify its air conditioning products by taking into account the unstable power supply and high temperatures. Eventually, the modified products were successfully launched.

In 2015, water pollution in India was becoming increasingly serious, and water treatment and water-related products received immense attention. The joint venture company saw huge opportunities for water treatment products and set its sights on the Indian water purifier market. The research and development of water treatment-related products started in 2015 and continued for nearly two years, before the products were officially launched in India in the fall of 2016. Due to various issues including hardness of water, low water pressure, large voltage fluctuations, and frequent water and power outages, the reliability requirements for water purifier products were higher in India than in China. The joint venture company's water purifier project team led by Wei had never done business in the Indian market before. At first, no one knew how to get in, and so they adopted a pragmatic approach. First, they observed how competitors made their products. They compared about 200 models of various competing products, performed in-depth analyses, and carried out 300 tests to evaluate all sorts of performance parameters. In order to create products that could tackle the low water quality in India, they also conducted a two-month national water quality survey in India and invested in a local laboratory.

The second challenge was that the institutional environments in China and India were vastly different, which brought high operating costs to Chinese companies. At present, the Indian government was inefficient. Although the Modi administration had simplified the government approval process, Chinese companies operating in India still faced many challenges. India's corporate income tax rate was high (more than 34%). Its road transport facilities were poor, which made overall logistics inefficient and increased operating costs. Under the same conditions, the warehousing and logistics costs in India were twice as high as those in China. All these factors combined had made the Indian market relatively harsh from the perspective of foreign companies.

The third challenge came from consumers' biased perceptions of Chinese brands. Overall, wealthy Indians desired corporate brands from Japan, South Korea, and Western countries. Therefore, most of India's mid- to high-end home appliance market was occupied by Japanese, Korean, European, and American companies. Local Indian companies mainly competed in the low-end market. Chinese home appliances were priced slightly above their Indian counterparts and slightly below their Japanese and Korean counterparts. Because of their low income, the purchasing power of consumers in the low-end market was low and they were highly sensitive to price, so the competition among Indian brands was fierce. In general, local manufacturers and consumers in India were not friendly toward Chinese companies and products.

The top management team of the joint venture company, including Krishan Sachdev and Wei Li, generally believed that as the strategic importance of the Indian market continued to increase, there were both opportunities and challenges for Chinese home appliance companies. In the near future, the Indian market was expected to become the fourth-largest consumer market after China, the United States, and Japan. Even though there were still many problems in the Indian market, the investment environment in India was gradually improving, and most of the renowned home appliance companies from around the world had entered the Indian market. However, the team members from Midea represented by Wei Li felt that the biggest factor hindering the development of Midea's brand in India was that the sales channels had not yet been established. They had previously relied heavily on the brand and sales channels of Carrier. However, according to the agreement between Midea and Carrier, more than 100 of Carrier's businesses were excluded from the joint venture. In other words, the joint venture company could not use those resources, which had led to many difficulties in the development of sales channels in the past few years. Another concern pertained to the abilities of team members. The start-up team of the joint venture company was mainly composed of old employees from Carrier and Midea and new ones recruited locally in India. But they were short-staffed and so some team members had to assume multiple roles to maintain the operations of the joint venture. Team members often held different opinions, which might becaused by cultural differences. All these factors affected the development of the joint venture in the Indian market.

Now that the global economy was showing signs of recovery, major multinational companies had begun to build their presence in the Indian market, but the uncertainty was great. How should the brands and products of the joint venture be adapted to the Indian market? How could the joint venture improve its sales in India? Should Midea maintain the cooperation with Carrier or seek to expand its own business in the India market? In the face of intensifying competition, how could Midea build and maintain a competitive advantage? Currently, there were two opposing voices within Midea's Indian team. One voice belonged to the Midea representatives led by Wei Li, who were striving to establish their own independent channels to vigorously develop Midea's own brand rather than rely solely on that of Carrier. The other voice came from the representatives of Carrier, who argued that Midea should continue to negotiate with Carrier to maximize the use of Carrier's sales channels. After all, Carrier had a strong brand and well-established sales channels, and their Indian joint venture had not tapped these advantages yet.

Amid these opportunities and challenges, what path should the company take in India? This was weighing on Krishan and Wei's minds on this hot afternoon. The Indian market was like a gold mine for many companies around the world, and yet striking gold in this market was no easy feat.

Exhibit 1: Financial Information of Midea Group

See Tables 1 and 2, Exhibits 2 and 3.

Table 1 Key Financial Information of Midea Group in Recent Years

	2017	2016	2015	2014	2013
Operating revenues (RMB'000)	240,712,301	159,044,041	138,441,226	141,668,175	120,975,003
Net profits attributable to shareholders of the company (RMB'000)	17,283,689	14,684,357	12,706,725	12,502,220	5,317,458
Net profits attributable to shareholders of the company before non- recurring gains and losses (RMB'000)	15,614,103	13,492,866	10,911,341	9,476,849	3,903,376
Net cash flows from operating activities (RMB'000)	24,442,623	26,695,009	26,764,254	24,788,512	10,054,196
Basic earnings per share (RMB/share)	2.66	2.29	2.00	1.66	1.15
Diluted earnings per share (RMB/share)	2.63	2.28	1.99	1.66	1.15
Weighted average ROE (%)	25.88	26.88	29.06	29.49	24.87
Total assets (RMB'000)	248,106,858	170,600,711	128,841,935	120,292,086	96,946,025
Net assets (RMB'000)	82,925,171	68,976,696	56,031,622	45,731,454	39,080,562
Net assets attributable to shareholders of the company (RMB'000)	73,737,437	61,304,298	49,201,852	39,470,499	32,847,431

Table 2 Midea group's statement of corporate profits in recent years

Items	2017 Consolidated	2016 Consolidated	2017 Group	2016 Group Company
I. Gross trading income	241,918,896	159,841,701	1,565,670	1,193,744
Including: Operating				
revenue Interest income	240,712,301	159,044,041	1,565,670	1,193,744
	1,206,582	789,414	—	—
Fee and commission	13	8,246	—	—
income Less: Cost of sales				
	(180,460,552)	(115,615,437)	(38,819)	(38,713)
Interest expenses	(250,925)	(439,607)	—	—
Fee and commission	(2,717)	(2,839)	—	—
expenses Taxes and surcharges	(1,416,428)	(1,077,119)	(26,607)	(29,741)
	(26,738,673)	(17,678,451)	—	—
Selling and distribution	(14,780,236)	(9,620,777)	(694,314)	(718,487)
expenses General and				
Add: Gains/(losses) from changes in fair value				
Income	(25,045)	117,376	—	22,618
Investment income	1,830,22	1.285.961	10,214,403	9.853.358
Including: Share of profit of associates	310,016	165,904	209,908	247,016
Gains/(losses) from disposal of assets	1,327,251	(111,874)		9,573
Other income	1.311.123	—	(95)	—
II. Operating profit	21,627,854	17,324,101	10,702,184	9,551,291
Add: Non-operating income	467,204	1,758,220	1,961	46,494
Less: Non-operating expenses	(240,284)	(167,718)	(1,216)	(2,139)
III. Total profit	21,854,774	18,914,603	10,702,929	9,595,646
Less: Income tax expenses	(3,243,584)	(3,052,691)	74,702	(16,183)
IV. Net profit	18,611,190	15,861,912	10,777,631	9,579,463
(I) Classified by continuity of operations				
Net profit from continuing operations	18,611,190	15,861,912	10,777,631	9,579,463
Net profit from discontinued operations	—	—	—	—
(II) Classified by equity ownership				
Attributable to equity owners of the company	17,283,689	14,684,357	10,777,631	9,579,463
Minority interest	1,327,501	1,177,555	—	—

V. Other comprehensive income net of tax	(310,628)	1,188,215	42,528	(30,075)
Attributable to shareholders of the parent company	(257,817)	1,084,276	42,528	(30,075)
(I) Other comprehensive income items which will not be reclassified subsequently as profit or loss	(31,132)	82,223	—	—
1. Remeasurements of post-employment benefit obligations	(31,132)	82,223	—	—
2. Share of the other comprehensive income of the investee accounted for using the equity method which will not be reclassified subsequently as profit and loss				
(II) Other comprehensive income items which will be reclassified subsequently as profit or loss	(226,685)	1,002,053	42,528	(30,075)
1. Share of the other comprehensive income of the investee accounted for using the equity method which will be reclassified subsequently as profit and loss	(36,017)	(73,811)	(24,431)	(30,075)
2. Changes in fair value of sellable financial assets	(240,597)	231,672	66,959	—
3. Effective portion of cash flow hedging gains or losses	318,553	199,356	—	—
4. Translation of foreign currency financial statements	(268,624)	644,836	—	—
5. Attributable to minority shareholders	(52,811)	103,939	—	—
VI. Total comprehensive income	18,300,562	17,050,127	10,820,159	9,549,388
Attributable to shareholders of the parent company	17,025,872	15,768,633	10,820,159	9,549,388
Attributable to minority shareholders			—	—
VII. Earnings per share				
Basic earnings per share (in RMB)	2.66	2.29	N/A	N/A
Diluted earnings per share (in RMB)	2.63	2.28	N/A	N/A

Source: Midea Group Co., Ltd., 2017 Annual Report, March 31, 2018,accessed June 30, 2018, 87–88.

Endnotes

1. Dong, J. Dong Mingzhu said, "If Midea has to build a factory in India, I'll stand aloof". Operators' World Network, July 5, 2017, accessed June 20, 2018. http://www.sohu.com/a/154656776_452858.
2. J. Liu, "India Becomes a Hot Place to Invest for Chinese Household Appliance Giants, and Midea Invested 1.27 Billion Yuan to Build a Science Park," First Finance, November 4, 2018, accessed November 30, 2018, https://www.yicai.com/news/100052439.html.

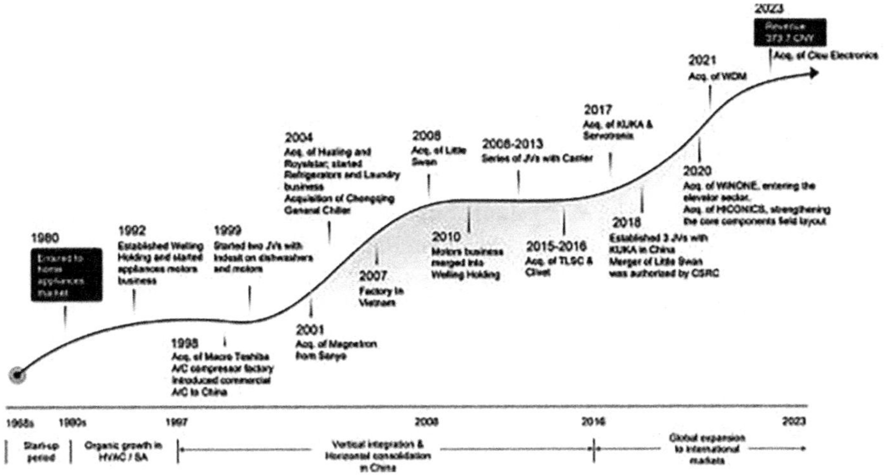

Exhibit 2 Internationalization process of midea group. *Source* "Presentations", Midea Official Website, September 2017, accessed June 30 2018, www.midea.com/global/investors/financial_investors/financial_statements/Presentations

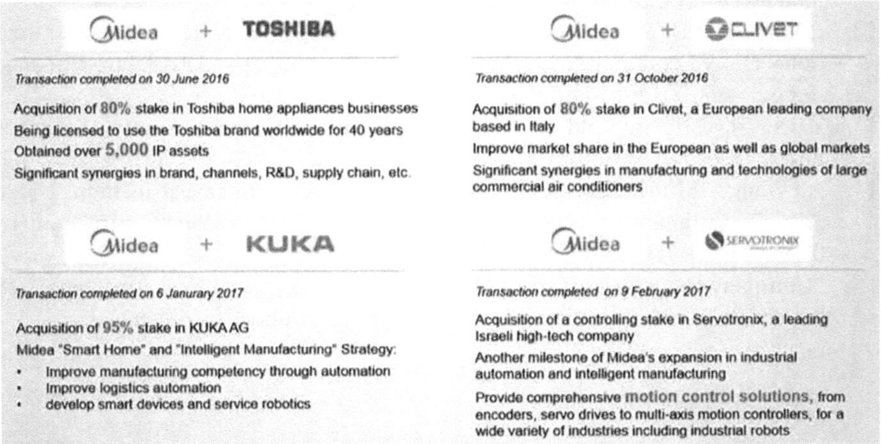

Exhibit 3 Midea Group's Recent Strategic Actions. Source: "Presentations", Midea Official Website, September 2017, accessed June 30 2018, www.midea.com/global/investors/financial_investors/financial_statements/Presentations

3. Midea Official Website, June 20, 2018, www.midea.com/midea-page/about-midea.html.
4. Y. Kang, "Analysis of the Internationalization of Midea Group," Modern Business 2 (2017): 153–154.

5. Y. Qu, "Midea Discusses Business Transformation after Acquiring Kuka and YASKAWA," Caixin, March 8, 2017, accessed August 30, 2018, http://companies.caixin.com/2017-03-08/101063917.html.
6. M. Cai, "Midea Enters E-commerce and Realizes Online and Offline Integration," Nanfang Daily Online Edition, November 10, 2014, accessed November 30, 2018, http://tech.southcn.com/t/2014-11/10/content_111872799.htm.
7. "GDP Ranking," The Word Bank, September 21, 2018, accessed November 1, 2018, https://datacatalog.worldbank.org/dataset/gdp-ranking.
8. Y. Mu, "Opportunities and Challenges for Investing in the Indian Home Appliance Market," China Economic News Network, April 24, 2018, accessed November 1, 2018, www.cet.com.cn/itpd/sdyd/2020236.shtml.
9. "Introducing Investment Environment in India," Global Taiwanese Business Service Network, December 2014, accessed September 2018, www.twbusinessnet.com/countryPage.do?id=9&country=IN.
10. India Average Daily Wage Rate. Trading Economic, January 1, 2018, accessed November 10, 2018. https://tradingeconomics.com/india/wages.
11. Y. Mu, "Only 40% of All Households in India Have TV Sets: Is India Household Appliance Market a Gold Mine?" China Household Electrical Appliances Network, April 26, 2018, accessed November 10, 2018, www.diankeji.com/guandian/41271.html.
12. P. Chen and D. Wen, "Midea's Experience in India Market: Product Localization," Daily Economic News, May 14, 2017, November 15, 2018, http://finance.ifeng.com/a/20170514/15374361_0.shtml.
13. Z. Li, "Investigating Indian Household Appliance Market to Dig Out Opportunities," Electrical Equipment 5 (2018): 36–37.
14. X. Wang, "Midea Electric Cooperates with Carrier to Invest in India," State Securities, January 9, 2012, November 12, 2018, http://money.163.com/12/0109/13/7NB48COA00253B0H.html#.
15. "Company Summary," Carrier Official Website, accessed November 15, 2018, https://www.carrier.com/building-solutions/zh/cn/about/fact-sheet.

Alibaba versus JD.Com: Strategies, Business Models, and Financial Statements

After more than ten years of development, two giants—Alibaba, the world's largest online marketplace operator, and JD.com (JD), China's largest online direct sales operator—towered over China's e-commerce industry. In 2014, Alibaba and JD were listed successively, and in the first half of 2015, they disclosed their first annual reports after listing (see **Exhibit 1: Simplified Financial Statements of Alibaba and JD**, Exhibits1.1, 1.2 and 1.3). The annual reports and overwhelming media coverage attracted the attention of Zhang Wei, an institutional account manager who had just graduated from a reputable EMBA program. Anticipating questions from his clients, he decided to study these two e-commerce companies. After gathering the relevant materials, he began to read over the reports, hoping to find some investment highlights.

1 JD and Alibaba's Listings

On January 30, 2014, JD took the lead to file to list in the United States. On May 22 of the same year, the company debuted on the Nasdaq under the symbol "JD." It sold 93.7 million American depositary shares at US$19 per share, above the expected US$16 to US$18 range. JD's shares opened at US$19 and hit a high of US$22.8 in the early morning before eventually closing at US$20.9, an increase of 10 percent on its market debut. JD raised US$1.78 billion through its initial public offering (IPO), the largest US listing by a Chinese company to date.[1]

Professor CHEN Shimin, Teaching Assistant PAN Dingwen and Case Writer Dr. HUANG Xiayan of China Europe International Business School developed this case. The case aims to provide the basis for classroom discussion rather than illustrate effective or ineffective handling of a management situation.

This case was the Nominated Case Award winner of 2019 Global Contest for the Best China Focused Cases.

China-Focused Cases, https://doi.org/10.1007/978-981-97-8580-3_10

	Alibaba (Year ended March 31, 2015)		JD (Year ended December 31, 2014)	
	¥ million	% of revenue	¥ million	% of revenue
Revenue	**76,204**	**100.00**	**115,002**	**100.00**
Retail	61,500	80.70	—	—
Wholesale	7,923	10.40	—	—
Cloud computing and Internet infrastructure	1,271	1.67	—	—
Others*	5,510	7.23	—	—
Online direct sales	—	—	108,549	94.39
Service and others	—	—	6,453	5.61
Operating expenses	**53,069**	**69.64**	**120,805**	**105.05**
Cost of revenue	23,834	31.28	101,631	88.37
Fulfillment expenses	—	—	8,067	7.01
Product development expenses	10,658	13.99	1,836	1.60
Marketing expenses	8,513	11.17	4,010	3.49
General and administrative expenses	7,800	10.24	5,260	4.57
Income from operations	23,135	30.36	–5,802	–5.05
Net income	**24,320**	**31.91**	**-4,996**	**-4.34**

Exhibit 1.1 Simplified income statements *Source* Created by the case authors based on data from iResearch. *Note* Other revenue mainly represents interest income generated from micro loans, revenue from online marketing and other services provided by UCWeb and AutoNavi, and SME annual fees received from Ant Financial Services. *Source* Collected by the case authors based on Alibaba's financial statements for fiscal year 2015 and JD's financial statements for fiscal year 2014

On March 16, 2014, just after JD filed its IPO application, Alibaba also announced its listing plan. On September 19 of the same year, Alibaba listed on the New York Stock Exchange under the symbol "BABA." The company released 368 million American depositary shares at US$68 a piece, at the high end of its proposed range. Alibaba's shares opened at US$92.7 shortly before noon eastern time and quickly rose to a high of US$99.7, before paring gains to close at US$93.89, an increase of 38 percent on its market debut.[2] Alibaba raised US$21.8 billion from its public offering, making it the largest U.S. IPO of all time.[3]

Even though JD is China's first major e-commerce company listing in the U.S. capital market, Alibaba's listing is more eye-catching. Alibaba and JD are giants

	Alibaba (As of March 31, 2015)		JD (As of December 31, 2014)	
	¥ million	% of assets	¥ million	% of assets
Cash and cash equivalents	108,193	42.36	16,915	25.44
Inventories	—	—	12,191	18.33
Total current assets	**142,109**	**55.63**	**49,942**	**75.11**
Investment inequity investees	33,877	13.26	587	0.88
Property, equipment, and software	9,139	3.58	2,408	3.62
Construction in progress	—	—	1,929	2.90
Goodwill	41,933	16.42	2,622	3.94
Total non-current assets	113,325	44.37	16,551	24.89
Total assets	**255,434**	**100.00**	**66,493**	**100.00**
Accounts payable	—	—	16,364	24.61
Other current liabilities	34,314	13.43	10,505	15.80
Total current liabilities	**39,672**	**15.53**	**28,995**	**43.61**
Non-current bank loans	1,609	0.63	—	—
Unsecured senior notes	48,994	19.18	—	—
Total non-current liabilities	**57,691**	**22.59**	—	—
Total liabilities	**97,363**	**38.12**	**28,995**	**43.61**
Additional paid-in capital	117,142	45.86	47,131	70.88
Retained earnings	24,842	9.73	–9,272	–13.94
Total shareholders' equity	**158,071**	**61.88**	**37,498**	**56.39**

Exhibit 1.2 Simplified Balance Sheets *Source* Collected by the case authors based on Alibaba's financial statements for fiscal year 2015 and JD's financial statements for fiscal year 2014

in China's e-commerce industry with different business models—one is the largest third-party platform, while another is the largest direct online retailer; one enjoys the most online traffic, while another has a strong fulfillment infrastructure. Both companies have strengths and weaknesses, growing with many opportunities while also facing various risks.[4]

	Alibaba (Year ended March 31, 2015)			JD (Year ended December 31, 2014)		
	¥ million	% of assets	% of revenue	¥ million	% of assets	% of revenue
Net cash provided by operating activities	41,217	16.14	54.09	1,015	1.53	0.88
Net cash used in investing activities	–53,454	–20.93	–70.15	–13,203	–19.86	–11.48
Net cash provided by financing activities	87,497	34.25	114.82	18,392	27.66	15.99

Exhibit 1.3 Simplified statements of cash flows *Source* Collected by the case authors based on Alibaba's financial statements for fiscal year 2015 and JD's financial statements for fiscal year 2014

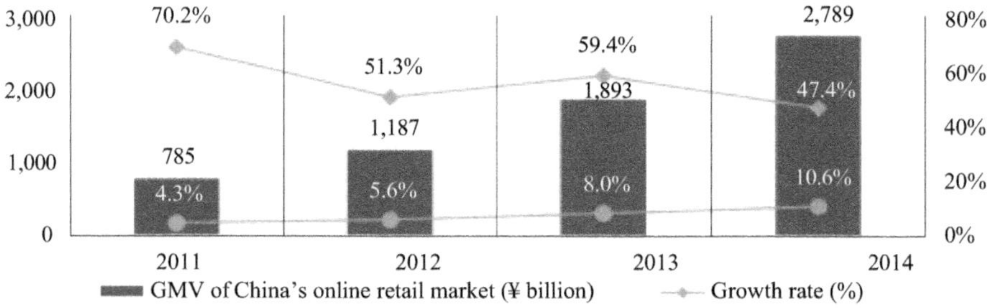

Exhibit 2 GMV of China's Online Retail Market from 2011 to 2014. *Source* Created by the case authors based on data from iResearch

2 China's Retail Industry

The Gross Merchandise Volume (GMV) of China's online retail market increased from ¥784.5 billion[1] in 2011 to ¥2.8 trillion in 2014, with a compound annual growth rate of 52.6%. With the rapid growth of GMV in the online retail market, its share of the total China's retail market had gradually increased from 4.3% in 2011 to 10.6% in 2014 (see Exhibit 2). In 2014, China's online shopping market entered a boom phase. The penetration rate of online shopping among netizens was as high as 55.7%. At the same time, the scale of online shopping through mobile commerce apps had also increased substantially. Among about 360 million online shoppers, mobile shopping users totaled 236 million, accounting for 65.6%.[5]

With the booming e-commerce economy, many excellent e-commerce websites had emerged in China. The technological improvement in online payment and

[1] ¥ = CNY = Chinese yuan renminbi; ¥1 = approximately US$0.1587, US$0.1540, US$0.1591, US$0.1640, US$0.1634, by the end of 2011, 2012, 2013, 2014 and 2015,respectively.

E-Commerce Platform		Support Behind the Platform	Business Ecosystem	
Retail	Wholesale			
Taobao	Alibaba.com	Alipay	UCWeb	Alibaba Health
Tmall	1688.com	Alibaba Cloud	Weibo	Xiami
Juhuasuan		Cainiao Logistics	AutoNavi	Alibaba Pictures
AliExpress			Laiwang	Youku Tudou

Exhibit 3 Major Components of Alibaba's Business Ecosystem. *Source* Created by the case authors based on information from Alibaba's annual report for fiscal year 2015. *Note* Some of Alibaba's businesses and acquired companies are not displayed in the image

logistics made it possible that e-commerce companies could make constant breakthroughs in technology and business model innovation, subverting traditional business practices.

3 Alibaba: Just an E-Commerce Operator?

3.1 "Broker" in the Business

Alibaba was founded in 1999 with a mission to make it easy to do business anywhere. It aimed to empower individuals and companies to change their approaches to marketing, selling, and operating, and to improve their efficiency. Therefore, Alibaba provided fundamental technology infrastructure and marketing reach to help businesses establish their online presence and conduct commerce with customers. As of fiscal year ended March 31, 2015,[2] Alibaba's core e-commerce businesses included Taobao, Tmall, and Juhuasuan. In addition to these three major domestic retail marketplaces, Alibaba also operated Alibaba.com, a global online wholesale marketplace, 1688.com, a China-wide wholesale marketplace, and AliExpress, a global retail marketplace (see Exhibit 3).

3.1.1 Retail Platforms

In 2003, Alibaba launched Taobao, a customer-to-customer (C2C) platform. Through online storefronts on Taobao, sellers could list their products and services and

[2] At Alibaba, an accounting year is a 12-month period that begins in April this year and ends on March next year. Alibaba names its fiscal year after the next year — for example, "FY2015" refers to the period from April 1, 2014, to March 31, 2015. At JD, the accounting year is the same as the calendar year.

complete transactions with buyers. As sellers on Taobao were primarily individuals and small companies, Taobao empowered them to serve their customers. Sellers were provided with data analytics for effectively converting shoppers to buyers, and were also given tools and enablers for better communication and storefront management. In the interests of buyers, sellers were required to comply with Taobao's return and exchange policy; buyers could seek compensation through a dispute resolution system in the case of disputes with sellers.

As a "broker" in the business, Alibaba was not involved in any trading process, but rather generated revenue mainly from sellers who purchased marketing services to direct traffic. In 2008, Taobao and Alimama merged. Alimama was an online marketing platform that offered sellers P4P (pay-for-performance) marketing and display marketing services through its auction and bidding system.

During the development of Taobao, many problems occurred concerning product quality control, intellectual property protection, and customer experience. In 2008, Alibaba launched at an opportune time Taobao Mall (later named Tmall), which served as a comprehensive business-to-customer (B2C) shopping website, catering to customers looking for branded products and a premium shopping experience. Different from Taobao, Tmall used a charging system. Sellers on Tmall were brands and retailers, who needed to pay commissions based on GMV (see Exhibit 4). Revenue was also generated from annual upfront service fees.

In 2010, Alibaba launched Juhuasuan, an online group-buying platform. Sellers on Taobao and Tmall could promote their products on Juhuasuan by paying placement fees for promotion slots and commissions based on GMV.

In addition to these domestic businesses, Alibaba also founded AliExpress in 2010. This global consumer marketplace enabled consumers worldwide can buy directly from wholesalers and manufacturers in China at attractive prices. The revenue was mainly from collecting fixed commissions and advertising promotion fees from sellers.

Platform	Region	Revenue items	Revenue model
Retail Platform	China (Taobao, Tmall, Juhuasuan)	P4P marketing	Sellers' bidding charge for specific spots on Taobao's page is subject to cost per click (CPC)
		Display marketing	Advertising fees are charged according to fixed prices or cost per mile (CPM)
		Value-added service fee	Provide storefront software to upgrade, decorate, and manage sellers' online storefronts
		Commissions	Taobao and Tmall's sellers pay 0.3% to 5% of GMV for transactions settled through Alipay

Exhibit 4 Revenue source of Alibaba E-commerce platform. *Source* Collected by the case authors based on The Founder Securities Research Institute's research report and Alibaba's annual report for fiscal year 2015

3.1.2 Wholesale Platforms

Alibaba.com and 1688.com, Alibaba's two major business-to-business (B2B) platforms, earned revenue mainly by collecting membership fees and providing Internet marketing services (see Exhibit 4). As Alibaba's first online commerce platform, Alibaba.com was a B2B platform focused on the global wholesale market. Chinese products on the website could be exported to the world. 1688.com offered a membership package for sellers in China's wholesale market.

3.2 Supporting Services Behind E-Commerce

In addition to these e-commerce platforms, Alibaba also established several systems such as payment service (Alipay), data service (Alibaba Cloud), and logistics service (Cainiao Network), to provide support for every facet of online trading (see Exhibit 3).

4 Financial Payment: Alipay

With the rapid development of Taobao, credit risk and security issues in online shopping payments had become increasingly prominent. Accordingly, Alibaba built up a new payment method called Alipay in October 2003. Alipay provided payment and escrow services for transactions. When a transaction began, funds from the buyer went to Alipay's escrow account, and Alipay released the funds from escrow to the seller only after the buyer confirmed receipt of the goods in satisfactory condition. Escrow service reduced the concerns of online shoppers and made shopping convenient and efficient to a large extent.

As an essential part of Alibaba's business ecosystem, as of fiscal year 2015, Alipay had become the main settlement method between buyers and sellers on Taobao and Tmall. However, Alibaba did not own any shares of Alipay. In July 2011, Alibaba and Alipay signed a framework agreement in which Alipay had to pay Alibaba 49.9% of pre-tax profits each year for intellectual property licensing and software service fees. In August 2014, Alibaba reached a new agreement with Small and Micro Financial Services Group,[3] which paid 37.5% of pre-tax profits to Alibaba every year.

[3] Small and Micro Financial Services Group was established in March 2013. Besides Alipay, it included assets such as Zhao Cai Bao and ZhongAn Online.

5 Cloud Computing: Alibaba Cloud

Due to the large volume of traffic and data generated on its online marketplaces, Alibaba had to spend millions of dollars each year to buy commercial equipment from IBM, Oracle, and EMC. However, such IT equipment was expensive and could not fully meet Alibaba's technical needs. In September 2008, Alibaba devised its cloud computing and data strategies and decided to develop Apsara, a large-scale distributed computing operating system, in order to create a data management platform. In September 2009, Alibaba Cloud Computing Co., Ltd. ("Alibaba Cloud") was formally established.

As of fiscal year 2015, a massive amount of data from Alibaba's platforms, its affiliated companies, and Alipay had run and been stored on Alibaba Cloud. In July 2011, Alibaba Cloud began to open its cloud computing services and become a data infrastructure provider. As of fiscal year 2015, Alibaba Cloud had provided cloud computing services to over 1.8 million customers, including enterprises, financial services, and government clients. On MaxCompute, the big data computing platform released by Alibaba Cloud, companies or institutions could conduct massive data analysis with payment of only a few hundred yuan.

6 Logistics Support: Cainiao Logistics

Alibaba's logistics shortage had become increasingly apparent during its expansion. As such, the Alibaba-led logistics project "China Smart Logistics Network" was officially launched in Shenzhen. Alibaba, along with Yintai Group, Fosun, Forchn Holdings, SF Express, STO Express, YTO Express, ZTO Express, andYunda Express, established a new company named Cainiao Network Technology Co. Ltd. (Cainiao Logistics).

Alibaba not only offered logistics but also launched a third-party logistics service system to create supply chain plans based on big data. Cainiao Logistics and third-party logistics providers reached a series of agreements on data sharing, transportation regulations, prices, and specific commodity logistics services, in order to build up a logistics platform. The platform provided real-time access to information and data for sellers, buyers, and logistics service providers. Moreover, Cainiao Logistics also offered additional services, including demand forecasting, inventory planning, plan-driven logistics, terminal distribution, customer service, and supply chain visualization. According to Alibaba's plan, Cainiao Logistics would become a transit center and settlement center based on big data.

6.1 Business Ecosystem and M&A

To maintain its market share and enhance profitability, Alibaba had to continuously optimize and expand the scale of its e-commerce platform and related services, and obtain access to more traffic sources in the meantime.

Searching was a vital traffic source in the age of personal computing. As early as 2005, Alibaba acquired all the assets of Yahoo! Inc.[4] (Yahoo), a well-known Internet website, and had the exclusive right to use the Yahoo brand in China. In return, Yahoo obtained 40% of Alibaba's economic benefits and 35% of voting rights. In 2012, Alibaba repurchased 20% of its shares held by Yahoo with US$6.3 billion in cash and US$800 million in preference shares in Alibaba. At the same time, Alibaba Group paid a lump sum of US$550 million in cash for Yahoo's technology and intellectual property licensing fees. Based on an agreement between the two, Alibaba retained the privilege to buy back half of Yahoo's remaining stock when it went public.[6]

With the popularity of mobile phones, the era of mobile e-commerce dawned. On mobile devices, traditional industries affecting daily life interacted with e-commerce. To create a diverse cross-industry chain and improve the business ecosystem, Alibaba sped up mergers and acquisitions in many industries, including online-to-offline (O2O) businesses, digital media, finance, logistics, culture, entertainment, and health.

Since 2010, Alibaba had accelerated the speed of investment in social applications, search engines, and location services in order to lock in more sources of traffic. To obtain more potential customers, Alibaba successively invested in a 100% share in UCWeb (China's largest mobile browser provider) and a 30% share in Weibo. In April 2013, the acquisition of AutoNavi was completed, making GPS the cornerstone of its marketing business. In October 2013, the social application Laiwang was launched. In addition, Alibaba released Alibaba YunOS to connect Alibaba Cloud services directly with mobile phone users.[7]

The boom in mobile-driven consumption opened up a sizeable O2O market. Taobao created a network around local life services, covering shopping, travel, catering, and entertainment, and formed a closed circuit of transactions through Alipay. Focusing on the "Double H" strategy,[5] Alibaba acquired 38.1% of shares in CITIC 21CN (later known as Alibaba Health) in order to compete in the health industry. Also, Alibaba acquired Xiami Music and Tiantiandongting, Cultural China (later known as Alibaba Pictures), and invested in Youku Tudou. Meanwhile, Alibaba bought UC Jiuyou to set up a platform for on-line games, and invested in Wasu to enter the Internet set-top box market.

---

[4] Sources of repurchase funds included Alibaba Group's own cash reserves, bank borrowings, convertible preference shares, and common shares. The China Development Bank provided a bank loan of US$1 billion for this transaction; eight international banks for this purpose also provided a combined US$1 billion in bank loans. In November 2014, Alibaba issued senior unsecured bonds to replace mature bank borrowings.

[5] "Double H" means "happiness" and "health". The former refers to the entertainment industry and the latter refers to the health industry.

7 JD: ARising Star

Unlike Alibaba's business model, which resembled that of eBay, JD was more like Amazon, with inventory in warehouses and delivery services under its direct control.

7.1 Largest Online Direct Sales Business

JD's primary business was online direct sales, which was different from Taobao. In the supply chain, JD was situated in the middle of suppliers and customers. On the one hand, it provided customers with products and a satisfying online shopping experience, and on the other hand, it offered suppliers a display platform and sales channels. According to the annual report released in the first half of 2015, JD was the largest online direct sales company in China in terms of transaction volume, with a market share in China of 49%. GMV from its online direct sales was ¥159.3 billion (US$25.6 billion) in fiscal year 2014 (for fiscal year ended December 31, 2014).

JD started selling computer products online in 2004 and significantly expanded its product offerings in 2008 with home appliances and a wide array of general merchandise product categories, such as home furniture, household goods, luxury goods, sports equipment, and mother and childcare products. In 2014, 15 product categories were provided, and the percentage of revenue from 3C (computer, communication, and consumer electronics) products decreased from 65.3% in 2012 to 54.1%. As 3C products were price-sensitive, JD's changing strategy of product category expansion not only exerted a positive influence on its gross margin but also enlarged its customer base from being heavily male-dominated to including a substantial number of females.

The slogan of JD was "selection, speed, quality, and value", and it emphasized customer experience and satisfaction. Product selection, competitive pricing, and customer service were crucial aspects for JD to achieve its strategy. For example, JD selected and negotiated with suppliers to guarantee authentic products and obtain the most favorable terms. JD offered discounted products on June 18 and November 11—promotional shopping days in China—in order to gain pricing advantages. Meanwhile, JD had a nationwide fulfillment infrastructure to deliver products on time, which was critical to the customer in online shopping.

7.2 The "Sugarcane Theory" and JD Logistics

In 2014, Qiangdong (Richard) Liu, Founder of JD, proposed a "sugarcane" theory to explain the "ten sugarcane sections" of the customer goods industry. That is, the value chains of the retail and customer goods industry covered ten links, including creativity, design, R&D, manufacturing, pricing, marketing, trading, warehousing, delivery, and after-sales service. Among them, the first five links related to brands, and the latter five to retailers.[8]

As a retailer, JD aimed to invest more in the last five sugarcane sections. It would not only serve as an online retailer, but would also expand to other fields like warehousing, delivery, after-sales services, and marketing. Its investment in fulfillment infrastructure aimed to "eat more sugarcane sections," which would support JD with long-term competitiveness.

As of December 31, 2014, JD had established fulfillment centers in seven major cities in China, and operated 123 warehouses in 40 cities and 3,210 delivery stations and pickup stations in 1,862 counties and districts across China, and had 35,282 delivery personnel, 12,580 warehouse staff, and 7,758 customer service personnel. Leveraging the nationwide fulfillment infrastructure, JD delivered a majority of the orders directly to customers itself—over 80% on the day of the order or the day after. JD provided same-day delivery in 134 counties and districts under the "211" program and offered next-day delivery in another 866 counties and districts across China.

However, the increasing expenses related to infrastructure hurt JD's profitability. Fulfillment expenses kept rising from 2010 and reached ¥4.1 billion in fiscal year 2014, accounting for 7% of total revenue. Meanwhile, logistics-related depreciation and amortization expenses were approximately ¥186 million and ¥293 million in fiscal years 2012 and 2013, respectively, but skyrocketed to over ¥1.65 billion in fiscal year 2014.

7.3 *Online Marketplace*

In October 2010, JD launched an online marketplace to attract third-party sellers. Different from online direct sales, the revenue of the online marketplace mainly included two parts. One was sales commissions, and the other was service fees from providing third-party sellers with value-added services such as delivery and warehousing. JD selected third-party sellers based on brand, reliability, volume, and price, and monitored their performance and activities closely to ensure product quality and customer service. The online marketplace business leveraged JD's brand recognition, customer base, transaction data, and fulfillment infrastructure, and greatly expanded its product offerings.

The past few years had witnessed the high-speed growth of JD's online marketplace. As of December 31, 2014, there were over 60,000 third-party sellers on JD's online marketplace, with GMV reaching ¥100.9 billion, an increase of 217% over the previous year. Although JD's revenue outside of online direct sales reached ¥6.5 billion in 2014, it only accounted for 5.61% of its total revenue. With the fast-growing marketplace, however, JD also faced challenges in areas like traffic resource allocation, system construction, seller selection, quality control, and service quality assurance. At the same time, it also competed with JD's online direct sales business.

How to coordinate its products and third-party offerings was an issue needing urgent resolution.

7.4 Strategic Cooperation Agreement with Tencent

On March 10, 2014, JD signed a five-year strategic cooperation agreement and an eight-year non-compete agreement with Tencent, China's largest Internet social enterprise. With the agreement, Tencent acquired 15% of JD's shares and agreed to purchase an additional 5% at the time of JD's IPO. As a payment, JD received US$240 million in cash and a 100% interest in Tencent's Paipai, QQ Wanggou online marketplace, and certain other assets such as logistics. As a result, JD's valuation jumped from US$8.03 billion to US$15.7 billion in merely three months.

After integrating Tencent's B2C QQ and C2C Paipai platforms into the company, JD relaunched Paipai in July 2014. To compete with Alibaba's Taobao directly, JD tapped into the C2C market and provided customers with more long-tail products.

As part of the strategic partnership, Tencent agreed to offer JD prominent direct access points in its mobile applications Weixin and Mobile QQ and to provide Internet traffic and support from other key platforms. Tencent users could directly access JD after one click on the home interface of Tencent's mobile applications. According to Tencent, Weixin had 500 million active users monthly. With support from Weixin, JD's active users increased from 56 million in 2014 fourth-quarter to 98 million in 2015 fourth-quarter. In addition, JD and Tencent agreed to cooperate in several areas, including mobile-related products, social networking services, membership systems, and payment solutions. For example, JD customers had direct access to Weixin payment.

Holding the annual reports and scanning the massive media coverage of Alibaba and JD, Zhang Wei was lost in deep thought: What were the differences between these two companies' strategies and business models, and how did these differences affect the financial statements? He knew that many of his clients would be interested in the e-commerce industry, but how would he advise them to choose between the two e-commerce giants? Before making up his mind, he referred to the two companies' financial statements to organize his analysis systematically.

Endnotes

1. Jack Freifelder, "JD.com makes US debut with $1.78b IPO." China Daily, May 23, 2014, accessed July 6, 2020, http://www.chinadaily.com.cn/kindle/2014-05/23/content_17536997.htm.
2. Eric Pannef lek, "The Alibaba IPO of September 19 2014." PGM Capital, September 20, 2014, accessed February 15, 2020, https://www.pgmcapital.com/nl/the-alibaba-ipo-of-september-19–2014/.

3. Seth fiegerman, "Alibaba Market Cap Tops $225 Billion on IPO Debut, Passing Facebook." Mashable, September 19, 2014, accessed February 15, 2020, https://mashable.com/2014/09/19/alibaba-ipo-day/.
4. He Shulong, "JD PK Ali, Who Is the Future," NetEasy Tech Channel, January 21, 2015, accessed February 15, 2020, http://tech.163.com/15/0121/08/AGFHVONB000915BF.html.
5. "Analysys: Analysis of Typical Enterprises in China's Online Retail Market in 2015", Useit, December 31, 2015,accessed February15, 2020, https://www.useit.com.cn/thread-11077-1-1.html.
6. Eric Sacitz, "Alibaba Group Closes $7.1B Buyback of Shares from Yahoo (Updated)", Forbes, September 18, 2012, accessed February 15, 2020, https://www.forbes.com/sites/ericsavitz/2012/09/18/alibaba-group-closes-7-1b-buyback-of-shares-from-yahoo/#3122dce3d448.
7. Xu Wen and Wang Qing, "Strategy and Ecosystem Clingers in the Mobile Age", Ping An Securities, December 15, 2014, accessed February 15, 2020, https://doc.mbalib.com/view/55896f81d3beae614d932a5f9f89f862.html.
8. "Liu Qiangdong: Interpreting JD.com's 'Ten Sections of Sugarcane Theory'", China Business News, August 1, 2014,accessed February 15, 2020, https://www.yicai.com/news/4001883.html.

Being United and Working Together: Qiangda Chilli Leads to a Win–Win Outcomes

The case was developed by Professor WANG Chongfeng, CAO Jiangxin of Qingdao University, CHAO Yixuan of PricewaterhouseCoopers Business Consulting (Shanghai) Co. Ltd, Qingdao Branch, GONG Jie, SUN Jing and MENG Xingchen of Qingdao University, ZHAO Yang of Jiaozhou Association for Science and Technology, LI Mingzhe of Jiaozhou Municipal Bureau of Administrative Services, with the helpful collaboration and support of Qingdao Qiangda Foods Co., Ltd. The case was developed to provide the basis of classroom discussion rather than to illustrate effective or ineffective handling of a management situation.

This case was the Nominated Case Award winner of 2020 Global Contest for the Best China Focused Cases.

In April 2019, Zhang Jingqiang, General Manager of Qingdao Qiangda Foods Co., Ltd.[1] (hereinafter referred to as Qiangda Foods), was at the construction site of China's first dedicated chilli-growing in Yujia Village, Jiaozhou City (see Exhibit 1). The main structures were finished already, and workers were busily engaged in the final six months of construction. The buildings were to be put into use at the beginning of 2020, and Jiaozhou would usher in a new era of development in the chilli industry.

The case was developed by Professor WANG Chongfeng, CAO Jiangxin of Qingdao University, CHAO Yixuan of PricewaterhouseCoopers Business Consulting (Shanghai) Co. Ltd, Qingdao Branch, GONG Jie, SUN Jing and MENG Xingchen of Qingdao University, ZHAO Yang of Jiaozhou Association for Science and Technology, LI Mingzhe of Jiaozhou Municipal Bureau of Administrative Services, with the helpful collaboration and support of Qingdao Qiangda Foods Co., Ltd. The case was developed to provide the basis of classroom discussion rather than to illustrate effective or ineffective handling of a management situation.

This case was the Nominated Case Award winner of 2020 Global Contest for the Best China Focused Cases.

China-Focused Cases, https://doi.org/10.1007/978-981-97-8580-3_11

Exhibit 1 Proposed Layout of Chilli Town. *Source* Meng Xin, "RMB 6 Billion in Jiaozhou to Build a 'Chili Town,'the Country's Largest Chili Museum," Qingdao News, November 8, 2017, accessed May 1, 2019, http://house.qingdaonews.com/content/2017-11/08/content_20044413.htm

Zhang couldn't conceal his pride and joy at the sight of such a busy scene. As one of the first of Jiaozhou's local entrepreneurs in the chilli industry, Zhang Jingqiang and Qianda Foods had witnessed the local chilli industry's arduous journey towards cooperation and win-win development. A few years earlier, both the industry and the company had faced a resource bottleneck, with cutthroat market competition and other problems that only piled on pressure.

1 The Journey from Nothing to Something

Zhang Jingqiang was born in 1964 in Bailan Village, Jiaozhou. His family made do with a few acres of barren land and had lived an extremely tough life for generations. He had six siblings, and as kids they rarely had enough food or warm clothes. Leaves of the pagoda trees and willows were the main food source of the family, so their hands and feet were often swollen. The dream of Zhang Jingqiang, toughing it out since childhood, was to escape poverty and have a good life with his family someday.

In autumn of 1986, Zhang Jingqiang learned by chance from a friend at the Jiao County Foreign Trade Department that a foreign merchant planned to buy chillies from Jiaozhou in large quantity, owing to its location next to the harbor. On learning this, he pondered over the possibility of the "red hot" chilli being a flourishing business venture. Jiaozhou had a long history of chilli production (see Exhibits 2, 2.1 and 2.2), so why not give it a try?

Zhang Jingqiang started right away with a simple chilli-purchasing business. The profit was as low as RMB 0.15 per kilogram to begin with, but it allowed him to gain substantial business experience. After a dozen years of operations, Qingdao Qiangda Foods Co., Ltd. was established in June 2004.

With Jiaozhou in Qingdao being China's largest chilli-processing and chilli-exporting hub, Qiangda Foods grew rapidly from 2004 to 2008. Its annual chilli product output quadrupled from 564,000 tonnes to 2.11 million tonnes, and its total

Exhibit 2 Overview of Jiaozhou's Chilli Industry

Location of base	Area of base (acres)	Main chilli variety	Annual production (tonnes)	Number of peasant households benefiting
Korla, Xinjiang	120,000	Sweet chilli and Jinta chilli	60,000	16,000
Aksu, Kashgar, and Hotan in Xinjiang	80,000	Sweet chilli and Jinta chilli	38,000	16,000
Northern Xinjiang	100,000	Jinta chilli	48,000	15,000
Kailu, Inner Mongolia	30,000	Beijing red chilli and Qianjin red chilli	16,000	4,500
Xinzhou, Shanxi	20,000	Beijing red chilli	10,000	4,000
Dezhou and Jinxiang in Shandong	25,000	Beijing red chilli and pod chilli	13,000	8,000
Luohe, Puyang, and other areas in Henan	75,000	Pod chilli	35,000	15,000

Exhibit 2.2 Statistical table of development of chilli bases driven by Jiaozhou's Chilli industry

processing and trade volume reached RMB 4.2 million, making it a major chilli product producer and exporter as well as a major Chinese manufacturer of advanced chilli-processing machines.

Category	Quantity (tonnes)	Output value (RMB)	Main destination country and region	Leading enterprise
Chilli	150,000	2 billion	Korea, Japan, Southeast Asia, E.U., U.S., and Mexico	Xintianfeng, Bo Lan, Qiangda, Hanxiangzi, Yunda, Liandahang, and Yongfa
Chilli seed	15,000	100 million	Korea, E.U., and U.S.	Shuntong, Qiangda, Hanxiangzi, Dafeng, and Liandahang
Chilli powder/ crushed chilli	100,000	2.2 billion	Korea, Japan, E.U., U.S., etc.	Hewang, BoLan, Dafeng, Shuntong, Qiangda, Hotmiso, Chuntianyuan, Liandahang,
Chilli sauce	50,000	400 million	Korea	Hewang, Shuntong, Bo Lan, Jin Guangjin, and Dongxuan
Paprika oleoresin	2000	500 million	Mainly exported to Europeand Americans	Tongxing Natural Pigment

Exhibit 2.2 Analytical and statistical table of output value of Jiaozhou's chillies. *Source* Case authors based on public information

2 Courage to Go Against the Stream

2.1 A New Approach to Dealing with Bottlenecks

Zhang Jingqiang was not satisfied with his now-comfortable life. He found that the company had surpassed profit maximization, driven by scale expansion and extensive operations. But it had no room to grow, due to land limitations and the depletion of chilli and other resources. Chilli-processing plants started popping up all over Jiaozhou, and some of the smaller ones lowered their prices to grab market share. Cost factors—such as scale, human and material resources, and machinery and equipment—meant that costs at Qiangda Foods were much higher than at small processing plants, which made it impossible to further penetrate the market with lower prices. Faced with internal and external problems, Qiangda Foods promptly needed to develop new strengths to stand out from numerous chilli-processing plants in Jiaozhou and achieve sustainable development.

Zhang Jingqiang convened a meeting with the marketing and R&D departments. "The company's future development prospects are in everyone's hands. I hope that we can conduct more market research and seek out new development opportunities," he said. Since almost all employees of Qiangda Foods were Bailan villagers, they were emotionally attached to the company, and treated it as if it were their own family business.

One afternoon, Zhang Jingqiang was looking at documents in his office. Cui Li from the Marketing Department knocked on the door and said cheerfully, "Sir, I have an idea to share with you! We are seeking a new profit growth target. Given limited local resources and chilli production being far from meeting demand, why don't we try other areas? Xinjiang has vast land for extensive cultivation, and its climate, water, and soil are more suitable for growing chillies than Jiaozhou." Zhang Jingqiang thought for a while, patted him on the shoulder, and said, "That's a bold idea, but Xinjiang is too far from us, and transportation costs alone will be around RMB 1,000 per ton. Let's check the transportation costs as well as other information on the advantages and disadvantages of cultivation in Xinjiang first, and then discuss it with the others." Embarrassed, Cui Li scratched his head and added, "Sir, I have just learned from a TV program that Xinjiang has vast land yielding good melons and fruits, which reminds me of growing chillies. I think we should give it a try if it's feasible."

2.2 *Initial Decision on Xinjiang after Careful Consideration*

Zhang Jingqiang started to give Cui Li's suggestion some thought. The purchase volume of chillies from Jiaozhou had not met demand for a long time, so the company had gradually expanded its purchase locations to bases in western Shandong, Jilin, Liaoning, Gansu, Heilongjiang, and other areas. If Xinjiang's water and soil could yield quality chillies, why not give it a try?

Zhang Jingqiang learned that Xinjiang not only had the sunshine and heat suitable for growing chillies, but also boasted an arid climate, fewer pests, and low pesticide residues and other harmful environmental pollutants, which made it an ideal production environment for green and organic chillies. Although Xinjiang was not suited to growing all edible chillies, it was good for growing chillies used for the extraction of pigment.

Paprika oleoresin—as a natural pigment extracted from chillies for pain and itch relief, anti-inflammation, anti-bacterial properties, anti-lipid peroxidation, myocardial protection, weight loss, and other functions—had been extensively used in processing, dining, pharmaceuticals, and foodstuffs, giving it very high commercial value. Chilli prices are determined by pigment value,[2] and an increase in each pigment value unit could result in a price increase of approximately RMB 1,200 per ton. Problems such as long distances and high transportation costs could be solved if the chillies planted in Xinjiang boasted high yields, a fine taste, and high paprika oleoresin content.

Zhang Jingqiang also noticed that Shandong Province, along with the municipal Party committee and municipal government of Qingdao, had been dedicated to Xinjiang aid programs,[3] striving to support livelihood projects and the development of feature industries in recent years. Xinjiang was situated in a core area of the ancient Silk Road, while Qingdao was both a major link of the New Eurasian Land Bridge Economic Corridor and a strategic hub for maritime cooperation, which laid a natural foundation for cooperation between the eastern city and the western province. Qingdao City had given an annual subsidy of RMB 30 million to this development corridor between Jiaozhou and Xinjiang from 2007 to 2010. If Qiangda could successfully enter Xinjiang, it could acquire quality raw materials, facilitate healthy development of the business, and help Xinjiang's farmers become wealthy.

Upon thorough investigation, Zhang Jingqiang summoned his team the following morning to discuss the idea. He convinced them to begin an exploratory investigation of a site in Cele County in Xinjiang. Situated in the southernmost part of Xinjiang, Cele neighbors the Kunlun Mountains to the south and the Taklamakan Desert to the north, and covers a total area of 31,600 km.[2] With a wide temperature difference between night and day, 1,705 annual sunshine hours above 10 degrees Celsius, and an effective accumulated temperature above 10 degrees Celsius of 4,375 hours, it is very suitable for growing chillies and other red crops.

3 A Journey of a Thousand Miles Started with the First Step

3.1 Field Investigation in Xinjiang Carried Out with Great Difficulty

On March 16, 2009, Zhang Jingqiang and a team of young, experienced growers left Jiaozhou to carry out extensive field investigations. Zhang Jingqiang was energized by the trip. He could imagine fields of Jiaozhou chillies taking root in the Gobi Desert, painting the vast landscape red in the near future.

After entering Cele County, the wild plains, low houses, ragged clothes, and otherworldly sights made a deep impression on Zhang Jingqiang, and gave him pause for thought. He felt, "We should really help each other: maybe I can make their lives better through the small business of chilli growing, and we can achieve win-win progress!"

During the study trip, although Zhang Jingqiang and his team found that Cele County had natural advantages for chilli growing, things didn't go smoothly. On one hand, there were communication difficulties. Exchanges and communication on growing chillies would be needed if a production base so far away from headquarters was going to work. But the main population of Cele County was made up of minorities, which led to a range of communication challenges. Insufficient communication would affect monitoring and quality control. On the other hand, the trust level between the communities was weak. Earlier, someone had convinced the locals to grow potatoes, but had failed to fulfill their commitment to purchase them, which shattered trust in any enterprise coming in from outside the county. In addition, the people of Cele County had been growing wheat and cotton for generations, and it seemed a bit risky to them to begin a new chilli-growing endeavor. They simply didn't dare to grow chillies much, and some people even told Zhang Jingqiang and his team, "If we grow corn, we can feed it to sheep if you don't want it anymore. But if we grow chillies, we can't feed them to the sheep in case of a breach of contract."

3.2 *Overcoming Difficulties with a Clear Mind*

Zhang Jingqiang stayed silent for a while in the face of such a situation. He thought that they could only cooperate in chilli growing by gaining locals' trust, and they could probably only gain their trust by giving them tangible benefits ...

Zhang Jingqiang introduced the situation in Qiangda Foods' QQ group, soliciting the opinions of his colleagues. Someone said that employing an intermediary, proficient in both Mandarin and the local dialect—Uyghur, could facilitate accurate exchanges and technical communication between the company and the locals. Others suggested that the intermediary should have public credibility, and that the effect would be better if a local official of high standing was involved.

Zhang Jingqiang was the kind of person who would undertake bold efforts based on any hint of a solution. To him, happiness came from the company could improve, and he was looking for a breakthrough with his team. Zhang Jingqiang used his connections to make contact with the local Party secretary. Muhammad Yiburehim was touched by Qiangda Foods' selection of Cele County as its Xinjiang chilli-growing base and was impressed by their study trip. He recognized that if chilli growing worked, it would provide an opportunity for locals to shake off poverty and achieve win-win development.

Chilli growing could increase locals' annual income. Since a lot of preliminary preparations needed to be made before a new economic crop was introduced, it would be a disaster in the case of failure. As Party secretary of the county, Muhammad had to protect the interests of the locals first, and he said after a while: "Mr. Zhang, I would like to express our gratitude to you for travelling from afar. But we have never grown chilli before, and know very little about what kind of chilli we should grow and how to grow it." Zhang Jingqiang replied: "I've thought about it. We will provide seeds and techniques, you can find some villagers proficient in Mandarin, and it will be alright as long as we can conduct smooth communication on techniques and receive supervision." Muhammad was persuaded, but he still felt unease. He looked at Zhang Jingqiang and said: "Mr. Zhang, thank you, I really appreciate that. But I need to go through the details and solicit others' opinions and reply to you tomorrow." The two parties went back for further planning after confirming the time, venue, and other matters for the next day's meeting.

As soon as Muhammad returned to his office, he reviewed the business conditions of Qiangda Foods immediately, and gathered interested villagers through an assembly to solicit their opinions. After soliciting villagers' reasonable concerns and doubts, he was more assured when he went to his meeting with Zhang Jingqiang the next day.

After greeting Zhang Jingqiang, Muhammad said: "Mr. Zhang, I had a discussion with others; we think it's indeed feasible, but it's better for us to sign an agreement. Villagers have a low annual income, and I just want to make them feel at ease." Zhang Jingqiang agreed with him, offered a minimum agreement price of RMB 8,000 per ton after internal discussions, and defined standards for quality and the production of chillies. The two parties started initial cooperation based on these terms.

They started right away! Zhang Jingqiang encouraged locals to conduct trial planting of chillies; the company would provide seeds of Spanish and Peruvian sweet chillies suitable for Xinjiang's water and soil as well as technical support, and would teach villagers how to grow chillies (see Exhibit 3). If the chillies complied with quality requirements, the minimum agreement price could cover the farmers' investment. Although most people still took a wait-and-see attitude after Zhang Jingqiang's introduction, some villagers had already been persuaded. They believed that since seeds and techniques would be provided by the enterprise, all they needed to provide was a piece of land. Besides, the selling of quality chillies was guaranteed by the local Party committee, which prevented the risk of the company's breach of contract and made it a feasible project.

Thus, the first year's trial planting was carried out with support from the villagers in Xinjiang, who started planting in mid-April. The company's personnel provided technical assistance, and Zhang Jingqiang waited for the harvest five months later with fingers crossed...

Exhibit 3 Cooperative chilli-growing process of Qiangda Foods and Xinjiang. Greenhouse seedling–transplantation–grow gradually–grow–harvest–drying–after drying–loading and delivery to plant–cargo arrival factory. *Source* Qingdao Qiangda Foods Co., Ltd

4 Long and Arduous Journey Completed Through Unremitting Efforts

4.1 Great Doubts in Harvest Season

In October of gold autumn, the supposed harvest season, Zhang didn't see the red fruits he had expected. According to the locals, the chillies all dried up and died because the farmers didn't know the habits of the plant. Experienced chilli growers all knew that chillies would not survive a flood, but would be fine in times of drought. After a special investigation, it was found that these chillies had died due to being waterlogged, rather than drought. Water from the Kunlun Mountains was the cause of great losses, which led to the death of numerous waterlogged chilli seedlings. In addition, this trial planting also revealed other problems—most farmers were scattered about and engaged in small-scale production. Decentralized management resulted in great difficulties in establishing a epidemic prevention system in particular. Conforming chillies had standardized criteria for Escherichia coli, iron powder (magnetic metal content), insect debris, and hair, and it was very hard for the scattered farmers to control them.

The outbreak of this problem gave the company intense pressure, and made it reconsider its decision to grow chillies in Xinjiang. Employees of Qiangda Foods had numerous private discussions. But Zhang Jingqiang wouldn't give up. He believed there was nothing wrong with the decision to set up operations there and maintained that it was feasible to grow chillies in Xinjiang. Since problems had occurred, a complete set of plans had to be formulated to continue the project. He decided to conduct a screening of existing problems, and revisit Xinjiang for detailed discussions after figuring out some possible solutions.

With respect to the problem of waterlogged chillies, specialists found, after a field study, that the installation of drainage and flood control devices could solve the problem. But given the large and scattered planting area, although the installation of drainage and flood control devices in each plot of land could guarantee a normal harvest of chillies, the dramatically increased cost would result in the failure of the whole project. If planting could be concentrated on a standardized chilli farm, the number of drainage and flood control devices installed could be greatly reduced, which would both guarantee chilli production and lower the cost. Moreover, the growing base could also benefit from centralized management and unified monitoring of farmers' growing process as well as adoption of a standardized process for chillies to meet organic food export standards, and the problem of food quality could be solved easily.

There were still many obstacles even after solutions were found. For example, would villagers in Xinjiang still trust Qiangda Foods? Would they still be willing to grow chillies on a large scale in the second year? Who should be made responsible for managements of operations in Xinjiang? Many problems were yet to be solved. Therefore, Zhang Jingqiang summoned all senior experienced employees to his office for a brainstorming session.

4.2 Rebuilding Trust Through Base Management

After brainstorming, they found the base could be managed by Xinjiang Production and Construction Corps ("XPCC" for short) if they could convince locals to keep growing chillies. Military approaches could more rigorously ensure the quality, and XPCC was respected by locals, so the idea of "business + base + farmers" came up.

Zhang Jingqiang and his team visited Cele County again with great trepidation. As they expected, everyone was hesitant about the project, and those engaged in the trial planting were sure that it wouldn't work out. Zhang Jingqiang had already taken such a scenario into consideration, so he started to give out written technical instructions, promised to send specialists for guidance on the planting process, undertook flood control and relief precautions to ensure chilli production, and pledged to purchase chillies at guaranteed prices. He resolutely reiterated to local villagers, "Please, have a look at the material. Our specialists will pay you a visit every month on a regular basis, and they will explain to Muhammad how to grow and take care of your chillies! I assure you that Qiangda Foods will purchase the lot during harvest! The failure last time was due to lack of drainage devices, scattered management, and improper safety precautions."

To further allay villagers' fears, Zhang Jingqiang decided to ask for support from the county Party committee and county government through Muhammad to convince villagers to grow chillies. However, it was not just the staff of Qiangda Foods that were under pressure from the new enterprise. Muhammad was also under huge stress as its guarantor, and he felt responsible for any failure. The villagers trusted him very much, but so far he had failed them.

Muhammad was hesitating to take in the lobbying and proposal from Zhang and his team, considering he couldn't make any commitment and disappoint the folks again. Zhang Jingqiang said slowly, "We are highly responsible for the failure. We started the trial planting without sufficient preparations. But we have drawn lessons from that, so please retain your trust in us, and we will cover villagers' losses incurred. Things will get better, please trust us and try again!"

His team also explained the detailed plan to Secretary Muhammad, who finally agreed to help Qiangda Foods make another attempt at chilli growing, owing to the company's persistence.

4.3 Achievement Built upon Perseverance

Villagers' confidence in getting wealthy through growing chillies was restored by means of the joint efforts of Zhang Jingqiang, Muhammad, the county Party committee and county government, the assurances of the military-base management of XPCC, the professional drainage devices installed, and the guaranteed purchase price. In the spring of 2010, Cele County's chilli-growing endeavor finally got on the right track.

Qiangda Foods' perseverance eventually paid off. Cele County was exceptionally beautiful in October 2010, with the farmlands covered in red chillies. Zhang Jingqiang purchased 1,200 tons of raw chilli materials with high paprika oleoresin content at the price of RMB 8,000 per ton, which both solved Qiangda Foods' difficulty in insufficient raw material procurement and reduced material costs. Muhammad expressed his gratitude on behalf of the villagers of Cele County for the opportunity given by Qiangda Foods. Cele County was a state-level poverty-stricken county, where people grew wheat and cotton for an income of around RMB 300 per acre, and they could only make several thousand RMB per year. Chilli growing increased their net income to RMB 3,000 per acre, and increased their annual income from several thousand RMB to nearly a hundred thousand RMB, which benefited the local villagers significantly. Based on the success of the initial cooperation, Qiangda Foods established reliable, stable long-term cooperation with them by means of execution of contracts for the production and sales of agricultural products.

5 Journey from "Lone Battle" to "Mutual Development"

5.1 Difficulty Dealing with Cut-throat Competition Alone

As the first batch of chilli-processing enterprises represented by Qiangda Foods conducted chilli-growing activities in Xinjiang, a great number of similar businesses in Jiaozhou wanted a piece of the Xinjiang pie. Meanwhile, the price war in the chilli industry didn't end, which severely affected large-scale chilli enterprises. Zhang Jingqiang's Qiangda Foods was no exception. In contrast to large enterprises' standardized production, small enterprises had lower machinery, plant, and labor costs. More importantly, they were not bound by the same rules. There was a tax refund in the chilli-exporting industry, but dried chillies were not eligible for tax refunds. As a result of incomplete random inspections of customs, small businesses could take advantage of the loophole, abandon their company after being caught up in an inspection, and change names to continue production afterwards. The tax refund offered a substantial income. On the other hand, enterprises with large shipments had limited tax refunds, had rules to follow, and pursued strong branding. Those differences made their costs much higher than those of smaller enterprises.

Zhang Jingqiang felt powerless in the face of the price war started by small enterprises, and the long-term price war against small enterprises would be a war of attrition for Qiangda Foods, which worried him greatly. It was also true for other businesses. Not only did Qiangda Foods encounter such a challenge, but several other large chilli enterprises in Jiaozhou also faced increasing pressures from cutthroat competition, and the entire chilli industry was stuck in intense low-price competition.

5.2 Cooperation for Co-existence and Win-win Development

To find a solution to this endless price war, Qiangda Foods not only had to tighten its internal policies of strengthening cost management, tightening internal control, and eliminating management loopholes, but also had to adopt proper strategies to respond to external realities. What kind of adjustments should it make in an environment of intense competition? Zhang Jingqiang and his employees had a brainstorm session to gather possible courses of action.

Zhang Jingqiang said: "Bolan, Hewang, Xintianfeng, and many other large- scale chilli enterprises in Jiaozhou want to have joint development, increase market concentration, accelerate the elimination of backward processing and production technologies, guarantee quality and price, and jointly move from the 'red ocean' to the 'blue ocean' instead of constantly lowering their price and hurting each other. What do you think about that?"

Cui Li from the Marketing Department couldn't agree more . "We should facilitate the cooperation. Of course, we need to reduce cost, but the urgent need of the chilli industry is increasing the price. We are exhausted in the price war, everyone pursues sales volume by constantly lowering costs, and nobody wants to spend money on quality improvements, which will certainly lead to abnormal development in the long run," he said.

Li Zheng, a production manager, said: "Jiaozhou's chillies can only become more popular through mutual cooperation, resource sharing, and a win-win situation rather than a no-win situation."

Zhang Jingqiang summarized, "We should be bound together for good or ill. To continue great development, the chilli industry needs to get rid of the 'law of the jungle' and achieve positive internal cooperation. We shall actively respond to the trends, and make contributions to facilitate healthy industry development."

5.3 "A Golden Opportunity" or "a Short-lived One"?

Zhang Jingqiang's proposal was recognized by Jiaozhou's chilli enterprises. And the number of enterprises with intentions to be a joint partner gradually increased from a very tiny amount. The realization of the need for mutual development and an end to the chaotic situation characterized by insufficient coordination and price war became a consensus. The Qingdao Chilli Industry Chamber of Commerce and Jiaozhou Chilli Industry Association were established in September 2012. Wang Yong, GM of Qingdao Hewang Foods, and Zhang Jingqiang served as President and Vice President, respectively.

The fundamental objectives in establishing the association were to promote uniform pricing among its members and avoid cutthroat competition and a situation in which "bad money drives out good." Meanwhile, the association established its website[4] and official WeChat account, allowing customers and enterprises to keep abreast of domestic and international spot chilli market demand, ensure access to information, and realize "point-to-plane" exchanges. In addition, the association walked the path of mutual cooperation and joint development through integration of members' resources, facilitated standardized development of the entire industry, and improved Jiaozhou's chilli industry.

Along with the development of the chilli association, many problems surfaced. The association seemed superficial and, to a larger extent, a mere formality. Although leaders of the association such as Zhang Jingqiang actively promoted and established their official accounts and portals, set up their offices, and organized substantial team-building and charity events, other enterprises in the association showed less interest. In terms of an organization initiated by enterprises without government regulation, no penalties existed if an enterprise violated the rules. The association could not enforce market regulation. Many small enterprises followed the chilli association's price management by unifying prices, but there were always some enterprises taking advantage of loopholes in the system or lowering their prices without authorization to improve their sales volume. Such problems hindered self-regulation of the industry.

6 ALong, Tough Road Ahead

Qiangda Foods benefited a lot from both horizontal and vertical cooperation, with profitability between 2016 and 2018 reaching as high as RMB 10 million.

However, there were still many challenges for the company. Among them, Zhang Jingqiang's biggest concern was over whether, without government participation, the chilli industry association could guarantee quality and price through industry self-regulation alone. How could the company further expand its cooperation with Xinjiang in chilli growing? Should the company build a processing base in Xinjiang, or should it attempt the fine processing of chilli products? Those problems, coming up one after another, made Zhang Jingqiang uneasy. Watching builders busily traveling at the construction site of Chilli Town, he looked anxious, despite trying to convey confidence. He couldn't help moving his eyes from the construction site to a place far away and deep in his thoughts world's market share. Although Jiaozhou was not a core chilli-growing area, it was the largest chilli-processing and chilli-exporting hub in China. In Jiaozhou, there were around 365 chilli-processing enterprises, 72 of which had export rights. With its chilli product export volume accounting for 80% of that of China, Jiaozhou had 25 enterprises with annual sales revenue over RMB 100 million, six province-leading enterprises, and more than 4,000 chilli- purchasing personnel and middlemen. Jiaozhou's chilli trade volume accounted for 70% of the national chilli market share, and its annual trade volume and total trade amounted to 600,000 tons and around RMB 12 billion. There was a saying that "China is the center of the world's chilli industry, while Jiaozhou is the center of China's chilli industry." Accompanied with the development of Jiaozhou's chilli industry, its enterprises had also gained strength, allowing them to establish new specialized processing bases that were "based in Qingdao, driving the development of Shandong, covering the whole country, and facing the world," effectively integrating "primary, secondary, and tertiary industries."

Endnotes

1. Official website of Qingdao Qiangda Foods Co., Ltd., accessed April 5, 2020, www. qiangdafoods.com.
2. Gradation of paprika oleoresin was mainly measured by pigment value and tone. According to the international trade pricing for the purchase of sweet red chillies, they were divided into three grades (A, B, and C). Grade A paprika oleoresin should reach 240 ASTA and above, Grade B paprika oleoresin should be 140–200 ASTA, and Grade C paprika oleoresin should be 70–140 ASTA. International trade pricing was normally calculated by the formula of 1 ASTA = USD 0.005678, which was followed by all paprika oleoresin manufacturers.
3. Qingdao's Xinjiang-aiding work had changed from "one-way support" to "mutual cooperation", had been upgraded from "transfusion support" to "hematopoietic support," and had developed from "governmental support" to "diverse social support".
4. www.chilliali.com.

KFC China: Building Competitive Advantages Through Digitalization

KFC was the first Western fast-food chain in China, entering in 1987 with its first restaurant in Beijing. Since then, KFC had seen remarkable success in the country and the Chinese market had grown to become one of the most important for Yum! Brands (see Figs. 1.1, 1.2 and 1.3). In 2015, Joey Wat was named Chief Executive Officer of KFC China and in the following year, Yum China (NYSE: YUMC) spun off from Yum! Brands and became an independent, publicly traded company.

The quick-service restaurant (QSR) industry had evolved significantly since 1987 and in order to take KFC China to the next level, including further expansion, Joey Wat had to navigate a rapidly changing and increasingly competitive landscape. A consumption upgrade had taken off in China, with consumers increasingly not only attracted to healthier and higher-quality products, but also looking for an enjoyable customer experience. At the same time, the proliferation of Chinese fast-food chains and snack choices was intensifying market competition. KFC China was burdened with a high employee turnover rate, as well as rising rental and labor costs. As Generation Z[1] became the largest consumer base,their demand for high-value, personalized experiences and a sense of engagement went beyond just affordable products. KFC China had highly standardized offerings and a stable ticket average, but the challenge facing the brand was how to successfully manage the different evolving trends whilst still achieving a strong performance.

Joey Wat saw digitalization as the answer and under her leadership KFC China began being referred to as "a tech company disguised as a fried chicken business."

[1] The concept refers to the demographic cohort after Millennials.

Professor LIN Chen and Case Writer ZHANG Chi of China Europe International Business School developed this case with the helpful cooperation and support of the case company. The case aims to provide the basis for classroom discussion rather than illustrate effective or ineffective handling of a management situation.

This case was the Nominated Case Award winner of 2019 Global Contest for the Best China Focused Cases.

China-Focused Cases, https://doi.org/10.1007/978-981-97-8580-3_12

Company	Market Share (%)	Brand
Yum China	15.8	KFC; Pizza Hut; East Dawning; Taco Bell; Little Sheep
McDonald's	6.1	McDonald's
Starbucks	3.9	Starbucks
Ting Hsin International	3.1	Dicos; Master Kong Chef's Table
Sichuan Haidilao	1.4	Haidilao Hot Pot
Shenggen Foods	1.2	A Little Milk Tea
Burger King	1	Burger King
UCC Ueshima	1	U.B.C Coffee
Quanjude	0.9	Quanjude
Kungfu	0.8	Kungfu
Morals Village	0.8	Morals Village; Rain Sentiment; Pure Green

Exhibit 1.1 Market Share of Yum China and Its Competitors (2016). *Note* The market share is calculated based on the sales revenue. *Source* CICC Research Division, QSR Leader Makes a Comeback (2017), accessed September 15, 2019, https://max.book118.com/html/2017/1106/139161379.shtm.

Exhibit 1.2 Most popular brands in QSR Industry. *Source* CICC Research Division, QSR Leader Makes a Comeback (2017), accessed September 15, 2019, https://max.book118.com/html/2017/1106/139161379.shtm

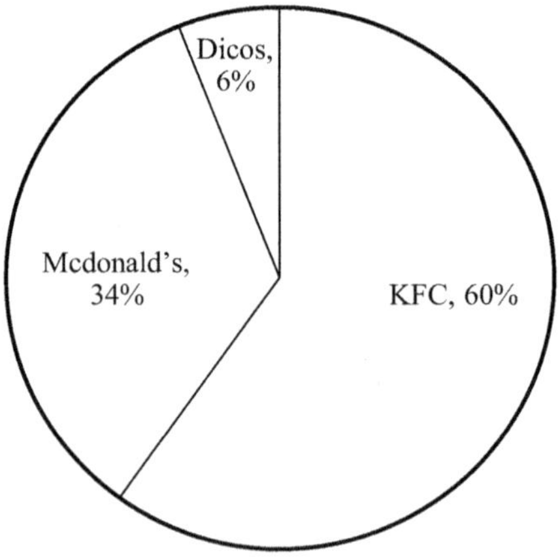

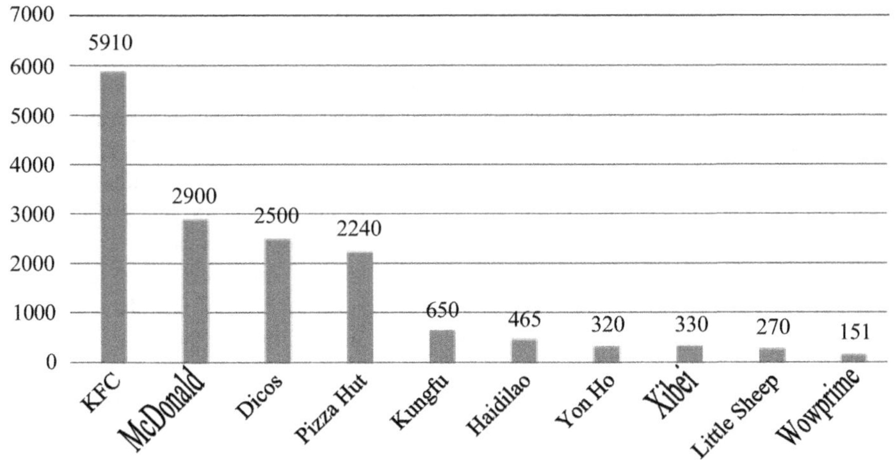

Exhibit 1.3 Store count of QSR brands in 2018. *Source* CICC Research Division, QSR Leader Makes a Comeback (2017), accessed September 15, 2019, https://max.book118.com/html/2017/1106/139161379.shtm

The brand started creating its digital ecosystem very early, accumulating powerful digital capabilities ahead of its competitors. KFC China made various attempts to drive productivity, reduce costs, and constantly improve the customer experience throughout the entire customer journey. All these efforts boiled down to an eight-word business mantra: "Good food, good fun, internal beauty, external beauty." To empower the digital strategy to better serve the brand, Joey Wat first needed to consider how disruptive technologies developed by KFC China could benefit future business. Would people be replaced by technology in the QSR industry? What role could technology play in enhancing the customer experience and fostering innovation?

1 The Rise of New Catering

The trend of New Catering blended the boundary between retailing and QSR. Convenience stores and other retailers began offering food services,[2] while QSR restaurants with intellectual property and futuristic stores[3] built their products in the same way that retailers did. Meanwhile, B2B service providers had started to emerge to

[2] Leveraging advantages in supply chains, retailers offered food processing, easy cooking, and takeaway services to increase productivity. Convenience stores leveraged their advantage of in-store traffic and sold takeaway snacks, fast food, and drinks, which saved on rental costs and expanded sales options.

[3] The QSR industry used new technologies to facilitate online and offline integration and enhance the customer experience. Intellectual property giants referred to food chain companies with good brand awareness who turned their offerings into products for trading outside physical stores. Futuristic

support small and medium QSR companies with supply chain, finance, and other operational management. In addition, new technologies were completely reshaping the traditional QSR industry, from customer acquisition to feedback and interaction. The application of big data transformed the way QSR businesses were started and managed by enabling data-driven user profiling, enhanced location decision making, and precision marketing and advertising campaigns. Meanwhile, membership programs further incentivized frequent consumption and built loyalty, while reviews and feedback from online platforms helped companies better understand customer behavior and adopt targeted menus and service improvements. Mature on-demand delivery services supported a variety of consumer scenarios and became the cornerstone of the seamless integration of online and offline channels.

Digital payment reinvented the purchasing process and brought about an improved buying experience. Upgraded supply chain management of both standard and semi-finished products drove efficiency, quality, faster delivery, and a stable supply.

2 KFC in China

2.1 Overview of KFC China

KFC China was the largest Western QSR chain in China. As of the end of December 2019, KFC China had 6,534 restaurants in over 1,300 cities across China, approximately two times as many outlets in China than its biggest competitor. In addition to KFC's original menu, KFC China offered an extensive localized menu featuring pork, seafood, rice dishes, fresh vegetables, soups, congee, and many other products that catered to local tastes. Chinese KFCs also adopted ubiquitous offerings with breakfast, home delivery, and 24 h operations.

An AC Nielsen survey in 2004 showed that KFC was the most "frequently visited" international brand in China and KFC was still overwhelming in 2019. But this success did not come easily and in 2014, KFC was burdened with performance setbacks and its same-store sales declined by 4%. (See Exhibit 2)

On August 20, 2015, Joey Wat was appointed CEO of KFC China.[1] Under Wat, KFC China launched several large-scale initiatives and when sharing her insights on the Chinese market Wat said that, "The inner self has been liberated. People care more about themselves and want to enjoy a simpler lifestyle and return to their true selves. Therefore, in 2016, KFC China sought to offer a place to BE YOURSELF …"[2]

Through a series of initiatives oriented around "Good food, good fun, internal beauty, external beauty," KFC China was committed to reinventing the brand as "young and relevant." KFC China set up its own digital team and IT Department a long time back and the success of its digital strategy played a pivotal role in

---

stores widely used new technologies to attract customers, including 24 h automated stores and augmented reality-themed concept stores.

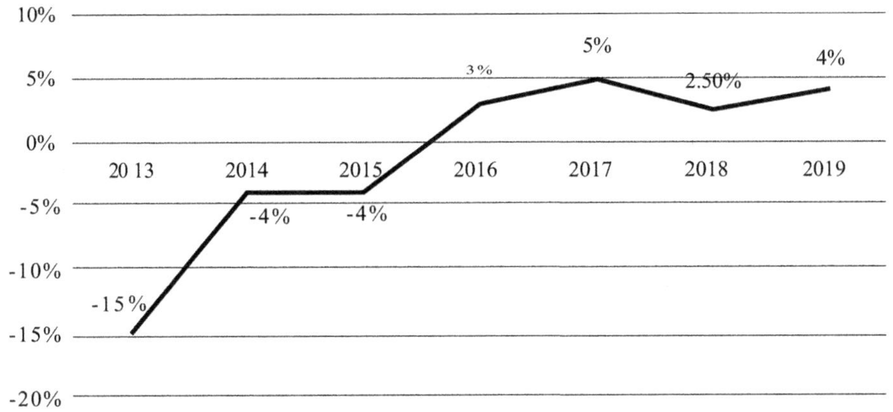

Exhibit 2 KFC China's same-store sales growth. *Source*: Based on YumChina, Fourth Quarter & Full Year 2017 Results Presentation (2018), accessed July 29, 2020, http://ir.yumchina.com/static-files/4b224d05-3cae-48be-a0fc-cdf8939bf1bd; Yum China, 2018 Annual Report, accessed November 11, 2019, http://ir.yumchina.com/static-files/4f1aaebb-c10c-48cf-bb53-256de7d1ac32; YumChina, Fourth Quarter 2019 Results Presentation (2020),accessed February 27, 2020, http://ir.yumchina.com/static-files/571a9284-70ee-4d55-90ab-3ed0fb652bc1

achieving its strategic ambitions (see Exhibit 3). Within the QSR industry and the broader retail industry, KFC China was one of the first to explore mobile ordering. With no precedent to follow, KFC China adopted the mindset of an Internet startup, prioritizing speed and a lean approach.

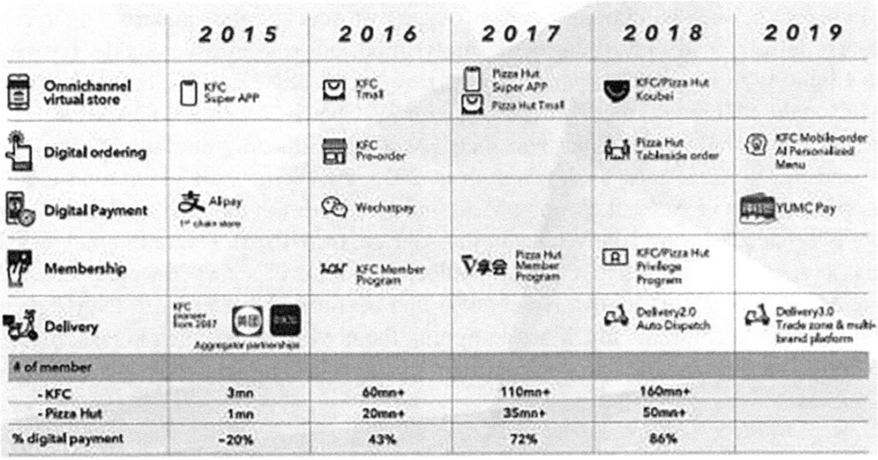

	2015	2016	2017	2018	2019
Omnichannel virtual store	KFC Super APP	KFC Tmall	Pizza Hut Super APP; Pizza Hut Tmall	KFC/Pizza Hut Koubei	
Digital ordering		KFC Pre-order		Pizza Hut Tableside order	KFC Mobile-order AI Personalized Menu
Digital Payment	Alipay 1st chain store	Wechatpay			YUMC Pay
Membership		KFC Member Program	Pizza Hut Member Program	KFC/Pizza Hut Privilege Program	
Delivery	KFC [illegible] Aggregator partnerships			Delivery2.0 Auto Dispatch	Delivery3.0 Trade zone & multi-brand platform
# of member					
- KFC	3mn	60mn+	110mn+	160mn+	
- Pizza Hut	1mn	20mn+	35mn+	50mn+	
% digital payment	~20%	43%	72%	86%	

Exhibit 3 Yum China's Digital Evolution. *Source* YumChina, Digital Transformation and Disruption, accessed July 16, 2019, http://ir.yumchina.com/static-files/cf0acc90-987f-4029-b8c0-a6e925092b3d

KFC China's initial steps towards digital transformation were not without challenges: "Digitalization started early at KFC China, way ahead of consumers.

The difficult part was to go in the right direction before consumers were used to the digital experience. It was also challenging to correct ourselves when we took the wrong path," said Joey Wat.

The good news was that KFC China had several senior executives with a strong IT background. They had an in-depth understanding of the latest technology trends and applications. Today (In 2019), Yum China owned the intellectual property rights for almost all its in-house-developed software and hardware. This gave KFC China a significant competitive advantage and more freedom in the application of digital technology.

In 2016, after spinning off from Yum! Brands, Yum China became an independent, publicly traded company on the New York Stock Exchange. It had exclusive rights to the KFC, Pizza Hut, and Taco Bell brands in the Chinese Mainland. At the end of 2016, KFC China reported an annual operating profit of US$645 million, up 29% year-over-year, and same-store sales had increased by 3%.

2.2 *Digital Steps by KFC's Competitors*

2.2.1 McDonald's

McDonald's began in the United States in 1955 and entered China in 1990. In 2019, China was McDonald's second-largest market and its fastest-growing market globally. As of June 2019, McDonald's operated over 3,100 restaurants in the Chinese Mainland, selling hamburgers, various types of snacks, and desserts.[3] In recent years, delivery had played an increasingly important role in McDonald's business in China, with a year-over-year delivery revenue increase of 75% in 2017 alone.[4] McDonald's China cooperated closely with WeChat in its digital development. It enabled payment via WeChat, launched a WeChat mini-program for ordering, and joined the WeChat card pack program in 2015. Now over half of its transactions were handled via WeChat. Among McDonald's 85 million members in China, 85% were registered through its WeChat mini-program. In 2016, McDonald's and WeChat cooperated to launch the first "McDonald's of the Future" smart concept restaurant. By August 2019, this innovative concept had beenrolled out in more than 70% of McDonald's restaurants in China, equipping them with touchscreen kiosks, mobile ordering, mobile payment, a double-function counter, membership points, and table services.[5]

2.2.2 Dicos

Dicos was a leading local brand providing Western fast-food services in China. Originally from Texas, Dicos was acquired in 1996 by Ting Hsin International Group.

Since Dicos started franchising in 2000, it had opened 2,500 stores in all provinces and major cities across China, and 85% of its restaurants were franchised.[6] Dicos's growth had been driven by a low-price strategy and the brand took the decision to first focus on less developed areas before gradually expanding into major cities. Dicos began its digitalization push in 2014 with a digital membership program. It joined the Maxiipoint Alliance System within the Ting Hsin International Corporation and integrated WeChat Pay and Alipay. Dicos today had over 40 million[7] Maxiipoint members and had applied data analytics to extend its menu, capture new selling points, and develop bestsellers such as the Dicos Craburger in June, 2019.[8] In 2016, Dicos launched its Premium Paid Membership Program, and upgraded the middle and background of its point-of-sale system. It also opened its first fully automated smart restaurant in December 2017.

2.2.3 Burger King

Burger King was founded in the United States in 1954. It was not until 2005 that its first restaurant opened in the Chinese Mainland. Fueled by a capital injection in 2012, Burger King China began a round of aggressive expansion in the local market. By 2018, Burger King owned over 1,000 restaurants in 140 cities in China and this figure was expected to exceed 2,000 by 2021.[9] Burger King initiated digitalization efforts in China in 2015, with two WeChat mini-programs and two Alipay mini-programs. The mini- programs on Alipay were very successful and attracted four million member registrations in 2019. In addition, Burger King offered flexible ways to order, including kiosks, mini- programs, and QR codes. Orders placed via the food delivery apps ele.me and Meituan contributed over 30% of Burger King's total sales in 2019.[1010]

3 Tapping into Digital Resources

At Yum China, the creation of a local data warehouse began in 2008. On top of that, Yum China built a databank in 2016 and by the end of 2019, the company had more than 240 million members (KFC China had about 215 million). Yum China was aggregating a massive inflow of data. With insightful data mining, Yum China established a sophisticated customer labeling and profiling model and constantly updated its algorithms to produce increasingly accurate forecasts.

3.1 Consumer Labeling

Yum China's data bank had numerous consumer labels and included a considerable number of data points such as location, address, habits, preferences, and other social

Exhibit 4 Data and AI Support Across the Business. *Source* YumChina, Digital Transformation and Disruption, accessed July 16, 2019, http://ir.yumchina.com/ static-files/cf0acc90-987f-4029-b8c0-a6e925092b3d

data.[4] Consumption behaviors had been the deciding factors in consumer labeling. For example, if a customer regularly bought a Kids' Meal, then it was likely that they had young children, and similarly those customers who regularly used delivery services might prefer to spend more time at home. Targeted recommendations could be shared with individual customers based on these insights. Armed with precise consumer labels, KFC China adopted intelligent marketing tactics to drive its sales performance and build consumer loyalty.

4 AI Applications in Operational Activities

KFC China boasted detailed data surrounding all transactions, both online and offline, and this massive data pool formed the basis of its algorithm models. Five variables were used by KFC China to conduct transaction volume and product forecasting. These included sales performance, location, promotions, holidays, and weather. Based on historical sales data over the past two years, a deep-learning algorithm model was created. Yum China's data science team ran a simulation on the AI platform, then used historical data to constantly verify, calibrate, and optimize the forecasts for higher accuracy. The benefits included reduced waste, lower inventory risks, and better labor scheduling. In addition, AI technologies were used in four business domains: intelligent marketing, intelligent stores, intelligent service, and intelligent enterprise. The application of AI led to greater efficiency in areas such as personalized menus and deals, media optimization, consumer insights, store operation and inventory management, dynamic delivery routing, site finding, store recruitment, risk management, and supply chain management (see Exhibit 4).

[4] Social data also included those came from consumer behaviors. For example, consumers could approach to KFC's various commercial ads via different platforms, video websites, WeChat, or Alipay. Their channel selections might make sense.

5 Heightening the User Experience Digitally

KFC China's digital ecosystem was initiated in 2015. Supported by digital technologies, KFC China embarked on a journey to modernize the user experience. After extensive research, KFC China defined the key moments in the customer journey as being: within three kilometers of the nearest KFC restaurant, six seconds before arrival, deciding whether to wait or leave, three minutes before pick-up, recommending KFC to others, placing orders from home, or sending KFC e-gifts during festivals. KFC China then conducted in-depth research into each touchpoint of the customer journey and designed specific digital products for each of them. To ensure full digital coverage for each touchpoint, full-time product managers were assigned to analyze the pain points and improve the customer experience at each particular point and oversee the entire lifecycle of digital products (see Exhibit 5). KFC China adopted the same practices as tech companies and took a project-based approach to product development. In typical projects, the demand side—usually the Marketing Department—would take the role of product managers. They led and managed the projects with support from other product departments and the IT Department. In July 2019, KFC China had thousands of project teams.

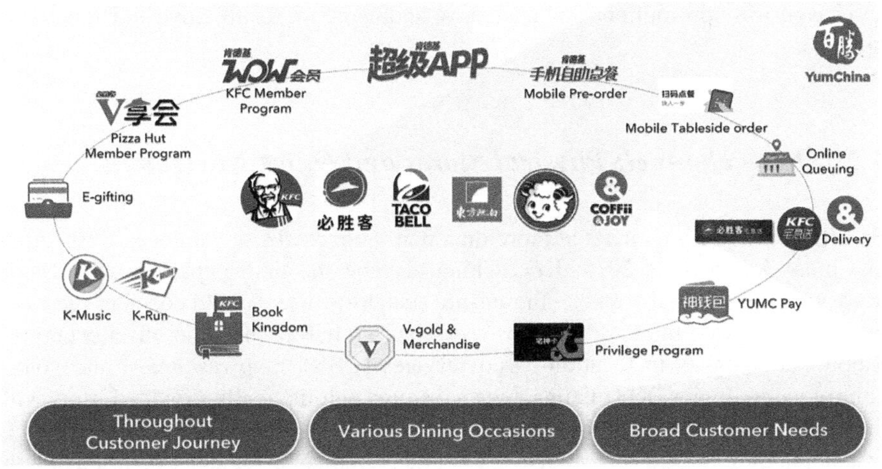

Exhibit 5 Yum China's Digital Ecosystem. *Source* YumChina, Digital Transformation and Disruption, accessed July 16, 2019, http://ir.yumchina.com/ static-files/cf0acc90-987f-4029-b8c0-a6e925092b3d

6 Before Arrival: Zero Moment of Truth[5]

6.1 Mobile Pre-Orders

In 2014, KFC China introduced mobile pre-orders.[11] Customers using the mobile pre-order service enjoyed a more convenient experience. When they arrived in the physical store for pick-up, their orders were already paid for online[6] and were given priority in preparation. These customers were able to skip the line through a fast-track system and the quality of food was always maintained.[12] The digital platform for this self-service ordering process was built independently by KFC China. Mobile pre-orders were most effective during the morning rush hour, as surveys showed that customers were extremely sensitive to the time spent on breakfast. KFC China engaged a design company to reshape the pre-ordering process. The design company gained insights by using an ethnographic approach: observing employee routines, analyzing data from stores and users, and conducting in-depth interviews to understand user' motivations and needs. Based on these insights, KFC China developed an integrated solution for a new version of the pre- ordering app including focusing on instant ordering and scaling back pre-orders and check-ins; satisfying the "fast" in fast-food ordering; simplifying menu and meal options; more intuitive and easy-to-use promotions and packages; and using more attractive and appetizing pictures.

6.2 Omn-ichannel: Physical Stores and Quick Navigation

By 2019, KFC China operated more than 6,500 physical stores in over 1,300 cities in China. As early as 2015, KFC China became the first to partner with Baidu Maps to build "virtual stores. " In real-life scenarios, users could consider the location, discount, and brand reliability of a restaurant before they chose it. Leveraging Baidu's advantages in location-based services (LBS), map resources, and voice-control technologies, KFC China's virtual stores automatically provided users with the information they cared most about. For example, if users wanted to go to a KFC restaurant, they could say "I want to eat a burger", which resulted in a certified official KFC-branded webpage popping up. Once the KFC virtual store was located, Nuomi, a Baidu group-buying platform, would recommend special offers and Baidu Maps and then direct users on how to pick up their food.[1313]

---

[5] The "Zero Moment of Truth", a term coined by Google in 2011, referred to the critical moment when a customer was ready to pull the trigger and buy.

[6] Online ordering included ordering from Tmall, the mobile app, mini-programs, or personal computers, or by scanning QR codes.

6.3 Online Virtual Stores

KFC China built a V-Gold Mall within its own Super App. Apart from KFC products, consumers could also purchase a variety of other merchandise, from beauty products, to digital devices, to electrical appliances. On Alibaba's Tmall, consumers could buy product coupons at KFC flagship stores and redeem them offline. There were also attractive discount campaigns during shopping festivals like the annual 11/11 festival.

During the Christmas season in 2018, KFC China developed a WeChat Lite App—KFC Pocket Store—which enabled people to open, design, and share their own Pocket Stores. Friends could order meals from each other's pocket store. For every order, both buyers and pocket store owners were rewarded with KFC discounts and products according to the amount spent and the number of orders. To respond to the development of social commerce, KFC China also launched a lite app for group buying where consumers could buy products at a very affordable group price. By the end of 2018, KFC China had more than 1.5 million pocket stores and daily active users peaked at two million.

6.4 Social Media Marketing

In December 2013, KFC China launched a campaign themed around the battle between its Original Recipe vs. Extra Crispy. Within eight weeks, the campaign had generated more than 20 million votes.[14] In July 2017, KFC China cooperated with Bilibili,[7] and customers who bought the Extra Crispy Bucket or Superstar Meal Box at designated KFC restaurants would get a limited-edition B Site badge. In December 2017, KFC China put a new breakfast offering on the menu, conpoy-shrimp congee.[15] To promote it, KFC China released a popular song called "Cheers Hero." The name of the song matched the Mandarin pronunciation of the word for congee. To meet the personalization that Gen Z consumers required, KFC China encouraged customers to post creative short music videos on the Chinese short mobile video platform TikTok. KFC China's official Weibo account had more than 2.42 million followers by September 2019, making it an important channel for releasing new products, promotions, and other information. Partnering with key opinion leaders, these campaigns triggered extensive reposts and media coverage.

[7] Nicknamed B Site, a video-sharing website with the themes of animation, comics, and gaming.

7 In-Store Digital: Creating an Enjoyable Dining Experience

KFC China opened its first "Original+" concept store in 2016. Joey Wat said in her opening ceremony speech: "The store combines good food, high-quality service, and a unique experience. What we want to do with this store is to showcase our goal: 'Good food, good fun, internal beauty, external beauty'..."[1616]

7.1 Ordering Options

In addition to mobile pre-orders, consumers could also order from digital menu boards or touchscreen kiosks. Yum China independently developed the hardware and software required for the touchscreen kiosks and held all the relevant patents. The kiosks provided both a Chinese and an English menu and were also kid-friendly, with a customized screen showing only the bottom half so that the height would be suitable for children. In Hangzhou's AI Town, KFC China unveiled a future store equipped with a Genius Bar. Children and elderly people could go to the Genius Bar for support if they didn't have or use mobile phones. Genius Bar services covered all steps in the customer journey, from ordering to pick-up.

As counters were gradually replaced by digital ordering, the KFC China store layout also changed. In 2015, KFC China stores had large ordering areas. By 2018, many of them became assembly areas. In Q4 2018, the revenue generated by digital ordering had increased to 54% of total revenue, an increase of over 50% year-over-year. The service efficiency was greatly improved, as hourly transactions[8] rose by 15% compared with 2013.

7.2 Digital Payment Options

In July 2015, KFC China became the first large brand to accept Alipay nationwide, giving Alipay access to 4,800 KFC physical stores in more than 1,000 cities. In January 2017, KFC China started to integrate WeChat Pay and in September 2017, Yum China introduced "Smile to Pay" facial recognition payment technology at its KPRO[9] by KFC restaurant in Hangzhou. This was the first restaurant in the world to accept facial recognition payment and was the first commercial application of this technology. In February 2019, Yum China partnered with UnionPay to launch

---

[8] Hourly transactions refer to the number of transactions handled per employee per hour.

[9] KPRO was a sub-brand tailored to white-collar individuals in China, featuring innovative menus, make-to-order food, and seasonal menu updates. It was positioned as trendy and dynamic and as advocating a green lifestyle and offering light food. It was the first restaurant in the world to accept facial recognition payment.

YUMC Pay,[10] which brought another convenient payment option to its customers. The introduction of digital payments greatly facilitated the checkout process. The average number of points of sale in KFC China stores was reduced from six to two or three. A 50% reduction in points of sale helped lower the risk of receiving counterfeit currency and saved on labor costs. In the past, KFC China's accountants needed to visit banks once a day to deposit cash, and now this only needed to be done once a week or even once a month. The significant savings realized on labor was directed towards offering new and improved services. In Q4 2018, the share of digital payments at KFC China increased sharply to 85% from 39% two years before.

7.3 Easy Pick-up

In addition to its fast-track system, KFC China designed a double-function counter that separated the order pickup area from the in-store ordering area.

7.4 Gamification[11]

KFC China stores leveraged new technologies to create a unique personalized experience. Customers could access free Wi-Fi in the store and could even customize in-store playlists by scanning the QR code on the table or via the K-Music digital jukebox.[17] In 2018, K-Music had about 80,000 songs were picked via K-Music monthly. In 2017, KFC China pioneered collaboration with a popular role-playing game, Onmyoji. KFC China incorporated 5,000 KFC locations into the game with the help of a location-based service (LBS) system and augmented reality (AR) (see Exhibit 6). Gamers who went to KFC stores could hunt down in- store exclusive ghosts with the LBS system. KFC China also launched a series of offline campaigns including Onmyoji-themed meal boxes and stores and limited- edition flashcards. The campaigns generated heated discussions and significant media coverage.

In the KFC Super App gift card section, users could select gift cards and send them out via text message. E-gifting helped KFC China create an emotional bond with users and Online Audio Books represented another impactful effort by KFC China to engage young readers.

Some disruptive futuristic technologies were also used in KFC stores. In 2018, KFC China launched a fully automated dessert station powered by artificial intelligence in Suzhou. During its first 100 days of operation, the station sold a maximum

---

[10] YUMC Pay refers to the payment app developed by Yum China in partnership with China UnionPay.

[11] Gamif ication refers to the practice of integrating a game's thinking with the game's mechanics in a non-game environment to guide user interactions and use, which can increase audience engagement, loyalty, and fun.

Exhibit 6 KFC Using AR Technology for Gamers to Hunt Down In-store Onmyoji Ghosts. Source: "Live News! Onmyoji × KFC Collaboration Caused Huge Sensation," 163.com, April 5, 2017, accessed February 28, 2020, http://help.3g.163.com/17/0405/11/CH8N86L800968CPU.html#from=relevant

of 300 ice cream cones per day. The robotic arms could scoop and serve the ice cream into cones just like human employees, and strictly followed operating instructions to make perfect ice cream cones of a consistent weight.

8 After Consumption: A Continuous Personalized Service

Exiting the store was not the end of the customer journey. KFC China undertook various measures to "let customers leave with rewards." "He will remember the rewards and the rewards will drive him back", said Head of Digital Marketing at KFC China.

8.1 Super App

In 2016, KFC China integrated all touchpoints into a single platform, the KFC Super App, which gave customers a single point of entry for delivery, mobile pre-orders, membership benefits, and coupons. The Super App was at the core of Yum China's digital ecosystem, serving as an all-inclusive platform for KFC China's over 215 million members (as of the end of 2019) with one- stop service including K-Gold redemption,[12] Members' Day, and other loyalty rewards. The Super App's functions were constantly being improved and enriched. Initially, the app only provided must-have services such as coupons and ordering, however, many interactive sections were soon added. Studies showed that once users began their sign-in they tended to complete all sign-in assignments, so the Super App introduced a sign-in section, which quickly became its most popular interaction point. Users were rewarded with V-Gold when they checked in. There were also other follow-up activities. For example, V-Gold could be redeemed as cash, and users could get a free coupon for a product after seven consecutive days of checking in.[13] Check-ins at physical KFC stores were rewarded with extra benefits, such as upgrades to more premium products. "When users check in in-store, they will usually buy something—a drink, coffee, or even a meal", said the Head of Digital Marketing of KFC China.

8.2 *WOW Membership System*

In 2016, the "KFC WOW Members" Program swept across China. As of the end of 2019, KFC China's memberships rocketed to over 215 million. The greatest result of the membership system was that it turned customers into frequent buyers. In the past, once customers exited a store, it was difficult to connect with them and encourage them to quickly return. The membership system ensured greater connections with potential customers. In 2018, the revenue generated by active members was 1.8 times greater than in 2016.

In 2017, KFC China launched Privilege Memberships to build loyalty and drive transaction frequency. Customers could subscribe to one service for ¥18[14] per month and choose Delivery Privilege, Breakfast Privilege, or K-Coffee Privilege.[15] In Q4 2018, transactions from the Delivery Privilege Program comprised 22% of its own channel's delivery transactions. Monthly spending increased by 2.1 times and monthly frequency was up by 2.4 times versus the previous year. Lunch participation increased from 37% in 2017 to 48% in 2018; breakfast and delivery participation increased from 15% to 21%.

---

[12] K-Gold refers to points collected from consumption after becoming KFC WOW members.

[13] Yum China integrated the membership systems of KFC and Pizza Hut in 2018 and KFC K-Gold became V-Gold. V-Gold could be used in both KFC and Pizza Hut.

[14] ¥ = CNY = Chinese yuan renminbi; ¥ 1 = approximately US$0.1537 by the end of 2017.

[15] Free delivery services twice a day, a 50% discount for one breakfast item per day, and a special offer for one coffee at ¥10 per day, respectively.

8.3 Personalized Membership Service

KFC China provided a number of quick and convenient ways to sign up for memberships, including at KFC stores, via the KFC Super App, WeChat, Alipay, and Tmall flagship stores. In the V-Gold Mall, members could get more gifts with points collected from their purchases. Members could also enjoy personalized services. For example, members had the opportunity to go to concerts for free and take part in the KFC marathon.[18]

8.4 AI+ Personalized Menu

It used to be difficult for traditional retailing to capture what consumers think and like, not to mention make informed decisions to attract and retain them. A one-size-fits-all approach to customers failed to meet the genuine, personalized needs of customers. KFC stores got closer to customers by collecting a large amount of masked data from customers and forwarded differentiated information to different customer categories based on customer labeling and AI (see Exhibit 7).

In the past, when ordering at the counter, most recommendations came from store staff, but customers were sometimes reluctant to hear staff recommendations. In the era of mobile ordering, recommendations suggested by e-commerce platforms such as Amazon and Taobao could serve as more effective reference points for many consumers and could generate more sales. However, businesses like KFC China needed to factor in the additional consideration of inventory supply. Yum China's Chief Technology Officer explained this further and gave an example: "If rice balls are very popular at breakfast time, we won't recommend it because it may be sold out

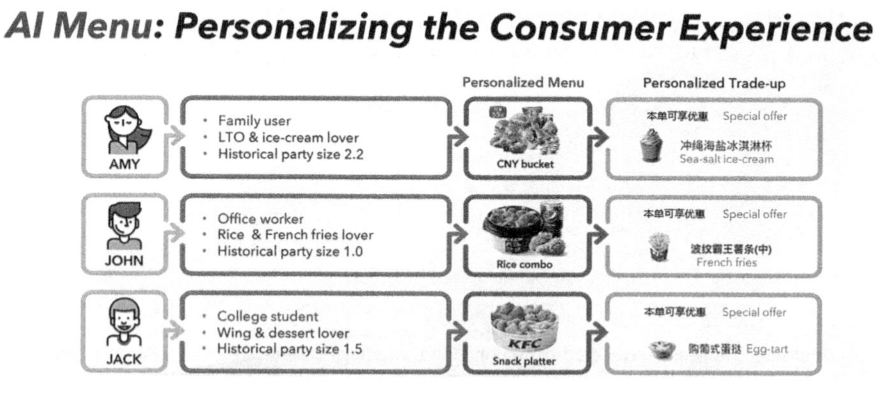

Exhibit 7 AI-Powered Personalized Menu and Trade-ups. *Notes* LTO refers to limited time offering. *Source* YumChina, Digital Transformation and Disruption, accessed July 16, 2019, http://ir.yumchina.com/static-files/cf0acc90-987f-4029-b8c0-a6e925092b3d

soon." To address this problem in 2019, one aspect of KFC China's efforts focused on connecting offline inventory and production with in-store and online sales. As a result, the system tracked production and inventory data in realtime and provided trade-up recommendations. For example, egg tarts and coffee would normally be insufficient supply, so they would be frequently recommended. All recommendations were powered by AI and big data.

8.5 Delivery Service

Besides in-store services, the delivery business was another important pillar of KFC China's strategy. KFC China started delivery services as early as 2006, more than half a decade earlier than Meituan and ele.me (which started in 2012). In 2007, KFC China rolled out its delivery service across China and was the first company in China to build up a delivery ecosystem integrating customers and mobile devices. This was what KFC China called restaurant-based Delivery 1.0, with the Call Center, products were dispatched manually and delivered by dedicated delivery persons. In 2014, Yum China decided to cooperate with the third-party platforms and became the first fast-food chain to join Meituan and ele.me. At that time, delivery technologies were not yet very advanced, and in 2017, Yum China acquired Daojia and Sherpa's, two food delivery companies focused on mid-to-high-end customers. Meanwhile, KFC China still owned its own exclusive delivery team. In 2018, KFC China embraced Delivery 2.0, which featured automatic dispatching, and in 2019, Delivery 3.0 was launched, which adopted an AI-powered dispatching system. In Q4 2018, 16% of KFC China's revenue was generated by deliveries, which represented a sales CAGR(Compound Annual Growth Rate) of over 40% from 2015 to 2018. Delivery had become an important driver of KFC China's business growth and a dynamic delivery system had enabled better labor scheduling and more efficient delivery route planning. Thirty-minute fulfillment increased from 69% in the first quarter of 2018 to 85% in the fourth quarter. Faster delivery guaranteed the taste and quality of delivered meals.

9 Digital Technology in the Future KFC

9.1 Remarkable Digital Transformation

Industry-leading data and digital capabilities had enabled Yum China to build a powerful digital ecosystem that encompassed the complete customer journey, multiple consumption scenarios, and personalized consumer needs, resulting in accelerated growth. Digitalization had helped KFC China fundamentally improve its business with lower labor costs, shorter lineups, and a greatly enhanced customer experience. As customers were able to place orders in flexible ways, there was an increase in orders; with production capacity increased and labor assignments optimized, customers were able to get their food in 90 s.

In Q4 2019, KFC China achieved 70% (51% in Q4 2018) digital ordering and 92% (85% in Q4 2018) digital payment. KFC China saw a 4% increase in same-store sales and a 11% increase in system sales in 2019.[16] KFC China's digitalization strategy had well and truly reinvigorated the business.

9.2 *The Future of Digitalization at KFC China*

In addition to AI, KFC China had adopted many other disruptive technologies such as fully automated dessert stations, KFC Intelligence in its Super App, facial recognition payment, and Music Charging Tables, to name just a few. While most of these technologies were initially limited to concept stores, could they play a greater role in the future?

As technology advanced, fully automated pick-ups or orders would one day become a reality. For instance, around two years ago, a fully automated ramen restaurant attracted widespread attention, but the craze quickly faded. The Head of Digital Marketing at KFC China said: "The purpose of the future digital model is not to save labor, but to offer a better customer experience, in which humans continue to play a role."

"Being customer-centric" was enshrined in Yum China's culture. The strategic purpose of digital transformation was to enhance the customer experience. As data became an increasingly important asset for Yum China, Yum China's Chief Technology Officer said: "My task is to leverage these data assets like financial assets and tap into their potential to create value. We should never simply view customers as a string of data or an ATM. If we serve customers well, profits will follow. It makes no sense to do things just for profits."

The emergence of 5G technology would empower the whole QSR industry by enabling higher-efficiency improvements, simplified programs, and an enhanced experience. In the digital era, when facing competition from McDonald's and Dicos, among others,how could KFC China translate its clear advantages into a sustained competitive advantage? What else could KFC China do to leverage technology to foster service innovation?

As KFC China pushed ahead with expansion plans, it needed to rethink and explore a business model that allowed the harmonious co-evolution of humans and technology.

Exhibit 1 Overview of Yum! Brands and Yum China

1. Yum! Brands

[16] All data listed excluded changes in currency exchange rates.

Yum! Brands was created on October 7, 1997, when PepsiCo, Inc. spun off part of its business and established Tricon Global Restaurants, Inc. The new company Tricon Global became the parent company of the KFC, Pizza Hut, and Taco Bell restaurant brands. In 1998, Tricon Global went public and changed its name to Yum! Brands, Inc. ("Yum! Brands"). In 2019, Yum! Brands operated three major brands: KFC, Pizza Hut, and Taco Bell. In 2019, Yum! Brands reported over US$50 billion in system sales.[17] In over 150 countries worldwide, it operated over 50,000 restaurants.

2. Yum China

Yum China was created following a spin-off from Yum! Brands in 2016 and went public on November 1, 2016 (NYSE: YUMC). Yum China held the exclusive right to operate and sub-license the KFC, Pizza Hut, and Taco Bell brands in China, and owned the East Dawning, Little Sheep, Huang Ji Huang, and COFFii & JOY concepts outright. By the end of March 2020, Yum China operated 9,295 restaurants in more than 1,400 cities and towns spanning every province and autonomous region across the Chinese Mainland. The company's values were:

Customer Mania, Entrepreneurship and Innovation, Thirst for Knowledge, Ethics and Integrity, Recognition and Encouragement, Trust and Support, Pursuit of Excellence, and Contribution to Society.[1919]

Notes

1. Han Lu, "KFC China CEO Joey Wat: A New Era for Deep-Fried and Baked Foods," 21st Century Business Review, August 21, 2015, accessed July 15, 2019, https://www.chinaventure.com.cn/cmsmodel/news/detail/282682.html.
2. "Good Food, Good Fun, Internal and External Beauty: KFC 'Original + ' Concept Store Opens," Jinbaonet, April 26, 2016, accessed September 14, 2019, www.sohu.com/a/71725474_259498.
3. "30 Years of History," McDonald's China, accessed July 28, 2020, https://www.mcdonalds.com.cn/index/McD/mcdonalds-china/MCD-in-China-2.
4. "Dismantling McDonald's Q2 Financial Report: Invest Heavily in Future Restaurants, and Increase the Number of Chinese Franchise Stores to 3,152," Baijiahao, July 30, 2019, accessed February 20, 2020, https://baijiahao.baidu.com/s?id=1640464118740437082&wfr=spider&for = pc.

[17] System sales is a term widely used in the franchise field. The franchisor of a certain brand provides franchisees with supply chain, marketing, and management services, and in return, shares a portion of their revenue. Meanwhile, franchisors may also run some self-operated stores. System sales refers to the total sales revenue derived from the use of the same brand, or the total revenue from self-operated and franchised stores owned by a franchisor. System sales is a convenient way to measure the growth of a franchise brand.

5. "CEO Interview: How Did McDonald's China Operations Become the Brand's Most Digitalized in the World?" Yicai, August 6, 2019, accessed February 12, 2020, https://www.yicai.com/news/100285340.html.
6. "Introduction," Dicos, accessed July 28, 2020, www.dicos.com.cn/join/introduce.html.
7. "Digital, Real-Time, Exclusive Services-Dicos Digs Deep on Member Data," Dicos, June 12, 2018,accessed February 12, 2020, www.dicos.com.cn/mediacenter/26.html.
8. "Shao Xinmou, Dingqiao Catering Service CEO: Promoting a New Dining Experience," iyiou, June 14, 2019,accessed February 12, 2020, https://www.iyiou.com/p/102761.html.
9. Burger King China, accessed July 28, 2020, https://www.bkchina.cn/trained/index.html.
10. Yang Jie, "Trillion Dollar Dining Industry: Burger King's Digital Transformation," 163. com, January 17, 2020, accessed February 12, 2020, http://www.dy.163.com/v2/article/detail/F3442CCD0519F5EB.html.
11. "No Need to Queue: KFC to Introduce Prepayment and Fast Collection," voc.com.cn, June 20, 2014, accessed June 24, 2019, http://www.epaper.voc.com.cn/sxdsb/html/2014-06/20/content_844234.htm?div = –1.
12. "The Internet Changes Life: Prepayment and Fast Collection Eliminates Queues," www.zjol.com.cn, June 19, 2014, accessed June 24, 2019, http://zjnews.zjol.com.cn/system/2014/06/19/020092959.shtml.
13. "KFC Teams Up with Baidu Map to Set Up 'Virtual Stores' in a Bid to Create New O2O Ecology," Beijing Youth Daily, November 30, 2015, accessed June 24, 2019, https://tech.huanqiu.com/article/9CaKrnJRSSI.
14. "KFC Meal Contest Ends: Original Recipe Beats Extra Crispy by a Small Margin," Chongqing Morning News, April 2, 2014, accessed September 17, 2019, http://news.cjn.cn/gnxw/201404/t2451668.htm.
15. "KFC Teams Up with TikTok to Offer Breakfast Meals," eastday.com, December 4, 2017, accessed September 17, 2019, http://mini.eastday.com/mobile/171204225342329.html.
16. "Good Food, Good Fun, Internal and External Beauty: KFC 'Original + ' Concept Store Opens," Jinbaonet, op. cit.
17. "KFC K-Music Themed Restaurant Debuts in Beijing," ChinaNet, August 2, 2017, accessed June 24, 2019, http://science.china.com.cn/2017-08/02/content_39066047.htm.
18. "How Did KFC Manage to Attract 50 Million Members in a Year?" Shenzhen Evening News, December 18, 2016, accessed October 15, 2019, http://wb.sznews.com/html/2016-12/18/content_3689170.htm.
19. Yum China, accessed August 9, 2019, www.yumchina.com.

Winner Technology: Big Data Disruption in the Retail Industry

It was a sunny day in February 2019. Mr. Zhang Hongjun, Chairman and CEO of Winner Technology Co., Ltd. (hereinafter "Winner Technology"), had just wrapped up a meeting with his executive team. At the meeting, they had discussed the challenges facing the company and how to cope with them.

Founded in 2004, Winner Technology focused on providing Chinese brick- and-mortar retailers with traffic analytics systems and related services. The company dominated this industry with a market share of more than 60% and steadily growing revenue (see Exhibit 1). With recent technological advancements and shifting consumer behaviors, the application of big data was widely considered the shape of things to come in the traditional retail industry. Zhang was keenly aware that simple traffic data collection and analytics could not keep up with retailers' growing demand for data. His company would need to change its business model.

At the end of 2018, Winner Technology rolled out its big data service, with a view to offering advice about operational efficiency and decision-making support to brick-and-mortar retailers. In the subsequent months, however, the service had garnered limited market reaction. Zhang and his executive team came up with two key questions. Firstly, to make it easier for customers to embrace big data services, what kind of revenue model should the company adopt while ensuring profitability? Secondly, since most traditional enterprises were unsure of the exact value of big data and were hesitant to pay, how should the company cultivate the market to tap into demand?

Professor XIANG Yi, Case Writer RUAN Liyang and Research Assistant LI Yanyu of China Europe International Business School developed this case with the helpful cooperation and support of the case company. The case aims to provide the basis for classroom discussion rather than illustrate effective or ineffective handling of a management situation.

This case was the Nominated Case Award winner of 2020 Global Contest for the Best China Focused Cases.

China-Focused Cases, https://doi.org/10.1007/978-981-97-8580-3_13

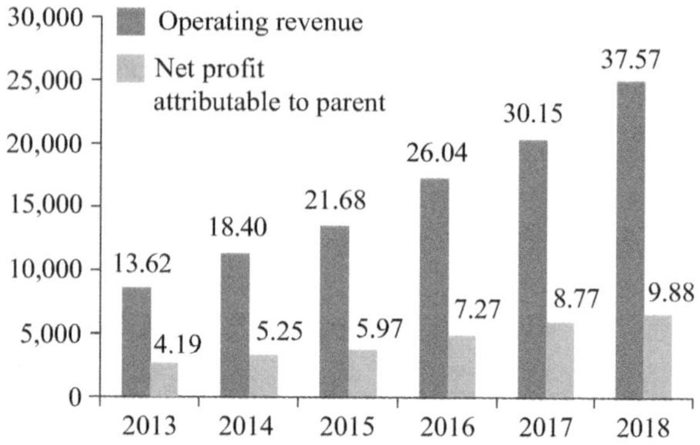

Exhibit 1 Winner technology's operating revenue and net profit (Millions of USD). *Source* Annual Report of Winner Technology

1 Brick-and-Mortar Retail: Change and Challenges

As consumers grew increasingly accustomed to shopping online, traditional retailers faced great challenges. For example, as consumers could compare prices through their mobile phones, many physical stores had become nothing but "showrooms" of e-commerce platforms.[1] While the Internet had a penetration rate of 58% in China,[2] online sales were only 20% of all retail sales, far lower than the share of physical retail sales.[3] These numbers drove home the importance of brick-and-mortar retail. In October 2016, Alibaba introduced the concept of "New Retail", which was considered a major trend in the next 10 to 20 years, replacing online-only e-commerce. The concept emphasized omni-channel integration and the consumer experience in physical stores. As e-commerce giants commenced efforts in the offline world—for example, Alibaba had invested heavily in large brick-and-mortar retailers such as Bailian Group and New HuaDu[4]—brick-and-mortar retail was gradually picking up after several years of decline.

The revival of physical retail did not mean that it could cling to the traditional model. With the development of technologies such as the Internet of Things and big data, the digital transformation of traditional retail was becoming a trend. However, unlike e-commerce, which was "born digital", physical stores faced challenges in data collection, processing, and application. Online consumer behavior, such as searches, clicks, and payments, yielded explicit data records. In contrast, in physical retail, it was hard to accurately digitally track complicated and ever-changing consumer behavior, including roaming, staying, touching, and so on.[5] The existing data for physical retailers was less than satisfactory. For example, offline data was collected in small samples and took a long time to gather, and industry-wide data was hard to come by. Applying big data in traditional retail was also much more complicated, as it required a broad understanding of retailing and a wealth of operational experience, coupled with access to online data and industry data. It seemed impossible for most traditional retailers to apply big data on their own. For one thing, they lacked the technical know-how; for another, big data application entailed high upfront costs. Therefore, they needed external big data services.

2 Big Data Application in Brick-and-Mortar Retail

China's big data industry was gathering momentum. Its total addressable market was ¥438.45[1] billion (US$ 66.26 billion) in 2018 and was expected to hit ¥ 807.06 billion by 2021.[6] The big data industry referred to all types of economic activity that focused on data sources, data management and analysis, and data application.[7] Primary big data sources in China included government agencies, Internet companies such as Baidu, Alibaba, and Tencent, and telecommunication companies; another important source was online data collected through web crawlers. Data management and analysis included data storage and security, as well as the use of mathematical models, artificial intelligence, and visualization tools for data analysis. Data application referred to applying the outcomes of data analysis to different industries. For example, in the financial industry, transaction data could be used to analyze financial risks and prevent fraud; in the healthcare industry, big data could be harnessed to analyze an epidemic so as to get it under control, evaluate users' health status, establish electronic medical records, and perform R&D and clinical trials to make diagnoses more accurate and drugs more effective.[8]

Big data also had applications in physical retail, including: (1) store location choice (a retailer could use big data on its target customers and trade areas to choose store locations); (2) category management (big data could be used to recommend the commodities a retailer should sell and determine the required quantity); (3) precision marketing (retailers could combine and analyze online and offline data to conduct precision marketing, such as targeted ads based on customers' locations); (4) in-store sales (such as intelligent shopping guides); and (5) operational optimization (such as analyzing changes in performance and suggesting improvements in operations).[9]

Traffic analysis was the basis of all these applications of big data to physical retail. Whether for e-commerce or brick-and-mortar retail, sales opportunities came with increased traffic. Retailers' top priority was to draw more customers into their stores and convert this traffic into sales. Therefore, it was critical for retailers to mine traffic data and manage traffic accordingly.

Physical retailers previously collected traffic data through the rudimentary manual counting of visitors. With technological progress, traffic analytics systems could be built using infrared light, gravity sensors, or video analytics. In recent years, innovations such as Wi-Fi probe requests, iBeacon, and facial recognition were increasingly applied to improve data accuracy and diversity. In developed countries, more than 90% of large malls and chain stores had adopted traffic analytics systems. In China, by contrast, these were still not widely used. By the end of 2017, there were more than 5,000 shopping centers across China,[10] of which only 2,000 had put in place such a system. Winner Technology dominated the traffic analytics system market for brick-and-mortar businesses in China, while 20 other players, such as Beijing Vion, Brickstream, and ShopperTrak, lagged far behind in market share.[11]

---

[1] ¥ = CNY = Chinese yuan renminbi; ¥ 1 = approximately US$0.1511 by the end of 2018.

3 Winner Technology

3.1 Company Development

Winner Technology was founded in 2004 by Zhang Hongjun, who was a typical technically minded CEO. Since the start of his company 15 years ago, he had thought about how to create more value for customers through innovative data services.

At its inception, Winner Technology developed a video-based traffic analytics system, and started providing customers with related products and services, including cameras, analysis software, and installation, operating, and maintenance services. With a dedication to technology and customer service, the company gradually established a strong reputation and attracted an increasing number of customers, including prominent commercial real estate developers.

In an effort to prepare for the company's transformation into a big data service provider, the company switched to the software-as-a-service (SaaS)[2] model in 2015, providing customers with cloud-based foot traffic analysis via the "winneryun.com" platform. In order to improve its big data capabilities, Winner Technology set up three R&D centers, invested in several technology startups, and forged R&D partnerships with universities in the fields of artificial intelligence, big data, and the Internet of Things.

In late 2018, Winner Technology launched enhanced big data services for retailers, offering advice about operational efficiency and decision-making support to managers in department stores and shopping centers. By the end of 2018, the company served more than 1,000 department stores and shopping centers, and more than 20,000 chain stores in 340 cities and regions. The over 200,000 data collection sensors[3] it deployed nationwide had counted tens of billions of store visits.

3.2 Customers

Winner Technology's customers mainly included commercial real estate developers (e.g., Wanda, Longfor, CapitaLand, and Hang Lung); brand chains (e.g., Apple, Watsons, and L'Oréal); some pavilions (e.g., Brazil Pavilion of 2010 Shanghai World Expo); and tourist hotspots.[4]

---

[2] SaaS refers to a mode of providing software services through the Internet. The vendor places software on its own server. Customers can place an order with the vendor for the required software services inline with their actual needs, access the services through the Internet, and pay fees based on the amount and length of services ordered.

[3] Data collection sensors usually refer to detection devices that can sense and measure required information and convert it into an electronic signal or other form of output so as to meet the needs of information transmission, processing, storage, display, recording, and control.

[4] Business from pavilions and tourist sites is not further discussed, as they accounted for only 2% of the company's total operating revenue.

Large and mid-sized commercial real estate developers were Winner Technology's key accounts. Many of them were located in first- and second-tier cities. Winner Technology mainly targeted department stores and shopping centers. Department stores focused on selling products and adopted a pool mode, i.e., leasing counters to merchants, relying on commissions from merchants' sales, and monitoring their transactions through a unified cash-register system. In comparison, shopping centers provided more comprehensive services including shopping, dining, and entertainment. Instead of taking commissions, shopping centers generally derived their revenue from rent and property management fees. In recent years, the boundary between department stores and shopping centers was getting blurred. Many department stores had added more dining and leisure businesses to attract customers. Furthermore, both department stores and shopping centers charged rent plus commissions, albeit in varying proportions. (Therefore, department stores and shopping centers are collectively referred to as "malls" in this case.)

The management of these commercial real estate came in three models. In the mainstream model, a developer set up its own business management company, which was responsible for the mall's operations, marketing, property, human resources, and so on. A few developers partnered with a third-party consulting firm, which directly sent out a management team to their malls. Increasingly, as operating commercial real estate required special management skills, some developers outsourced their malls to a third party, which took charge of the overall management.

In daily operations, the mall management team generally consisted of a General Manager, a Deputy General Manager, an Operations Department, a Marketing Department, a Merchants Department, a Property Management Department, and an Administration & Human Resources Department. Responsibilities and performance metrics varied across different departments. For example, the Merchants Department was mainly responsible for bringing proper brands into the mall, and was evaluated based on indicators such as store occupancy and vacancy rates on each floor. The Marketing Department focused on increasing foot traffic in the mall through public relations and promotions, and was evaluated based on indicators such as daily footfall and vehicle traffic, membership growth, and member activity. The Operations Department was mainly responsible for helping merchants boost sales so that rent could be increased, and constantly optimizing the brand and business portfolios within the mall to increase footfall, usually through adjusting, merging, or splitting stores. The performance indicators assigned to the Operations Department included the monthly sales efficiency of merchants (sales per square foot), the percentage of rent arrears (arrears/receivables), and the rent-to-sales ratio.

The mall's revenue and costs depended on the performance and efficiency of each department. Revenue generally comprised the rent charged to merchants, sales commissions, service charges (e.g., promotion fees and property management fees), operating revenue (e.g., retail space rental income and ad space rental income), parking revenue, and others (see Exhibit 2). Among these, rent and sales commissions made up the bulk, with the former relying on the mall's reputation and participating brands and the latter relying on operations and marketing. The main costs for the mall included marketing, operations management, property maintenance, and IT.

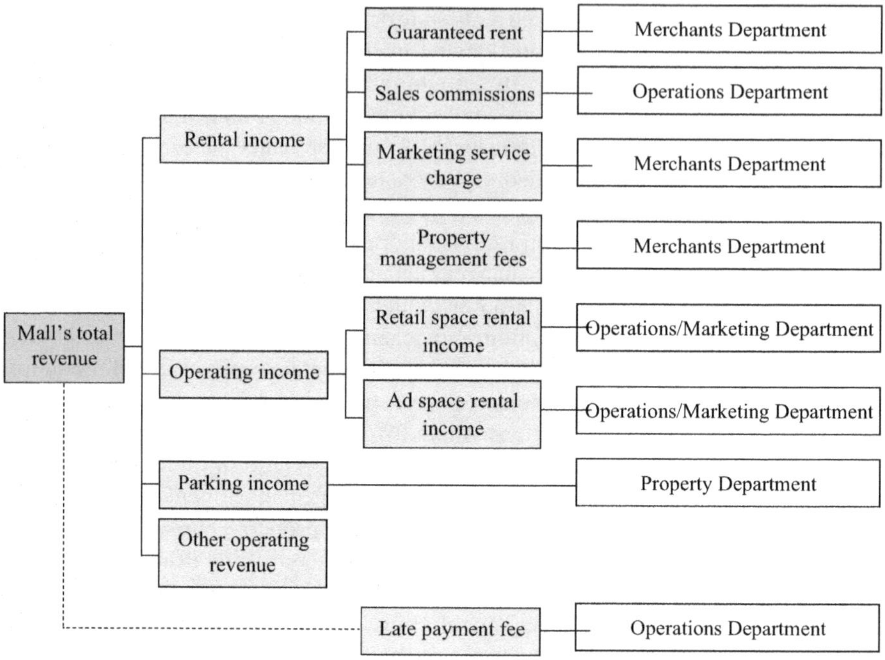

Exhibit 2 Composition of Mall's revenue by department. *Source* Winner Technology

The marketing costs generally accounted for 5–10% of rental income, and the cost of operations made up about 5%; the property management fees balanced out the property costs, or even produced a small surplus; and the IT costs varied drastically each year, depending on the demand for system operations and maintenance.

3.3 Traffic Analytics System and Data

In order to help retailers collect foot traffic data, Winner Technology developed the Intelligent Pedestrians Video Analysis (IPVA) system. This system worked on the principle of collecting video images of pedestrians through cameras, identifying and analyzing the characteristics of their body, position, and gait to accurately calculate foot traffic. After 2013, Winner Technology started leveraging Wi-Fi probe requests, iBeacon, and facial recognition technologies in the system.

In its data collection process, Winner Technology took a three-pronged approach. First, it installed cameras at mall entrances to count customers entering and exiting for overall real-time traffic data. Second, more cameras were installed in each section of the mall and in passageways on each floor to track the distribution of shoppers and identify the patterns of crowd movement in each area. Third, cameras could also be installed for each store in the mall to capture the foot traffic dynamics and footfall.

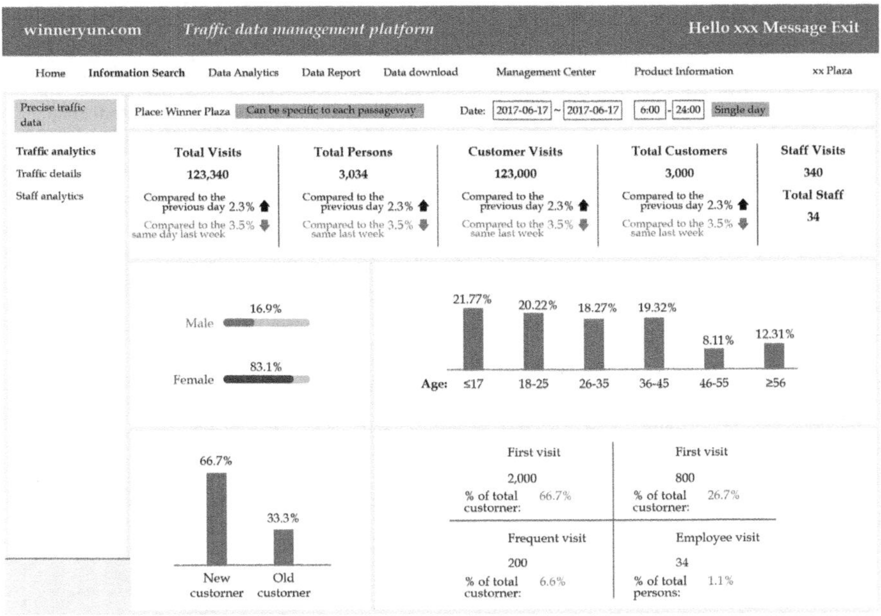

Exhibit 3.1 Foot traffic analysis

The data collected was processed to generate a report (see Exhibit 3: Excerpts of reports on winneryun.com, Exhibits 3.1 and 3.2), which could help mall managers better monitor traffic changes and distribution in realtime.

On top of malls' own traffic data, Winner Technology also provided in- depth data insights for its SaaS subscribers through winneryun.com. This platform marshaled three types of data: traffic data from all participating customers, proprietary data authorized by these customers (e.g., customer relationship management data and operational data), and third-party data such as mobile operator data, and customer location data and user profiles from other Internet companies. With careful data privacy management, winneryun.com broke through "data silos" to achieve industry-wide data integration and sharing and make data application more valuable.

3.4 Core Big Data Services

Zhang and his executive team devised the basic value-creation model surrounding winneryun.com (see Exhibit 4). As Zhang noted, each mall was, in essence, a hub for local traffic attraction and re-distribution; the primary sources of revenue for the mall were rent and commissions, which depended on store sales. In terms of the determining factors, sales could be described by the following equation:

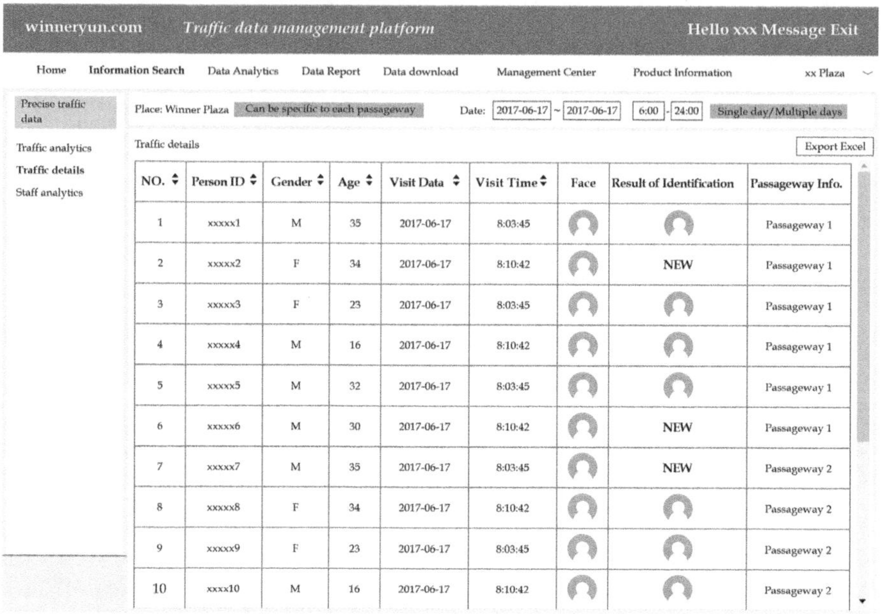

NO.	Person ID	Gender	Age	Visit Data	Visit Time	Face	Result of Identification	Passageway Info.
1	xxxxx1	M	35	2017-06-17	8:03:45			Passageway 1
2	xxxxx2	F	34	2017-06-17	8:10:42		NEW	Passageway 1
3	xxxxx3	F	23	2017-06-17	8:03:45			Passageway 1
4	xxxxx4	M	16	2017-06-17	8:10:42			Passageway 1
5	xxxxx5	M	32	2017-06-17	8:03:45			Passageway 1
6	xxxxx6	M	30	2017-06-17	8:10:42		NEW	Passageway 1
7	xxxxx7	M	35	2017-06-17	8:03:45		NEW	Passageway 2
8	xxxxx8	F	34	2017-06-17	8:10:42			Passageway 2
9	xxxxx9	F	23	2017-06-17	8:03:45			Passageway 2
10	xxxx10	M	16	2017-06-17	8:10:42			Passageway 2

Exhibit 3.2 Details about foot traffic. *Source* Winner technology

$$\text{Sales} = \text{Foot Traffic} \times \text{Percentage of Store Visitors} \\ \times \text{Conversion Rate} \times \text{Per Customer Transaction}$$

Therefore, increasing the foot traffic, percentage of store visitors, conversion rate, and per customer transactions would help boost store sales. For example, a mall could pull in more customers through adjusting brand portfolios within the mall and undertaking various marketing campaigns. Once store sales rose, the mall would not only earn more commissions, but would also enjoy higher commercial value, which would enable it to bring in more merchants and raise rent.

Without support from data insights, the aforesaid decisions were made by managers on the basis of instincts. Winner Technology could harness big data to improve decision making. Based on the data resources on winneryun.com, Winner Technology provided four types of big data services. Take Mall A as an example.

3.4.1 Foot Traffic Benchmarking

Most mall managers wanted to better understand the competitive landscape and their position in the industry. Managers used to send people to the entrances of competing malls for head counting or relied on business connections for regular updates on competitors and the overall market. These approaches not only yielded information that was low quality, incomplete, and delayed, but also incurred high labor costs. To

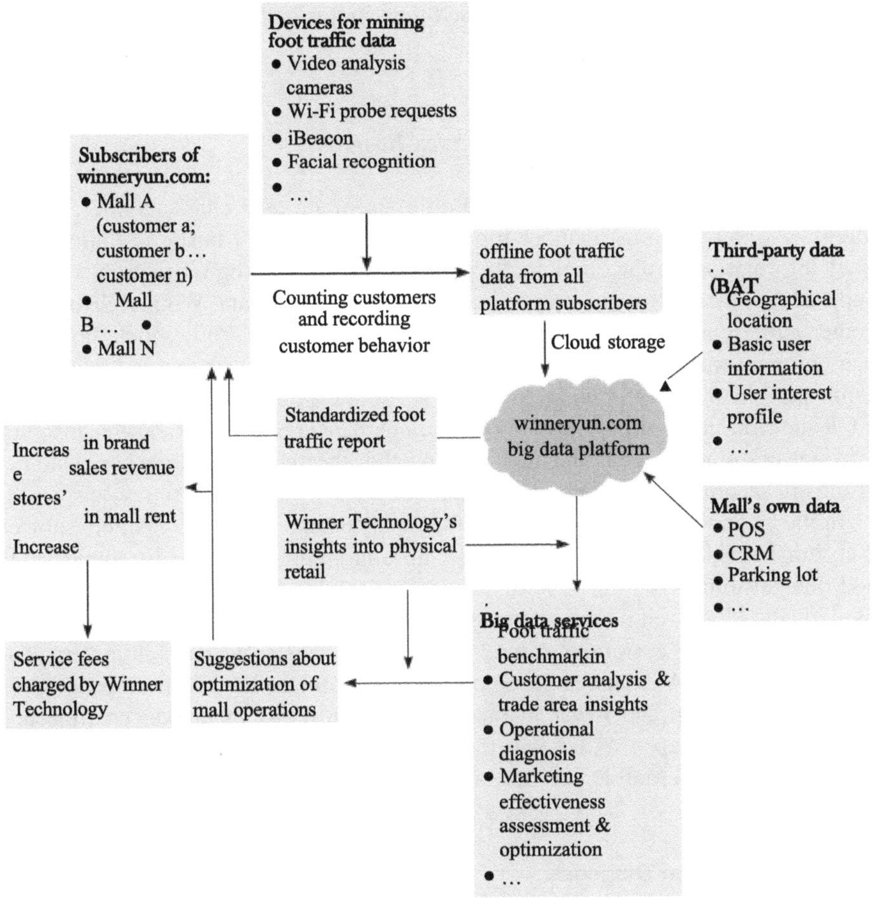

Exhibit 4 Logic behind Winner Technology's Big Data Services. *Note* POS = Point of sale; CRM = Customer relationship management; BAT = Baidu, Alibaba, and Tencent. *Source*: Case authors

address these concerns, Winner Technology launched a big data- based foot traffic benchmarking service that compared a mall with its peers and the entire industry index based on indictors such as foot traffic, ability to attract customers (foot traffic divided by leased area), and average visits per visitor (average number of stores each customer visited each time). These three indicators measured very different dynamics. Take average visits per visitor as an example. The higher the indicator, the higher the probability of customers entering stores and the more sales opportunities the merchants enjoyed.

The foot traffic benchmarking analysis showed that Mall A drew in 30,900 customers daily on average, better than 57% of malls in Shanghai; it pulled in 0.21 shoppers/m^2 daily on average, better than 14% of malls in Shanghai; and it saw each customer visit 3.52 stores daily on average, better than 35% of malls in

Shanghai. These three indicators revealed that Mall A had moderate foot traffic, but its operations left much to be desired.

3.4.2 Customer Analysis & Trade Area Insights

In order to understand its customer profile and trade area characteristics, a mall might have to rely on its membership system and managers' business connections. Such information was incomplete. By combining data from the Wi-Fi probe requests and facial recognition system in the mall and third-party data, Winner Technology could help a mall obtain a more comprehensive customer profile, including basic demographic characteristics, purchasing power, hobbies, and shopping preferences. Third-party data could provide information about customers' residential neighborhood and working district, supplying the mall with location-based trade area insights. Through customer analysis and trade area insights, the mall could target key customer groups in specific areas for precision marketing.

In the example of Mall A, the customer analysis and trade area insights showed that female customers aged 19–45 made up a large proportion of its shoppers. In addition, customers in Mall A were mostly single, white-collars and middle-income individuals. Moreover, most customers lived mainly in three particular districts, and around 80% of the customers came from within a radius of eight kilometers. The influence of Mall A extended along one particular metro line, with its penetration higher in the north and lower in the southeast. In terms of market position and competitive landscape, Mall A was the most popular with residents living within a radius of 3 km, and Mall B was its main competitor.

3.4.3 Operational Diagnosis

When making operational decisions, mall managers usually relied on their management intuition and historical data. Winner Technology, by contrast, used the Wi-Fi probe requests to attain data about the stores that customers visited, the sections, floors, and stores that experienced the most traffic, and changes in foot traffic. Therefore, it was able to find popular and unpopular areas within the mall, analyze synergies between stores, and offer traffic forecasts. Thus, more detailed advice about portfolio optimization, rent assessment, store adjustment, and marketing optimization could be provided. For example, store visit data could shed light on a brand's contribution to footfall in the mall. Based on these analyses, the mall's Operations Department could offer rent discounts to the stores that drew in more customers and charge higher rent to those that pulled in fewer shoppers. Also, the Merchants Department could seek merchants based on the contribution a brand or business had made to traffic.

According to the operational diagnosis, Mall A had 11 premium stores that featured high foot traffic, high sales, and a high conversion rate; 146 stores would need to increase footfall considering their high sales but low footfall; and 33 stores, where high footfall generated low sales, would need to increase their conversion rate by improving store clerks' selling skills. Also, an early warning should be given to 16 stores because of their low footfall and low sales. In terms of business type, Mall A's strong businesses included jewelry, digital goods, general merchandise, cosmetics, footwear, food, and dining, while an early warning should be given to businesses providing virtual reality experiences and beauty services.

3.4.4 Marketing Effectiveness Assessment and Optimization

According to Zhang, a large mall usually carried out hundreds of marketing campaigns annually, including dozens of large-scale events. When evaluating the effectiveness of these marketing activities, the mall's managers had been using simple measures such as sales and footfall and using subjective interpretations. Winner Technology, however, provided multi-dimensional assessment indicators, such as changes in visitor profiles, sales conversion during campaigns, and changes in category sales and brand sales. By comparing these indicators with intended marketing objectives, historical performance, and competitors, a mall could evaluate the effectiveness of marketing activities more accurately. The assessments could enable the mall to adjust its marketing events in real time, optimize budgets and marketing plans in the mid-to-long term, and build campaign portfolios and translate marketing experience into knowledge in the long term.

During Mall A's marketing campaign featuring an animated movie, Winner Technology noticed that the number of customers from upscale residential neighborhoods increased substantially, and new customers accounted for 9% of all shoppers during the campaign. Overall, the event boosted footfall by 8.8%, bringing more shoppers to stores that provided dining and child-focused services. It was China-Focused Cases: Selected Winners of the CEIBS Global Case Contest II concluded that parent-child activities significantly drove foot traffic to child-focused stores, especially children's retailers and casual dining restaurants. However, the sales promotion during this event was too simple. It was found that Mall A should organize theme-oriented sales promotions to translate foot traffic into sales.

3.5 Marketing Strategy at Winner Technology

Winner Technology adopted a direct-sales model for its traffic analytics system and big data services, where a sales team and a marketing center directly worked with clients. Other functional departments, such as the R&D center, provided technical support. The company mainly relied on sales visits, existing connections, and referrals for customer acquisition, supplemented by trade shows, the company website, and calls from potential customers. Promotions were mainly undertaken through participating in various trade shows and industry salons, as well as running ads and advertorials in mainstream industry media.

In the early days, Winner Technology charged customers a unit price of ¥5,000 for its traffic analytics cameras and required a system maintenance fee of 10% annually. Customers would be granted access to their traffic data and analytical reports based on this data. After the switch to the SaaS model, a similar service, called the basic package, required an installation fee (¥1,000/camera) and a data service fee (¥500/camera/year). The total costs of the traffic analytics system for a single mall ranged from ¥100,000 to 200,000 per year. Besides the basic package, the company provided additional big data services, and the overall price varied significantly depending on customers' subscriptions.

Account management was based on the size and operating scale of clients. Customers with nationwide operations, such as Wanda, were considered national accounts. Winner Technology signed non-binding agreements with these clients for strategic procurement and negotiated detailed contracts for specific projects or malls. Customers with a more regional focus were considered local accounts. Winner Technology usually communicated with key decision makers of these clients directly. The company channeled resources into projects/malls based on their operating scale—that is, small size (less than 50,000 square meters),medium size (50,000–100,000 square meters),large size (100,000–200,000 square meters), or extra-large size (over 200,000 square meters).

4 Challenges Ahead

According to relevant reports, the traffic analytics system market was capped at ¥1.2 billion to 1.6 billion.[12] Thus, growth in the sales of the IPVA would stall one day. To achieve sustainable growth, Winner Technology had therefore rolled out big data services for brick-and-mortar retailers. However, after several months of marketing, the market reaction was nowhere near the firm's expectations. Zhang thought the company would face two major challenges.

5 Revenue Model

Winner Technology derived more than 80% of its profit from the sales of the traffic analysis system. The gross margin of the system was about 70%. The company hoped to make big data services its primary source of profit, but its current sales team—built for marketing its traffic analytics system over the past decade—would need adjusting.

The first thing to consider was the change in those to whom Winner Technology sold services. The traffic analysis system was sold mainly through an competitive bidding or was directly purchased by customers through private negotiations. Winner Technology only needed to contact the mall's key decision-makers, mostly the IT and Procurement Departments. To pay for the system, the mall put aside a portion of its annual budget for IT-related fixed assets. However, when selling big data services, Winner Technology needed to approach multiple functional departments and managers, including General Managers, the IT Department, the Merchants Department, the Operations Department, and the Marketing Department. Each department tended to purchase big data services based on its own needs. For example, General Managers were more concerned about three key benchmarks about the mall; the Marketing Department would ask for event evaluation reports; and the Merchants Department and Operations Department required operational diagnosis reports. The budget for big data services usually came from the mall's Operations and Marketing Departments. As a result, the sales of big data services grew more complicated. On top of that, there might be conflicts of interest among departments, managers, and merchants. An indicator might benefit one party at the expense of another. Meanwhile, as some commercial real estate owners entrusted mall operations to a third party, a clash of interests might also arise. Therefore, Winner Technology needed to think over how to perform a balancing act among the stakeholders to reduce their resistance to big data services. Zhang was considering whether the company should offer mall managers more "soft" advice based on data analysis instead of providing them with hard numbers and key performance indicators.

In addition, Zhang thought the pricing strategy for big data services would need adjusting. The service fee now depended on the specific items selected by customers. For example, the benchmarking service, which involved three indicators, cost ¥10,000/indicator/year. As this service was highly valued by customers, the latter felt comfortable with the price of ¥30,000/year. Some customers even argued that the benchmarking service should be offered for free, as ¥30,000/year was a paltry sum for Winner Technology. Other big data services were priced higher. Customer analysis and trade area insights cost ¥98,000/year; marketing effectiveness assessment was priced at ¥200,000/year. Zhang had thought such a fee was not high, compared with the rental income for the mall. He explained, "The annual rental income for malls averages around ¥10 million nationwide. However, the number rises to ¥40–50 million for shopping centers in third- and fourth-tier cities and ¥100 million for those in first- and second-tier cities. Some large shopping malls might even spend ¥100 million a year on marketing." The problem was that clients might find it hard to put a figure on the value of big data services. If a single service incurred ¥200,000 per year, this accounted for 2% of the annual total cost of ¥10 million on average. Most customers felt disappointed that big data services might not bring about an immediate increase in their revenue. Winner Technology agreed that the existing strategy was not good enough, but what new strategy should be adopted?

6 Market Cultivation

So far, more than 3,000 shopping centers across China were running without a traffic analytics system. Big data service subscribers were the minority. Zhang thought the main reason for this was that the value of big data was still not clearly recognized.

Winner Technology's customers were mostly large and mid- sized malls and brand chains with foresight. Big data services failed to find favor with small customers in Central and West China and lower-tier cities, where operational managers relied heavily on personal experience instead of data for daily management. This held back the growth of the traffic analytics system market, not to mention big data services. How to nurture the market to help customers recognize the value of big data posed a challenge to Winner Technology.

Zhang hesitated. Market cultivation entailed considerable investments, and competitors would likely stand to gain. Nevertheless, Zhang was deeply aware that if big data services gained traction in the market, winneryun.com would marshal more data and build higher competitive barriers. Since the company began to promote winneryun.com in 2015, customers had had many misgivings about putting their data on this platform, and had lacked a strong desire to value and pay for SaaS services. By the end of 2018, the platform had brought in only 1,000 customers. Although Winner Technology possessed the largest sample of foot traffic data ever from brick-and-mortar retailers in China, Zhang was well aware that such a data volume was still far from enough. He emphasized that the company would need to access a larger sample (ideally 2,000 customers) as soon as possible; otherwise, there would still be a sample bias. He believed that with a larger data sample available on winneryun.com, the platform would increasingly demonstrate its value.

While nurturing the market, Winner Technology also needed to stay alert to competition. Winner Technology dominated the market for traffic analytics. However, this industry attracted more and more companies, including Internet heavyweights and tech-savvy startups. Internet heavyweights such as Alibaba and Tencent were particularly well positioned to provide overall solutions to retailers and guide them through digital transformation, as they had abundant data resources and technology in their ecosystems.[13] Meanwhile, with the application of emerging technologies such as facial recognition and 5G, the technical advantages of Winner Technology would be partially diminished and customers would likely dismiss Winner Technology's traffic analysis system as somewhat outdated, though it was efficient and cost-effective.

In order to cultivate the market and seize business opportunities as soon as possible, Zhang was considering free installation of the traffic analysis system and free access to winneryun.com among potential customers. In exchange, Winner Technology would have access to more customer data and could hopefully profit from high-quality big data services in the future. Was this idea feasible?

Facing these challenges, Zhang intended to call a meeting with his executive team as soon as possible to discuss the revenue model for big data services and the company's approach to cultivating the market.

Endnotes

1. "'New Retail' Comes into Its Own amid Waves of Traditional Department Stores Shutting Down," thepaper.cn, September 7, 2019, accessed February 14, 2019, www.ebrun.com/20170907/245691.shtml.

2. Xin Ling, "CNNIC Internet Report: The Number of Chinese Internet Users Hits 800 Million, with a Penetration Rateof 57.7%," tech.sina.com, August 20, 2018, accessed February 14, 2019, https://www.ithome.com/html/it/377972.htm.
3. iyiou.com and zmeng.cc, New Ecosystem for Offline Data, New Engine for Real Economy: Research Report on Offline Big Data Industry 2018 (May 2018), http://www.199it.com/archives/730110.html.
4. Fang Yan, "Metro China Is Next for Alibaba?" tech.qq.com, February 15, 2019, accessed February 18, 2019, www.ebrun.com/20190215/320346.shtml.
5. "Big Data Will Drive Technological Change in Retail Industry," Tencent, April 18, 2018, accessed February 17, 2019, https://cloud.tencent.com/developer/article/1102061.
6. CCID Consulting, White Paper on China's Big Data Industry 2019 (March 2019).
7. Ibid.
8. "Big Data Application in Four Areas," dtinone.com, July 13, 2018, accessed May 23, 2019, https://cloud.tencent.com/developer/article/1381906.
9. iyiou.com and zmeng.cc, op. cit.
10. "Report on Development of China's Shopping Centers in 2018 Paints Grim Picture of Dining Industry," qianzhan.com, November 18, 2018, accessed February 24, 2019, https://www.qianzhan.com/analyst/detail/220/181115-9f1a62c6.html.
11. Ping An Securities, Winner Technology, a Leader in Foot Traffic Analytics, Harnesses Intelligent Retail to Drive Its Robust Growth (November 10, 2017), accessed February 23, 2019, http://pdf.dfcfw.com/pdf/H3_AP20171110102847 4658_1.pdf.
12. "Report on Development of China's Shopping Centers in 2018 Paints Grim Picture of Dining Industry," qianzhan.com, op. cit.
13. "Digital Transformation Expert in New Retail Era," aliyun.com, accessed February 24, 2019, https://www.aliyun.com/solution/ecommerce?spm=5176.8142029.388261.64.3dbd6d3eQAUOjr.

Appendix

Awards Cases List 2015—2022 Contest for 30 **2015—2022“** 中国工商管理国际最佳案例奖”获奖案例

获奖案例第一作者所在院校	2015 竞赛	2016	2017	2018	2019	2020	2021	2022	Total
中欧	3	5	2	4	8	5	6	5	38
上海其他平台院校	1	1	2		2	8	6	3	23
国内其他院校或机构		1	2	4	1	2	3	2	15
海外院校	5	2	2		1		1	2	13
总计	9	9	8	8	12	15	16	12	89
其中中欧获得过的最佳奖	1	1	1	2	1	1	0	0	

Note

— 2021 竞赛香港理工大学–CEIBS co-branding: “利丰: 上市还是私有化(A)(B) Li and Fung: Stay Public or Go Private (AB)计入中欧”

— 2022 竞赛香港理工大学–CEIBS co-branding: “科劲国际:掘金纳米纤维新风口(A/B) King’s Flair International: A Big Future in the Nanofiber Opportunity? ”(A/B)计入中欧

Award List of The Global Contest for the Best China–Focused Cases (2015—2022) 2015—2022 中国工商管理国际最佳案例奖历届获奖名单(2024.03.13 更新)

序号	竞赛年份	英文标题(梳理后)	作者英文名(梳理后)	作者机构英文(梳理后)	奖项英文(核对后)
2022 中国工商管理国际最佳案例奖获奖名单					
1	2022	A Dispute over Year-end Bonuses (A/B/ C/D)	HAN Yulan//LEUNG Chi Wai//LI Wenqing	Shanghai University of Finance and Economics	Best Case Award

(continued)

China-Focused Cases, https://doi.org/10.1007/978-981-97-8580-3

(continued)

序号	竞赛年份	英文标题(梳理后)	作者英文名(梳理后)	作者机构英文(梳理后)	奖项英文(核对后)
2	2022	AstraZeneca (China): Promoting Social Innovation with Holistic Disease Management Solutions throughout the Patient Journey	CHEN Weiru// LIU Geng	China Europe International Business School	First Prize
3	2022	King's Flair International: A Bright Future in the Nanofiber Opportunity? (A/B)	Justin LAW// CHEN Shimin// Pamsy HUI// Anthony PANG/ /Alex WONG	The HongKong Polytechnic University// China Europe International Business School	First Prize
4	2022	ZUIG's Tender Offer Takeover of Zhenxing Biochem (A/B): Barbarians at the Gate/ Barbarians Enter the Gate	HUANG Sheng/ /HUANG Xiayan//MENG Yuan	China Europe International Business School//The Chinese University of HongKong	First Prize
5	2022	INFRA: Digital Transformation Defining New Third-party Logistics	ZHAO Xiaomin//YU Xiaoyu//LI Jiahui//JIANG Yin	Shanghai University	First Prize
6	2022	China Mengniu Dairy Company Limited (B/C): The Regulatory Clearance Question/ Stay or Quit	Mukund Ramarao Dixit// Rajendra Madhavamurti Inamdar	Independent Researcher// KLS Gogte Institute of Technology	Second Prize
7	2022	Luckin: Rising from the Ashes	LIANG Chao// ZHU Qiong	China Europe International Business School	Second Prize
8	2022	ROOTCLOUD: Customization vs. Standardization at an Industrial IoT Platform	CHEN Weiru// WANG Jiexiang// GONG Yitong	China Europe International Business School//Zhejiang Gongshang University	Second Prize
9	2022	Sinopec EasyJoy's Private Brand "Dolma Spring": Exploring a Benchmarking Model from Product Selection and Test Marketing to Shareholding	SUN Daojun// YING Wenchi// ZHANG Shuo// LI Hong//HUO Liwen	Communication University of China// Beijing Jiaotong University//Sinopec EasyJoy Sales Co., Ltd	Second Prize

(continued)

(continued)

序号	竞赛年份	英文标题(梳理后)	作者英文名(梳理后)	作者机构英文(梳理后)	奖项英文(核对后)
10	2022	Is Tencent's Strategic Investment a Good Medicine for Sunline?	TANG Songlian// ZHOU Shanyu	Donghua University// East China University of Science and Technology	Second Prize
11	2022	Xing Guang Photography: Leveraging Cultural Resources to Become an Industry Champion	WU Haining// SHUAI Ping// LU Xinyi// WANG Yutong// XU Liu// ZHANG Yuxuan	SILC Business School, Shanghai University	Second Prize
12	2022	Xinjiang Goldwind: Growing into a Global Wind Energy Business	Bo Bernhard Nielsen//Wei Li	The University of Sydney	Second Prize
2021 中国工商管理国际最佳案例奖获奖名单					
1	2021	SHEIN: Redefining Global Fast Fashion	Syeda Maseeha Qumer	ICFAI Business School, Hyderabad	Best Case Award
2	2021	Antigal: Strategy and Succession Challenges in a Family-Owned Vineyard with Global Ambitions	Lucia Pierini// Martin Roll// Gianfranco Siciliano//CAO Zhijing	China Europe International Business School//Martin Roll Company	First Prize
3	2021	Budweiser APAC Spinoff (A/B): The Financial Strategy for Localization	CHEN Shimin// David Hendrik Erkens//XUE Wenting	China Europe International Business School	First Prize
4	2021	Geek + : Challenges and Growth in the World of Autonomous Warehouse Robotics	XUE Yixi// LONG Zhengqin//YU Xiaoyu	Shanghai University	First Prize
5	2021	Desperate to Survive: Bankruptcy Reorganization at CNNC Titanium Dioxide (A/B/C)	YANG Bin// ZHANG Chaomin// ZHOU Fangsheng//LI Juan//XU Hui//ZHOU Qi// SHEN Feng	Nankai University// China Enterprise Reform and Development Society//Beijing Yining Culture Communication Co., Ltd	First Prize
6	2021	Li and Fung: Stay Public or Go Private (A/B)	Justin Law// CHEN Shimin// Li Jiang// Anthony Pang	The HongKong Polytechnic University// China Europe International Business School	Second Prize

(continued)

(continued)

序号	竞赛年份	英文标题(梳理后)	作者英文名(梳理后)	作者机构英文(梳理后)	奖项英文(核对后)
7	2021	NEIWAI: Brand Growth Based on New Feminist Values	ZHANG Mo// WANG Pei// JIN Yuan	Shanghai Maritime University	Second Prize
8	2021	Canyou Group: Creating a Sustainable Social Enterprise	Byron Yee Sing Lee//ZHAO Liman//Peter Moran	China Europe International Business School	Second Prize
9	2021	Bull Group's Path to Pre-IPO Dividend Windfall	WU Linman// ZHAO Taike// HU Peng//LIU Shengqiang	Chongqing Technology and Business University	Second Prize
10	2021	From Traditional FMCG Brand to New-category Thought Leadership: OATLY's China Venture	FAN Xiaojun// LI Xin	Shanghai University	Second Prize
11	2021	From Lianjia to Beike: Key Choices During Platform Transformation	XU Hui//XIAO Jin	Shanghai Maritime University	Second Prize
12	2021	Implications of Kingsoft's Serial Spin- off Listing	FANG Zong// ZHOU Yiran	Shanghai University	Second Prize
13	2021	AstraZeneca(China): Leveraging Offline Doctor-Patient Relationships in Online Healthcare Service Platform	LIN Chen//LIU Geng// CHIANG Jeongwen	Fudan University//China Europe International Business School	Second Prize
14	2021	Fenced Walls Built then Demolished? Amendments to China Baoan's Anti-takeover Clause	ZHU Lei// LONG Xuefang// YU Xiaotong// MAHaixin// WANG Chunyan	Shandong University of Finance and Economics	Second Prize
15	2021	Wuling Hongguang MINIEV: A New Breed of Chinese Automaker	WANG Gao// ZHU Qiong	China Europe International Business School	Second Prize
16	2021	CHINT: New Talent Inventory Post- digital Transformation	YAN Shumin// BI Wenlin//MA Yujie//SHASha/ /XIE Xianmei	Tongji University// CHINT	Second Prize

2020 中国工商管理国际最佳案例奖获奖名单

(continued)

(continued)

序号	竞赛年份	英文标题(梳理后)	作者英文名(梳理后)	作者机构英文(梳理后)	奖项英文 (核对后)
1	2020	Daddy Lab: AChinese Social Enterprise's Dilemma	Daniel Han Ming Chng// ZHAO Liman// Byron Yee Sing Lee//Peter Moran// SUN Heming	China Europe International Business School	Best Case Award
2	2020	Navigating EtonHouse through Crises: The Paradoxical Leadership of Ng Gim Choo	Jean Siew Kim Lee //JU Huirong	China Europe International Business School	First Prize
3	2020	Cabbeen Fashion: Strategic Decisions under the Pandemic (A/B/C)	ZHENG Xin// CHEN Honghui	Lingnan College, SunYat-Sen University	First Prize
4	2020	Keep: Commercializing China's Mobile Fitness Unicorn	FAN Xiaojun// LI Xin	Shanghai University	First Prize
5	2020	Making Bricks Without Straw: Newlink's Push to be the Energy Industry's Alibaba	XUE Yixi//REN Jie//YAN Hui	Shanghai University	First Prize
6	2020	Smart Health: "Internet + " Healthcare in Xiamen	CHEN Hong// ZHUANG Weifeng	Shanghai Advanced Institute of Finance, Shanghai Jiaotong University//Xiamen University	First Prize
7	2020	Ant Forest: Starting from Environmental Protection	RUI Meng// ZHU Qiong	China Europe International Business School	Second Prize
8	2020	SAIC Maxus: Pioneering the C2B Model in China's Auto Industry in the Digital Era	FANG Yue// QIAN Wenying	China Europe International Business School	Second Prize
9	2020	H&H Group: A Global Firm with Chinese Origins (A)	Emily M.David/ /XUE Wenting	China Europe International Business School	Second Prize

(continued)

(continued)

序号	竞赛年份	英文标题(梳理后)	作者英文名(梳理后)	作者机构英文(梳理后)	奖项英文(核对后)
10	2020	Information Disclosure Reviews for Registration-based IPOs: ACase Study of National Silicon Industry Group	LI Yuanqin//HUANG Yu//LI Ting//YU Xiaoyu	Shanghai University	Second Prize
11	2020	Perfect Diary: How E-commerce Brands Come Down to Earth?	LI Qianqian//ZHAO Chen	Shanghai University	Second Prize
12	2020	Buy42: Charting a Business Model Roadmap for Chinese Charity Stores	REN Shengce//ZHANG Mo//JIN Yuan//LI Jie	"Tongji University//Shanghai Maritime University//Xi'an Jiaotong-Liverpool University"	Second Prize
13	2020	AInnovation-Driven Renovation: Commercial Adventures of SenseTime	FAN Xiaojun//TANG Xinwei	Shanghai University	Second Prize
14	2020	The Rise of Bilibili: From AcFun Fallback to Flourishing Content Ecosphere	XU Hui//CHEN Zhiwu// MAO Jian	Shanghai Maritime University	Second Prize
15	2020	The Futures of Apples: Great Expectations	WANG Hongsheng//ZHU Yan//XU Jiayi	Shandong Agricultural University// Central University of Finance and Economics	Second Prize
2019 中国工商管理国际最佳案例奖获奖名单(来自获奖案例信息表)					
1	2019	Chasm Security: Facing the Technology Startup's Dilemmas (A/B/C)	Vincent Wen-Ching Chang//ZHAO Liman //S. Ramakrishna Velamuri	China Europe International Business School	Best Case Award
2	2019	Baman Tech (A/B): Breaking the Boundary of Catering/Building Competitive Barriers in the Supply Chain	ZHAO Xiande//RUAN Liyang//WANG Liang	China Europe International Business School	Nominated Case Award
3	2019	KFC China: Building Competitive Advantages through Digitalization	LIN Chen//ZHANG Chi	China Europe International Business School	Nominated Case Award

(continued)

(continued)

序号	竞赛年份	英文标题(梳理后)	作者英文名(梳理后)	作者机构英文(梳理后)	奖项英文(核对后)
4	2019	Alibaba vs. JD.com: Strategies, Business Models, and Financial Statements	CHEN Shimin//PAN Dingwen//HUNAG Xiayan	China Europe International Business School	Nominated Case Award
5	2019	LinkDoc: Commercial Exploration of Healthcare Big Data (A/B)	ZHANG Hua//QIAN Wenying//LI Shuyang	China Europe International Business School	Nominated Case Award
6	2019	Winner Technology: Big Data Disruption in Retail Industry	XIANG Yi//RUAN Liyang//LI Yanyu	China Europe International Business School	Nominated Case Award
7	2019	Voles System's Bribery Accusations in China	Daniel Han Ming Chng//PI Xin//ZHAO Liman	China Europe International Business School	Nominated Case Award
8	2019	WeDoctor: Strategically Reengineering Healthcare Process	JIN Xiaoling//YIN Mengjie//ZHANG Xiaojie//ZHOU Zhongyun	Shanghai University//Tongji University	Nominated Case Award
9	2019	Being United and Working Together: Qiangda Chilli Leads to a Win–Win Outcomes	WANG Chongfeng//CAO Jiangxin//CHAO Yixuan//GONG Jie//SUN Jing//MENG Xingchen//ZHAO Yang//LIMingzhe	Qingdao University//PricewaterhouseCoopers Business Consulting (Shanghai) Co.Ltd, Qingdao Branch//Jiaozhou Association for Science and Technology//Jiaozhou Municipal Bureau of Administrative Services	Nominated Case Award
10	2019	Chow Tai Fook: AChinese Jewellery Giant Changing Tactics	V. Namratha Prasad//Koti Vinod Babu	ICFAI Business School, Hyderabad	Nominated Case Award
11	2019	Capillary: An Indian Startup Deepening Its Presence in China	Shameen Prashantham//RUAN Liyang	China Europe International Business School	Special Recognition Award
12	2019	The Road of Chinese LiNing's Taking Off: From the Traditional Sports Brand to the TopicKing in Chinese Fashion World	FAN Xiaojun//ZHAO Wenyu	Shanghai University	Special Recognition Award

(continued)

(continued)

序号	竞赛年份	英文标题(梳理后)	作者英文名(梳理后)	作者机构英文(梳理后)	奖项英文(核对后)
2018 中国工商管理国际最佳案例奖获奖名单					
1	2018	Freshippo: A New Species in Chinese Retail (A/B): Business Model Evolution/ Data-Driven Core Competencies	Vincent Wen-Ching Chang // ZHU Qiong	China Europe International Business School	Best Case Award
2	2018	Xihaner Car Wash: Building a Sustainable Social Enterprise in China	Daniel Han Ming Chng// ZHAO Liman// SUN Heming	China Europe International Business School	Best Case Award
3	2018	JD.com (A/B): New Chief Human Resources Officer/ Culture Consolidation and Talent Review	Jean Siew Kim LEE//HAN Jian//ZHAO Ziqian//LONG Yu//Tan Ruofeng	China Europe International Business School//Tsinghua University//JD.COM	Nominated Case Award
4	2018	Midea in India	XU Yuehua// CHEN Honghui//LAI Hongyu// HUANG Xinyi	SunYat-sen University	Nominated Case Award
5	2018	Wei De Medicare: Strategic Transformation from OEM to Chinese Smart Manufacturing	DAI Jian// YANG Lingwei	GIC Consulting	Nominated Case Award
6	2018	Vatti Co., Ltd. 2018 WorldCup "If France Wins, Get a Full Refund" Campaign: Promotion Effect and Risk Control Strategy Based on Option Hedging	CHEN Qi'an// ZHANG Guohong// ZHAO Xu	Chongqing University	Nominated Case Award
7	2018	The Digital Revolution of Fresh Food Supply Chain: A Case of Songxiaocai	YAO Yanfei// FU Wenhui// GUO Hongdong//JIA Fu	Zhejiang University// South China Normal University//University of York	Nominated Case Award
8	2018	Yiliu Tech: Exploring Logistical Transparency (A/B)	ZHAO Xiande// QIAN Wenying/ /WANG Liang	China Europe International Business School	Nominated Case Award
2017 中国工商管理国际最佳案例奖获奖名单					

(continued)

(continued)

序号	竞赛年份	英文标题(梳理后)	作者英文名(梳理后)	作者机构英文(梳理后)	奖项英文(核对后)
1	2017	Jinhuobao: AB2B E-commerce Platform for FMCG in the New Retail Era	ZHANG Hua// QIAN Wenying/ /LI Shuyang	China Europe International Business School	Best Case Award
2	2017	TECNO Mobile's Growth Strategies in Africa	Syeda Maseeha Qumer// Geeta Singh	ICFAI Business School, Hyderabad	Nominated Case Award
3	2017	Why Didn't the SF Heike Project Succeed?	ZHENG Gang// HU Shan	Zhejiang University	Nominated Case Award
4	2017	The Evolution of Opple Lighting's E-commerce Business	CHEN Weiru// QIAN Wenying/ /HWANG Yuhchang// SHEN Fei	China Europe International Business School	Nominated Case Award
5	2017	Haidilao's Crisis Management: Threats, Opportunities and Corporate Values	SHU Chengli// ZHENG Shaoting	Xi'an Jiaotong University	Nominated Case Award
6	2017	Budget Management at KPMC R&D Center	TAN Huiling	Shanghai University of Finance and Economics	Nominated Case Award
7	2017	Grapes, Wine, and the Wise Old Vine: The Application of the Valuation Adjustment Mechanism to BlueFocus' Acquisition Activities	FANG Zong// JIANG Xiaoying	Shanghai University	Nominated Case Award
8	2017	Wolf Warrior 2: The Marketing and Stock Market Stories	HU Gang// CHEN Ting'en/ / HUANG Jingjing//LIU Chenhan//SUN Mengwei// WU Anqi	HongKong Polytechnic University	Nominated Case Award
2016 中国工商管理国际最佳案例奖获奖名单					
1	2016	FamilyMart: "Internet Plus" Strategy	LIN Chen	China Europe International Business School	Best Case Award

(continued)

(continued)

序号	竞赛年份	英文标题(梳理后)	作者英文名(梳理后)	作者机构英文(梳理后)	奖项英文(核对后)
2	2016	Can Starbucks Sustain its High Prices in China?	Debapratim Purkayastha//Benudhar Sahu//S Venkata Seshiah//Trilochan Tripathy	ICFAI Business School, Hyderabad//XLRI, Jamshedpur	Nominated Case Award
3	2016	Can Huawei Overcome Roadblocks in its Quest for Global Markets?	Muralidhara GV//Hadiya Faheem	ICFAI Business School, Hyderabad//Freelance Casewriter	Nominated Case Award
4	2016	From a Product Brand to a Platform Brand: The Business Evolution Logic of the Internet Brand Handu	HE Jiaxun//ZHU Liangjie	East China Normal University	Nominated Case Award
5	2016	ofo: A Bike-Sharing Company from Campus	Wang Rui//QIAN Liping	Peking University//Chongqing University	Nominated Case Award
6	2016	Midea Group: Founder-CEO Succession in a Chinese Home-Appliance Maker	Jean Siew Kim Lee//ZHAO Ziqian	China Europe International Business School	Nominated Case Award
7	2016	Solar Flare: The Rise and Fall of Suntech Power Holdings	Daniel Han Ming Chng//ZHAO Ziqian	China Europe International Business School	Nominated Case Award
8	2016	Struggle to Balance: Supply Chain Practices of China Resources Henan Pharmaceutical Company (A/B)	ZHAO Xiande//YU Feng//WANG Liang	China Europe International Business School	Nominated Case Award
9	2016	Shenzhen SJET Co., LTD. (A/B): Supply Chain Intergration and Supply Chain Financial Integration Solution/ Information System and the Establishment of an "Ecosystem"	ZHAO Xiande//SONG Hua//Jerry Wei//HUANG Qiuping//LU Qiang	China Europe International Business School//Renmin University of China//University of Notre Dame//South China University of Technology	Nominated Case Award
2015 中国工商管理国际最佳案例奖获奖名单					

(continued)

(continued)

序号	竞赛年份	英文标题(梳理后)	作者英文名(梳理后)	作者机构英文(梳理后)	奖项英文(核对后)
1	2015	OnePlus: A Chinese Tech Start- up Aiming to Disrupt the Global Smartphone Market	Syeda Maseeha Qumer, Debapratim Purkayastha	ICFAI Business School, Hyderabad	Best Case Award
2	2015	O2O Transformation in Rongchang Laundry Chain Services: Incubating an “e-Washing” Platform	CHEN Weiru// CHEN Chuang// LIN Ciwu	China Europe International Business School//Xiamen University	Best Case Award
3	2015	“Three Squirrels”: An Online Brand’s Rapid Rise to Success	HE Jiaxun// WANG Haili	East China Normal University	Nominated Case Award
4	2015	Yum! Brands in China: Facing Brand Fatigue?	Doris Rajakumari John	Amity Research Centers, Headquarter, Bangalore, India	Nominated Case Award
5	2015	Luxury Retailer Louis Vuitton in China: Losing Lustre or Adding Colour?	Punithavathi Srikant	Amity Research Centers, Headquarter, Bangalore, India	Nominated Case Award
6	2015	World’s Largest Retailer in the World’s Most Populous Country: Wal-Mart in China	Geeta Singh	ICFAI Business School, Hyderabad	Nominated Case Award
7	2015	Defying High Barriers to Entry: The Marketing Mix of 759 Stores	Ailie Tang// Monica Lo	The University of HongKong	Nominated Case Award
8	2015	KEMET’s Chinese Integration Team (A/B/C/D)	Katherine Rong Xin// ZHONG Jin	China Europe International Business School	Nominated Case Award
9	2015	LI-NING Co.Ltd: ALeading Chinese Company Stumbles	Daniel Han Ming Chng// ZHAO Ziqian	China Europe International Business School	Nominated Case Award

GPSR Compliance

The European Union's (EU) General Product Safety Regulation (GPSR) is a set of rules that requires consumer products to be safe and our obligations to ensure this.

If you have any concerns about our products, you can contact us on ProductSafety@springernature.com

In case Publisher is established outside the EU, the EU authorized representative is:

Springer Nature Customer Service Center GmbH
Europaplatz 3
69115 Heidelberg, Germany

Batch number: 10725971

Printed by Printforce, the Netherlands